Review for The Art of Forecasting using ~~Sol~~ ~~~~~

"Books on solar returns, like those on electional astrology, are far and few between. For many years the practice of solar returns has been more an option for astrologers rather than a necessity, and this is primarily due to the lack of adequate and researched texts on the subject. As a result, the subject has been caught up in contradictory methods and fraught with complications such as whether or not to precess or to relocate annual or monthly returns. But now Anthony Louis has come to the rescue and has produced a work that both builds upon and tests the sources of much of our original knowledge of returns, that of Jean-Baptiste Morin and his 20th century follower Alexandre Volguine.

In The Art of Forecasting using Solar Returns, Anthony Louis provides the reader with a solid historical background on the technique and lays out clearly how Morin, one of the greatest astrologers of all time, used it in the 17th century. He then proceeds to test this methodology rigorously with example after example – most from recent history featuring recognizable celebrities and also a few persons known to the author. Every aspect of return interpretation is raised and examined, including those promoted by the few modern-day writers on the subject. By the end of this dense and thorough book the reader is offered a methodological summary and worked example.

To my knowledge, nothing this complete has ever been published and a serious reader will find the work to be all they need to guide them through the interpretation of solar and lunar returns, as well as their progression through time. Louis also tackles the thorny problem of precessed returns - do they work and what does one do with them? Unlike other authors who take an either-or view on this topic, Louis shows the uses of both in example after example. Unfortunately, Louis does not engage in the same level of testing in regard to the relocation issue, though he mentions it as a technique used by both Morin and Volguine, the primary sources for his exposition of return techniques.

Overall this is a complete work and one that I would enthusiastically recommend as the one book to acquire on this subject."

— Bruce Scofield - November 2006 (http://onereed.com)
(Author of Astrological Chart Calculations and other texts on astrology)

THE ART OF FORECASTING

USING

SOLAR RETURNS

Anthony Louis

The Wessex Astrologer

Published in 2008 by
The Wessex Astrologer Ltd
4A Woodside Road
Bournemouth
BH5 2AZ
England

www.wessexastrologer.com

ISBN 9781902405292

A catalogue record of this book is available at The British Library

Cover design by Iris de Leeuw

Printed and bound in the UK by Biddles Ltd, Kings Lynn, Norfolk.

Unless otherwise stated in the text, all astrological charts and calculations
were done using the program Solar Fire Deluxe v.6.0.32 by Esoteric
Technologies Pty Ltd.

About the Author

The author is a psychiatrist who writes under the pen name Anthony Louis. He has been a student of astrology since his teens and has lectured internationally and published numerous articles and books on the topic. His widely acclaimed text on horary astrology first appeared in 1991 and was revised and reissued in 1996. His book *Tarot Plain and Simple* has become a perennial favorite. Anthony Louis has written the text for reports on vocation, secondary progressions, and solar returns for Halloran software's *AstrolDeluxe Report Writer*. In addition to writing his own texts, he has translated into English Morin's *Book 18* of *Astrologia Gallica* on the strengths and weaknesses of the planets. Anthony Louis is a member of NCGR and the Astrological Society of Connecticut.

...the revolution either brings forth or inhibits the effect of the nativity,
and it can only bring it forth from a similarity of figures...
Jean-Baptiste Morin, Book 23, *Astrologia Gallica*

Permissions

Grateful thanks to the following for permission to cite their work:

American Federation of Astrologers (AFA) – Morin's *Astrolgia Gallica* (translated by James Holden)

Robert Corre – *Forum On Astrology*

James A. Eshelman - *Interpreting Solar Returns*

Esoteric Technologies Pty Ltd – *Solar Fire Deluxe*

Robert Hand – *Whole Sign Houses: The Oldest House System*

Deborah Houlding - *The Houses: Temples of the Sky* (skyscript.co.uk)

Bob Makransky – *Primary Directions* (www.dearbrutus.com)

David McCann – skyscript.co.uk

Ray Merriman – *The New Solar Return Book of Prediction*

Marc Penfield – *Solar Returns in Your Face*

Mary Fortier Shea - *Planets in Solar Returns*

Celeste Teal - *Eclipses*

Alexandre Volguine (1903-1976), whose work on solar returns is referenced in this text, died in 1976 and his book has been out of print in English for many years. I primarily used copies of his book on solar returns in French and Spanish as background for my research. Volguine was an influential teacher and writer of the last century, and the height of his influence was from the mid-1930s until his death in 1976. Volguine's many students taught his techniques to subsequent generations of astrologers. If there is anyone who feels they own the copyright to this information, I would welcome contact with them.

Dedication

This book is written in honor of Jean-Baptiste Morin de Villefranche (1583-1656), one of the truly great minds in the history of astrology, and also in loving memory of my friend Don.

Contents

Preface

What if there were a method that would enable you to learn how the promise of your birth chart would unfold in the year ahead? What if that method would allow you to utilize everything you already know about astrology and simply apply it from a new perspective? Well, there is such a method and it is called a Solar Return (or Solar Revolution, to use a more antiquated terminology).

This book is about Solar Returns, specifically about how to use your Solar Return in conjunction with your birth chart annually to forecast the major themes and events of your life. The focus of this text is on technique. It is decidedly not a cookbook, plenty of which already populate the market, though you will find cookbook-like sections that catalogue information for easy reference. By the time you finish reading this book, you will have a solid foundation in delineating a Solar Return chart within the context of the nativity. Our approach will be to study the techniques of the masters who have devoted themselves to understanding solar revolutions, and the outcome will be an enhanced ability to think like an astrologer and also a greater appreciation of the potentials inherent in the birth chart.

The approach in this book is not dogmatic. In astrology as in much of life there are many ways to skin a cat (my apologies to cat lovers), and we shall consider several of them. I have selected for inclusion techniques from the literature that have proved useful in my own experience, and I have added a few methods of my own for the reader to try. Learning is best by doing, and many example charts are included for study. From these well-documented cases the reader will be able to judge whether these procedures are valid.

I come to Solar Returns from horary astrology. Having spent considerable time learning the techniques of traditional horary, particularly the method of William Lilly, I became fascinated with the ideas of Jean-Baptiste Morin, a brilliant French contemporary of Lilly. So great was my interest that I translated into English Morin's *Book 18* on the dignities and debilities of the planets. This text represents my own struggles to piece together traditional ideas with modern astrological concepts while remaining grounded in empirical reality and the evidence of verifiable case histories. These cases are based on well-documented stories that make excellent illustrations of technique.

After completing the manuscript, I noticed an unintentional emphasis on death, accidents, life-threatening injuries, murders, and similar misfortunes. Such a focus on the dark side occurred in part because these types of events are common in the traditional textbooks, especially the writings of Morin. It is likely that I am drawn to such themes because of the prominent Pluto and Saturn in my own nativity, and indeed my entrance into astrology was characterized by a study of the planetary conditions active at the time of my mother's untimely death. Yet a deeper reason may underlie the focus on issues of mortality in this text. Only after finishing the first draft of the manuscript did I have the "aha" experience that the Taurus Ascendant of my 2005 Solar Return, which was active during the year that I was writing this book, was drawing my attention, outside of my awareness, to my natal 8th house with its Taurus cusp. Ah, the wonders of astrology!

Acknowledgements

I wish to thank you, the reader, for taking the time to consider what I have written about Solar Returns and I hope you find it worthwhile. I also wish to thank all those who have helped directly or indirectly in the writing of this book. My wife Linda and my two sons, David and Aaron, were, as usual, supportive of my efforts. Carolyn Egan (http://weathersage.com/) graciously read the original manuscript and offered many valuable suggestions. Celeste Teal gave helpful feedback on eclipses and the USA chart of Evangeline Adams. John Halloran worked diligently to program many of the ideas presented here into his *AstrolDeluxe Report Writer*, for which I wrote the interpretive text on Solar Returns. Robert Corre, James Holden, and John Frawley gave generously of their time and intellects as I was translating *Book 18* of Morin's *Astrologia Gallica*, which has formed the backdrop for my understanding Morin's ideas about Solar Returns. Over the years Bruce Scofield, Rob Hand, and Luis Lesur, in public lectures and private discussions, challenged the very utility of tropical Solar Returns, which prompted me to investigate more deeply the theoretical basis and limitations of this technique. The calculations in this book were made easy by the fine program *Solar Fire Deluxe* from Esoteric Technologies. I am also grateful to the many astrologers who have written about solar revolutions and whose works are cited in this text. Modern authors who have especially influenced my thinking about Solar Returns include James Eshelman, Ray Merriman, Bob Makransky, Marc Penfield, and Mary Shea. Finally, I must thank all those whose charts appear as case examples in this book. The proof of the pudding is always in the eating, and without actual charts we would be but spinning tales in a world of fantasy and illusion.

1
Some Basic Ideas

The use of Solar Returns has become a staple among the forecasting techniques of Western astrology. Some astrologers swear by them, but others view return charts as unreliable and difficult to interpret. In addition, there is no consensus about how to calculate a Solar Return. Should it be cast for the birthplace, the current place of residence, or the actual location of the client on his or her astrological birthday? Should one take precession into account? Should one use the tropical or the sidereal zodiac? Can return charts be interpreted in isolation or do they always refer back to the natal chart? How does one distinguish figure from ground in a Solar Return figure? These are some of the questions we will be addressing in the following chapters.

Let me be clear from the outset that this volume will deal only with Solar Returns in the Western or tropical zodiac. It's not that sidereal techniques are any less valuable but rather that combining the two systems (tropical and sidereal) would take us too far afield. You may recall that the sidereal zodiac defines its astrological signs with reference to the actual constellations of fixed stars in the heavens whereas the tropical zodiac defines the zodiacal signs mathematically with reference to the four seasons.

Welcome to the Tropics
Tropical Solar Returns have been used as forecasting techniques in Western astrology for at least 1200 years. Why are they called tropical Solar Returns? Geographically speaking, the tropics are the regions on earth between the Tropic of Cancer (23°26' North latitude) and the Tropic of Capricorn (23°26' South latitude). The word "tropic" itself comes from the Greek word *tropikos*, which refers to a change in direction of the Sun's apparent motion with respect to the Earth's equator at the time of the summer and winter solstices when the Sun appears to stand still (Latin: *sol*, Sun – *sistere*, to stand).

Astrology developed in an Earth-centered (geocentric) universe. To the ancients the Sun appeared to travel around the earth on its annual journey. The path of the Sun was known as the Ecliptic because eclipses occur on that imaginary circle in the sky. A belt of constellations of fixed stars along the Sun's path resembled certain animals, objects, and human figures. The term zodiac comes from the Greek *zodiakos*, which means a circle of animals. The imaginary belt in the heavens on either side of the Sun's apparent path was divided mathematically into twelve equal parts called the signs of the zodiac, named after constellations of stars. The constellations had various lengths but the zodiacal signs all measured exactly 30 degrees.

The Sun's annual journey around the earth renews itself each year at the vernal equinox, the first day of spring. Equinox (Latin: *equi*, equal – *nox*, night) refers to equal lengths of day and night. Twice a year, at the beginning of spring and the beginning of fall, the Sun's path "crosses" the equator, giving twelve hours of daylight and twelve hours of darkness. Ancient Western astrologers took the vernal equinox as the starting point of the Sun's path; and they began measuring the zodiac beginning at the vernal equinox, which they called 0° Aries. The astrology of the Western world became a study of the symbolic meanings of the mathematical relationships between the Sun's apparent path in the sky, the Ecliptic, and the Earth's equator projected into the solar system as the Celestial Equator.

Astral Omens

The precursor of Western astrology was the omen lore of Mesopotamia, whose priests looked to the heavens, among other places, for messages from the gods. In his doctoral dissertation, Lester Ness states: "the omens themselves tended to deal with the country as a whole, or with the king, who represented the country to the gods, not with private individuals – an important difference from the astrology of the Hellenistic period."[1] The Hellenistic period of Greek history extended from the death of Alexander the Great in 323 BCE until the Roman annexation of the Greek peninsula and Greek islands in 146 BCE. During Hellenistic times, astrologers combined a sophisticated mathematical understanding of astronomy with the ancient omen lore to give birth to modern astrology. The first extant calculated horoscope similar to a modern chart dates from April 29, 410 BCE, almost a hundred years before the death of Alexander the Great. It was during the Hellenistic era that astrologers began to interpret horoscopes of everyday individuals rather than just those of kings and entire nations. A vast literature developed about the meaning of the birth chart and its implications for the character and destiny of the native.

A basic premise of Hellenistic astrology is that the birth chart is the fundamental starting point for any predictive technique. The natal chart is like a seed that grows into the individual person whom it represents. A modern metaphor would be that the birth chart is the astrological DNA of the person – a blueprint for all that is to follow during development. If you understand the birth chart, you have a good idea of what lies ahead for the individual. All predictive techniques are but a footnote to the birth chart because such techniques simply forecast when the natal potential will manifest during the life of the native. *In other words, all predictive techniques, including Solar Returns, are essentially timing devices that allow the astrologer to forecast when a particular facet of the birth chart will be activated in the life of the native.*

The Planets in Solar Returns

The good news about Solar Returns is that you can use what you already know about natal astrology to help you interpret the return chart. In this section we will review some basic meanings of the planets. In later chapters we will cover the significance of the astrological signs and houses as they relate to Solar Returns.

The English word "planet" derives from the Greek word *plançtçs,* meaning a wanderer. In Latin *planeta* refers to a planet or wandering star. Certain stars appeared to wander against the panoply of fixed stars in the night sky. Traditional astrology used seven "planets," namely, the two Lights or Luminaries, the Sun and the Moon, and the five visible planets – Mercury, Venus, Mars, Jupiter, and Saturn. Current astrology includes the modern non-visible planets Uranus, Neptune, and Pluto; the planetoid Chiron, which orbits between Saturn and Uranus; and countless asteroids. In 2006 the International Astronomical Union reclassified Pluto as a "dwarf planet" and has included Ceres and Eris in its list of dwarf planets. Regardless of whether or not we view Pluto as a dwarf planet, its astrological effect in a chart remains formidable. To avoid complicating the process of delineating a Solar Return, we will limit ourselves to the seven traditional planets and the three modern planets. Below is a list of these planets and some key associations about their general nature, based on centuries of observations of the roles they have played in the horoscope. In addition, we must always be aware that, in any given chart, the house(s) that a planet occupies and rules determine the specific significations of the planet in that chart.

Keywords for the Planets:

Sun: The Sun is the center and source of energy of the solar system. It rules Leo, the 5th sign of the zodiac. The Sun represents the father, the life-force, vitality, power, confidence, ego, personal identity, individuality, the outer you, creativity, personal growth, procreation, significance, prominence, leadership, awareness, authority, nobility, prestige, honor, pride, self-importance, the need for attention, warmth, illumination, fame, celebrity, promotion, public recognition, rewards, advancement, important contacts, powerful people, superiors, authorities, royalty, nobility, the heart. The Sun acts to illuminate, invigorate, empower, vitalize, individualize, make prominent, and elevate.

The house containing the Sun and any house(s) containing the sign Leo, especially those houses with Leo on the cusp, determine the particular significations of the Sun in a given chart.

Moon: The Moon receives and reflects the light of the Sun. It rules Cancer, the 4th sign of the zodiac. The Moon symbolizes feelings, emotions, the receptive mother, sensitivity, emotional responsiveness, fluctuation, the tides, the ebb and flow of life, changing conditions to which we must adapt, maternal instincts, caring, protective urges, habits, past influences, females, women's issues, the breasts, nurturing, being nurtured, food, alimentation, nursing, family matters, domestic concerns, the home, support, emotional ties with others, helping other people, receptivity, reactivity, moods, emotional security, interest in music, public support, publicity, popularity, public opinion, the masses. The state of the Moon in the Solar Return is closely linked to one's health and personal relationships in the year ahead.

The house containing the Moon and any house(s) containing the sign Cancer, especially those houses with Cancer on the cusp, determine the particular significations of the Moon in a given chart.

Mercury: Mercury, the messenger of the gods, rules Gemini and Virgo, which are respectively the 3rd and 6th signs of the zodiac. Mercury is connected with speaking, writing, knowledge, communication, reporting, correspondence, short trips, literary matters, learning, ideas, details, classification, routines, movement, travel, transport, comings and goings, mobility, variety, curiosity, intellect, wit, cleverness, analysis, logic, reason, language, news, gossip, rumors, sharing information, mental pursuits, commerce, sales, agents, go-betweens, business, busy-ness, a fast pace, restlessness, nervous energy, students, siblings, tricksters, young people, quicksilver.

The house containing Mercury and any house(s) containing the signs Gemini or Virgo, especially any houses with these signs on the cusp, determine the particular significations of Mercury in a given chart.

Venus: Known as the "lesser benefic" and goddess of love, Venus rules Taurus and Libra, respectively the 2nd and 7th signs of the zodiac. Venus signifies love, tenderness, attraction, courtship, romance, marriage, flirtation, affection received, social ties, the approval of others, looking good, happy occasions, parties, comfort, sexual pleasure, indulgence, laziness, luxury, attractive women, young women, esthetic sense, the fine arts, peace, harmony, cooperation, diplomacy, agreements, refinement, beauty, values, money, income, gifts, favors, pleasant surprises, the granting of wishes, the desire to please, sweets, tact, decoration, adornment, grace, teamwork, protection, good fortune.

The house containing Venus and any house(s) containing the signs Taurus or Libra, especially any houses with these signs on the cusp, determine the particular significations of Venus in a given chart.

Mars: Traditionally called the "lesser malefic," Mars rules Aries and Scorpio, respectively the 1st and 8th signs of the zodiac. Mars – the god of war – represents energy, heat, courage, passion, impulse, rage, burning desire, militant aggression, fights, battles, assertiveness, boldness, decisiveness, headstrong tendencies, athletic prowess, physical exertion, muscles, action, haste, rashness, thrusting, pushing, penetration, drive, initiative, new enterprises, mechanical devices, masculinity, virility, warriors, young men, the phallus, sexual arousal, lust, competition, aggression, hunting, territoriality, confrontation, opposition, resentment, anger, threats, weapons, guns, knives, sharp instruments, cars, speed, accidents, wounds, cuts, burns, fires, conflagrations, surgery, the use of force.

The house containing Mars and any house(s) containing the signs Aries and Scorpio, especially any houses with these signs on the cusp, determine the particular significations of Mars in a given chart.

Jupiter: Traditionally called the "greater benefic," Jupiter rules Sagittarius and Pisces, which are respectively the 9th and 12th signs of the zodiac. Jupiter signifies growth, abundance, benevolence, generosity, good luck, expansion, prosperity, acquisition, increase, optimism, faith, confidence, generosity, friendliness, a sense of humor, philanthropy, protection, reward, profit, advantage, exaggeration, enthusiasm, risk-taking, overextension, excess, (irrational) exuberance, tolerance or intolerance, philosophical insight, spiritual beliefs, long journeys, desire for adventure, publishing, expanded horizons, belief systems, farsightedness, opportunity, avuncular persons, fat cats, professional work, and matters related to religion or the law. Although Jupiter is generally quite fortunate, astrologers have noted that it is often prominent in the Solar Return of the year of one's death – perhaps symbolizing one's final extended journey into the unknown.

The house containing Jupiter and any house(s) containing the signs Sagittarius or Pisces, especially any houses with these signs on the cusp, determine the particular significations of Jupiter in a given chart.

Saturn: Traditionally called the "greater malefic," Saturn rules Capricorn and Aquarius, which are respectively the 10th and 11th signs of the zodiac. Saturn is associated with constriction, contraction, maturity, stability, patience, persistence, endurance, structure, self-control, responsibility, economy, a "time is money" mentality, planning, tradition, conformity, dogma, lack, limitation, hardship, privation, the reality principle, duty, order, caution, skepticism, obstructions, coldness, hardening, old age, longevity, consolidation, crystallization, discipline, testing, lessons learned, restriction, deprivation, death, delay, organization, administration, concentration, ambition, authority, high office, desire for public recognition, receiving one's just deserts, wisdom from experience, parental figures, supervisors, bosses, separation, loss, fears, falls, depression, darkness, being between a rock and a hard place, misfortune, taskmasters, the grim reaper. Saturn and Pluto are the two planets most closely associated with death.

The house containing Saturn and any house(s) containing the signs Capricorn or Aquarius, especially any houses with these signs on the cusp, determine the particular significations of Saturn in a given chart.

Uranus: Sometimes called the "higher octave of Mercury," Uranus co-rules Aquarius, the 11th sign of the zodiac. Uranus is linked with freedom, autonomy, liberation, rebellion, surprises, novelty, deviation, originality, uniqueness, invention, creative genius, willfulness, awakening, breakthroughs, sudden awareness, shocking events, jarring surprises, one-of-a-kind experiences, exciting relationships, sparks, lightning bolts, flashes of insight, excitement, disruption, discontinuity, sudden attachments, divorce, breakups, severing of old ties, breaks from the past, waywardness, shattering of familiar structures, experimentation, unexpected twists of fate, innovations, new methods, progressive thinking, unpredictability, rebelliousness, unanticipated changes, accidents, explosions, astrology, electricity, and modern science.

Uranus was exactly at the top of the chart crossing the Midheaven at Hiroshima, Japan, when the first atomic bomb exploded on August 6, 1945 at 8:15 in the morning. When Uranus is prominent in a Solar Return, you can expect the unexpected. A bolt from the blue will disrupt the status quo. It is often a time of shocking surprises – something you have taken for granted may suddenly disappear or no longer be available.

The house containing Uranus and any house(s) containing the sign Aquarius, especially houses with Aquarius on the cusp, determine the particular significations of Uranus in a given chart.

Neptune: Sometimes called the "higher octave of Venus," Neptune co-rules Pisces, the 12th sign of the zodiac. Neptune is associated with mystery, dreams, intuition, illusion, poetic imagination, altered states of consciousness, inspiration, compassion, idealism, glamour, spirituality, inner space, faith, music, myths, artistic endeavors, acting, hidden matters, mysterious circumstances, vagueness, evasion, confusion, carelessness, lack of clear boundaries, fog, clouds, liquids, gases, chemicals, hypnotics, drugs, role playing, make-believe, artifice, gullibility, unreality, lack of structure, merging, fusion, psychic experiences, seclusion, solitude, privacy, resignation, clandestine affairs, confinement, hospitalization, undiagnosed illness, hypersensitivity, hidden ailments, substance abuse, escapism, self-undoing, dissolution, fading away, sacrifice, selfless service, mysticism, otherworldliness, conspiracy, veiled motives, intrigue, fraud, cheating, misinformation, deception, careless mistakes, misrepresentation, con artists, scandal, the underdog.

The house containing Neptune and any house(s) containing the sign Pisces, especially houses with Pisces on the cusp, determine the particular significations of Neptune in a given chart.

Pluto: Sometimes called the "higher octave of Mars," Pluto co-rules Scorpio, the 8th sign of the zodiac. The god of the underworld, Pluto is connected with crises, powerful forces, life-changing events, the urge to reform, metamorphosis, transformation, transmutation, empowerment, research, investigation, depth understanding, penetration, sexuality, intense feelings, compulsions, upheaval, breakdown, eruption, near death experiences, fated events, turning points, once in a lifetime experiences, mass movements, power within a group, regeneration, rebirth, release, letting go, elimination, purging, purification, profound healing, waste removal, decay, refuse, surgery, débridement, invasive therapy, the need for repair or healing, atomic power, control, manipulation, pressure tactics, domination, terrorism, jealousy, resentment, love/hate relationships, abuse, extremes of behavior, fatal attraction, undercover activity, power brokers, matters of life and death, criminality, violence, clearing out the old to make way for the new.

When Pluto is prominent in a Solar Return, it often marks the year as a turning point that divides one's life into before and after, a time of major transformation. You may need to repair that which has broken down, to clear away the old and make way for the new.

The house containing Pluto and any house(s) containing the sign Scorpio, especially houses with Scorpio on the cusp, determine the particular significations of Pluto in a given chart.

Astrological Aspects in Solar Returns

As with the planets, you can use what you already know about astrological aspects when interpreting a Solar Return. By way of review, Ptolemy recognized as especially significant certain aspects or angular separations between signs or planets around the horoscope wheel. Pythagoras before him had discovered that particular measurements of length of cords corresponded to musical tones.

Certain numerical ratios appeared to recur in nature and form a fundamental part of the universe. For Ptolemy, the ratios of the musical notes on the scale became the basis for his understanding of astrological aspects. The Ptolemaic aspects (sextile, trine, square, opposition) represent the same ratios that are found in the tones of the Western musical scale – hence, the music of the spheres. Technically the conjunction is not an aspect but refers to two planets having the same longitude on the ecliptic, the path of the Sun along which measurements are made in the zodiac.

The *sextile* (60 degrees) and the *trine* (120 degrees) are often called soft or harmonious aspects; they represent an easy flow of energy. The *square* (90 degrees) and *opposition* (180 degrees) are called hard or stressful aspects. The hard aspects represent the dynamic interaction of energies and commonly result in some type of event or manifestation in physical reality. The *conjunction* (0 degrees) brings two energies, be they harmonious or conflicting, into direct contact. The effect of a conjunction depends on the natures of the planets involved and how their energies combine. Minor aspects such as the *semi-square* (45 degrees) and *sesqui-quadrate* or *sesqui-square* (135 degrees) resemble the square aspect in their effects.

Modern astrologers have mistakenly called the *quincunx* (150 degrees) an aspect. Ptolemy, however, regarded signs that are adjacent (*semi-sextile*, 30 degrees apart) or *quincunx* (150 degrees apart) as having no aspectual relationship because there is no analogous ratio in the Western musical scale. Instead Ptolemy called such relationships "*inconjunct*," "*disjunct*," or "*alien*." He regarded the inconjunct as an unfortunate state of being unable to be meaningfully joined – as when two people find they have nothing in common. Basically the astrological aspects unite planetary energies much as musical chords join together distinct notes of the musical scale. Just as certain musical notes are unable to combine their tones into a meaningful chord, signs that are inconjunct are unable to combine their energies in any valid astrological relationship. To quote Ptolemy (italics mine):

> "'Disjunct' and 'alien' are the names applied to those divisions of the zodiac which have none whatever of the aforesaid familiarities with one another. These are the ones which belong neither to the class of commanding or obeying, beholding or of equal power, and furthermore they are found to be *entirely without share in the four aforesaid aspects, opposition, trine, quartile, and sextile, and are either one or five signs apart*; for those which are one sign apart are as it were averted from one another and, though they are two, bound the angle of one, and those that are five signs apart divide the whole circle into unequal parts, while the other aspects make an equal division of the perimeter.[2]"

Experience has shown that the inconjunct (disjunct) relationship – being 30 or 150 degrees apart – is highly stressful, as if something were out of joint. Signs that are inconjunct bear 6th, 8th, or 12th house spacing from one another. Inconjuncts (semi-sextiles and quincunxes) in Solar Returns and in horary astrology herald stressful situations, illness, isolation, the need to let go, and sometimes danger of death. When the ascending sign of a Solar Return is disjunct the natal ascending sign, the native can expect a trying year. Although the semi-sextile is called "mildly favorable" in many modern textbooks, progressions and directions involving 30- and 150-degree angles tend to produce nasty results.

Paranatellonata (parans), measured on the Prime Vertical, are a special type of "diurnal" or "mundane" aspect formed between planets when each planet conjoins an Angle (ASC, DSC, MC, IC) of the chart. Often overlooked is the paran-square, which occurs when one planet lies on the horizon (east-west or ASC-DSC axis) and another planet lies on the meridian (north-south or MC-IC axis). Two such planets may or may not be in zodiacal square on the ecliptic but they are 90 degrees apart in the coordinate system involving the horizon and meridian. Because the planets are both angular on the ecliptic, paran-squares are powerfully stressful configurations. More will be said about parans when we discuss the work of James Eshelman on Solar Returns.

Parallels of Latitude and Declination

It is important to realize that aspects are measured on a circle called the ecliptic, which lies in a two-dimensional plane. In reality the planets are located in space in three dimensions and only rarely do planets travel in the plane of the ecliptic, which is the path of the Sun around the earth in a geocentric frame of reference. The horoscope used by astrologers is a two-dimensional map of a three-dimensional solar system. Astrologers have for millennia used additional methods to take into account planets traveling in planes other than that of the ecliptic. For example, the Hellenistic astrologer Dorotheus of Sidon, writing in Greek in the first half of the first century, stressed the importance of considering the latitudes of planets in addition to their location on the ecliptic.

Celestial latitude is a measure of how much the orbit of a planet is angled with respect to the ecliptic, the path of the Sun. Since the Sun travels on the ecliptic, it has 0 degrees of celestial latitude. The measure of a planet's celestial latitude together with its location along the ecliptic locates that planet on a grid in three-dimensional space. Two planets that share the same celestial latitude are said to be in *parallel of latitude*, which has a similar effect to being in conjunction. When two planets have equal but opposite celestial latitudes, one above and the other below the ecliptic, they are said to be in *contra-parallel of latitude*, which resembles being in opposition.

Similarly, *declination* is a measure of how much the orbit of a planet is angled with respect to the celestial equator. The measure of a planet's declination together with its location along the celestial equator (measured in *right ascension*) locates that planet on a grid in three-dimensional space. Two planets that share the same declination are said to be in *parallel of declination*, which is similar to being in conjunction. When two planets have equal but opposite declinations, one above and the other below the celestial equator, they are said to be in *contra-parallel of declination*, which resembles being in opposition.

Antiscia and Contra-antiscia

Yet another way planets can combine their energies is through conjunctions with each other's antiscia and contra-antiscia. More will be said about these points in a latter chapter. Suffice it to say here that antiscia are reflections of a planet's zodiacal position across the cardinal axis on which the Sun's solstice points occur. Similarly, contra-antiscia are reflections of a planet's zodiacal position across the cardinal axis on which the equinoxes occur. The contra-antiscion of a planet lies directly opposite its antiscion. Antiscial contacts are considered harmonious, and contra-antiscial contacts are considered stressful.

Predictive Techniques

Astrology has many ways to foretell when the potential of the birth chart will unfold in the life of the native. In this text we will be making use of the following:

• 	*Transits*. This refers to the actual daily movement of the planets in the solar system and the aspects that transiting planets make with points and planets in the natal or return chart. Morin paid special attention to transiting phenomena such as the equinoxes, the solstices, eclipses, New Moons, Full Moons, transits to fixed stars, and so on.

• 	*Directions*. The method of directions shifts the entire chart forward or backward (converse) by a particular angular distance (arc) that symbolically correlates to a certain date in one's life. In *primary directions*, according to Ptolemy, one degree of movement of the Midheaven, measured along the equator as the Earth turns after birth, correlates to one year of life; and the whole chart is carried forward at this rate. Morin preferred to calculate his primary directions at a slightly different rate, namely, the mean daily motion of the Sun along the equator (the Naibod rate). In *solar arc directions*, we calculate the difference between the position of the secondary progressed Sun and the natal Sun on a given day. Then we add this solar arc to every planet and point in the chart. Because the Sun travels about one degree per day, the number of degrees in the solar arc is more or less the same as the age of the native. Similar to solar arc directions, *Ascendant-arc* directions add the angular distance (arc) between the natal Ascendant and the secondary progressed Ascendant on a given day to each point and planet in the natal chart.

• *Progressions*. The method of progressions, like transits, is based on the actual motion of the planets except that the rate of motion is proportional to the actual daily motion by some formula such as one day after birth corresponds to one year of life (*secondary progressions*).

• *Returns (Revolutions)*. Every planet eventually makes a complete circuit of the horoscope wheel and revisits its original position in the zodiac. The new chart, cast for the exact moment and place on Earth when a planet makes a complete 360 degree revolution of the zodiac, is known as its return chart. The moment of completion of the planet's revolution is considered significant in unlocking the potential of the birth chart. The reader is referred to Celeste Teal's book *Identifying Planetary Triggers* for a good discussion of the various planetary returns as predictive techniques.

• *Eclipses*. During an eclipse the Earth, Sun, and Moon come into alignment. In a solar eclipse the Moon prevents the Sun's light from reaching the Earth. In a lunar eclipse, the Earth prevents the Sun's light from reaching the Moon. Traditional astrologers paid close attention to eclipses. Superimposing the chart of an eclipse on the natal or return chart is useful for forecasting. I have found that the chart of the first solar eclipse following the Solar Return is especially informative when laid upon the chart of the Solar Return.

• *Arabic Lots or Parts*. The so-called Arabic Lots or Parts are an ancient technique from pre-Hellenistic times. The Arabic Parts are particular points around the horoscope wheel that have special significance. They are derived from the positions of other points and planets in the chart by means of a formula such as: Part of Fortune = ASC + Moon – Sun, by day; and ASC + Sun – Moon, by night. The online encyclopedia *Wikipedia* says the following about interpreting the Part of Fortune:

> "... the *Lot of Fortune* was used to represent the body, fortune, health – in short, everything over which a person has little control in life. It was also used in place of the Ascendant thereby

changing the house-numbering, to find out more about these un-controllable factors. Lilly and his contemporaries used the Lot of Fortune as a simple indicator of material well-being and, in horary charts, a marker of success."[3]

In a later chapter we will also consider a useful modern part called Emerson's Point of Death.

•   *Fixed Stars.*[4] The interaction of a horoscope's points and planets, especially by conjunction or opposition, with particular fixed stars has always had predictive value in astrology. Due to precession of the equinoxes the fixed stars appear to move forward along the ecliptic at a rate of one degree every 72 years. Although there are countless fixed stars in the heavens, only a small number appear repeatedly in the literature and we will be meeting some of them later in this text.[5] Below are listed nine commonly used fixed stars in order of their 2010 positions on the ecliptic. To determine their ecliptic position in any other year, adjust the 2010 position by 50" (seconds) of arc for each year before or after the year 2010.

Caput Algol at 26° Taurus 18' is a nasty fixed star associated with misfortune, violence, disaster, beheading, murder, and sudden death.

Alcyone of the Pleiades at 00° Gemini 08' is one of the weeping sisters; she gives you something to cry about. Alcyone has been associated with violent death and with loss caused by fire or by one's enemies. The seven sisters of the Pleiades at 00° Gemini 06' are associated with accidents, violence and blindness.[6]

Sirius, the "Dog Star," at 14° Cancer 13' in the year 2010, is the largest most brilliant star in the heavens. A binary star, Sirius was known in ancient Greece and Egypt as "the Brightly Radiating One." Astrologically Sirius is linked to eminence, fame, high office, renown, wealth, ambition, worldly influence, and honors beyond the grave. The Dog Star is also connected with dog bites – go figure! Some astrologers have attributed America's role as a 20th century superpower to the conjunction of the Dog Star with the U.S. July 4, 1776 natal Sun. At the end of World War II the zodiacal longitude of Sirius was 13° Cancer 19' – the exact position as the USA Sun in the 5:10 PM Sibly Sagittarius rising chart for the Declaration of Independence. In the year 2018, Sirius will be at 14° Cancer 19', a full degree past the USA natal Sun (Sibley), perhaps marking the decline of the United States as a world superpower as Sirius moves beyond the traditional one-degree orb for conjunctions with fixed stars.

Regulus at 29° Leo 58'. William Lilly regarded Regulus (the heart of the Lion) as a fortunate royal star associated with glory, power, status, wealth, honors, connections with important people, and high positions in life – especially when conjoined with Jupiter. Robson attributed to Regulus "violence, destructiveness, military honor of short duration with ultimate failure, imprisonment, violent death, success, high and lofty ideals and strength of spirit."[7]

Vindemiatrix at 10° Libra 04' is associated with widowhood, falsity, disgrace, stealing, and wanton folly.

Spica at 23° Libra 59' and *Arcturus* at 24° Libra 22' are a pair of fortunate stars associated with good luck, wealth, fame, success, and honor.

Antares at 9° Sagittarius 54' is a royal star at the heart of the constellation Scorpio. It is linked to honors, riches, adventure, military acumen, dare-devil behavior, self-destructive obstinacy, eye problems, and violent injury or death.

Scheat at 29° Pisces 31' has been tied to misfortune, loss of life in catastrophes, murder, suicide, and drowning.

A Note on Notation

The literature refers to Solar Returns in various ways. The following terms are used more or less synonymously:

Solar Return
SR chart
Annual chart
Solar revolution
Return chart (this term refers to the return of any planet to its natal position)

Similarly, the literature has many names for the birth chart, including:

Birth chart (figure, map)
Nativity (the chart of the native)
Geniture
Radix (from the Latin *radix* meaning root)
Radical chart (chart of the radix)
Natal chart

An Essential Lock and Key Metaphor

As you read this book, keep in mind the following metaphor, which captures the traditional idea of how Solar Returns function as forecasting tools. *The Solar Return is a key that, in any given year, unlocks certain potentials of the birth chart.* Imagine that you find a key on the sidewalk. You can study that key and make educated guesses about what type of lock it fits and what type of building it opens. Sometimes the key alone can be quite informative; but a complete picture will not emerge until you find the corresponding lock, insert the key, open the door, and go inside. As a key, the Solar Return of each year will fit certain facets of the natal chart and will allow the astrologer entry to identify those birth potentials that are likely to manifest in the year ahead. Many modern astrologers forget this basic principle and try to solve the mystery of the return chart by studying the key without its corresponding lock – considering only the annual chart without reference to the nativity. How much more could they learn if only they were to look at the entire picture!

In the next chapter we will formally define the Solar Return and take a preliminary look at the method used by the French astrologer Alexandre Volguine to unlock its secrets. The Solar Return has a long and rich tradition in Western astrology. We will need to consider many ideas and methods from centuries past, especially the teachings of another French astrologer, the brilliant Jean-Baptiste Morin de Villefranche. Along the way we will study numerous charts to critique these methods and bring the ideas to life. Unless otherwise specified, all Solar Return charts illustrated in this book will be in the *non-precessed tropical* format. Because so many astrology programs are available for personal computers to generate return charts, we will not be giving detailed instructions for the manual calculation of a Solar Revolution.

NOTES

1. Lester J. Ness, Miami University Oxford, Ohio, *Astrology and Judaism in Late Antiquity*, 1990, at http://www.smoe.org/arcana/diss1.html.
2. Claudius Ptolemy. *Tetrabiblos I: 16, Of Disjunct Signs*. F.E. Robbins translation. Loeb Classical Library, 1940, pp. 77-79.
3. http://en.wikipedia.org/wiki/Arabian_Parts.
4. Detailed information about the meaning of fixed stars in astrology can be found online at http://www.winshop.com.au/annew/.
5. See Anthony Louis, *Horary Astrology Plain & Simple*, Llewellyn, 1998, pp. 241-245.
6. A useful listing of fixed stars and their astrological associations can be found online at http://www.astrologycom.com/fixedstars.html.
7. Vivian Robson quoted at http://www.winshop.com.au/annew/new_page_1.htm.

2

Many Happy Returns - The Technique of Alexandre Volguine

We have all heard the expression "many happy returns," but how many of us have paused to consider its meaning? Eastern cultures may use this phrase to refer to the idea of reincarnation and to wish happiness in a next life. In the western tradition, however, astrology for centuries has attached special significance to a complete revolution of the Sun, that is, the return of the Sun to its original position in the birth chart. In a sense each year we are "born again" at the moment the Sun returns to its birthplace.

Our birthdays are typically occasions for celebration with family and friends. As we mark another year of life, we reflect on where we have been and where we are going. Astrology seeks to determine the special significance of each birthday by use of a specialized chart – the Solar Return – cast for the exact time that the Sun returns to its original position at the time of our birth. In theory the state of the heavens at the moment of our Solar Return will reflect the current year's astrological significance, that is, which parts of the natal chart will be highlighted in the year ahead. The Solar Return is the annual key that unlocks certain potentials of the birth chart.

In any given year the Solar Return – your astrological birthday – may fall on the same day as your regular birthday, or it may be a day or two earlier or later. This discrepancy occurs because the civil year of 365 days (366 days during leap years) differs in length from the astronomical year (the time it takes the Sun to make a complete revolution in its apparent motion, which is about 365 ¼ days). For example, a child born at 00.00 AM on New Year's Day in 2006 experiences a Solar Return at 5:45:53 AM a year later on January 1, 2007, because it takes the Sun about a quarter of a day longer to return to its original zodiacal position of the year before. [1]

The 12th century Jewish astrologer Abraham ben Meir ibn Ezra of Spain used the difference in the length of the calendar and astronomical years to develop a simple yet remarkably accurate technique for calculating Solar Returns. David McCann says of Abraham ibn Ezra:

"One ingenious idea is his method of calculating Solar Returns. One year is approximately 365 days, 5 hours, 49 minutes in length. This means that the first return occurs 5 hours 49 minutes after the birth time and each successive return is later than the previous one by the same amount. Using this method, Abraham could get reliable returns, by-passing the inaccuracy of the old ephemeredes. Even for a middle-aged client, the error was only 10 minutes; by contrast, the error in the returns of Lilly and his contemporaries could be half an hour or more."[2]

As with most astrological techniques, the method of Solar Returns is a theme with many variations. In calculating Solar Return charts astrologers may argue for and against using a particular zodiac, a particular house system, the precession of the equinoxes due to the wobble of the earth's axis, and so on. Rather than engage in such theoretical arguments, this book will take as its starting point the well-researched and empirically validated method of Alexandre Volguine,[3] who developed his method within the tradition of the 17th century French astrological giant, Jean-Baptiste Morin de Villefranche. We will repeatedly test the observations of our astrological forebears against current charts to see if their findings still hold water.

Alexandre Volguine and his book: *The Technique of Solar Returns*

Volguine was one of the leading figures in 20th century French astrology. Born in the Ukraine, he moved to France in his youth. In 1938 Alexandre Volguine founded an influential astrological journal, which he continued to publish until his death in 1976. His many interests included the use of decanates, Hindu navasmas, Arabic parts, multicultural astrological traditions, chart rulers, Solar Returns , and planetary containment (encadrement). According to Gavin Kent McClung, Volguine "placed special emphasis upon the sequence into which natal planets fall when proceeding through the zodiacal wheel in a horoscope"[4]

Volguine's book, *The Technique of Solar Returns*, which first appeared in 1937, summarized a decade and a half of meticulous research into how Solar Returns functioned in the lives of his clients. After first publishing this book in French in 1937, Volguine continued to test and revise his findings, presenting his new material on Solar Returns in subsequent editions. Fortunately for us, the result was a system of interpreting Solar Returns that has undergone decades of testing and refinement by Volguine and his students. After his death in 1976 the book went out of print and may be difficult to find. One of my hopes with this volume is to preserve Volguine's method, developed in the tradition of Morin de Villefranche, and to make it more accessible to modern astrologers.

Volguine's Basic Assumptions

The remainder of this chapter will review Volguine's basic assumptions and caveats about interpreting Solar Returns. Rather than simply making theoretical points about Solar Returns, Volguine emphasized a method that was reliable and tested in countless charts of actual clients. He did not argue against the validity of other methods but instead presented his technique, which he had substantiated through experience.

It would be a mistake to conclude that because his methods were rooted in the astrology of the early 20th century, Volguine would be opposed to more modern methods. If anything, he was open-minded and welcomed new ideas. Nonetheless, his ideas are of early 20th century French astrology and some of them may seem a bit antiquated to the modern reader. The proof of the pudding, however, is in the eating. Outlined below are the core assumptions and recommendations that form the basis of Volguine's method.

• *Volguine used Placidus Houses.* Volguine based his findings on the Placidean system of houses, which was in vogue in early 20th century France. A key factor in Volguine's system is the interpretation of the relationships between the Solar Return houses and the natal houses of the horoscope. Further research would be needed to determine whether other systems of house division give equally valid results. Many modern astrologers continue to use Placidus houses. Eshelman, a sidereal astrologer, favors the Campanus system. Penfield prefers the house system of Porphyry. Volguine's predecessor, Jean-Baptiste Morin and his British contemporary William Lilly were strong proponents of Regiomontanus houses. Morin provides many compelling examples of the use of Regiomontanus houses in his own classic text on solar and lunar revolutions. Morin also used information from the Whole Sign house system, which consists of using each sign of the zodiac as a house where the Ascendant indicates which whole sign represents the first house.[5] We will study Morin's contributions in more detail later in this text.

• *Volguine used the tropical zodiac.* Based on the seasons of the year, the tropical zodiac is the one that readers are familiar with from daily horoscopes in the newspaper. The apparent circular path of the Sun around the earth in the course of a year is divided mathematically into twelve equal parts called the signs of the zodiac. Each season of the year (spring, summer, fall, and winter) consists of three consecutive zodiacal signs. These tropical signs derive their names from the constellations of fixed stars that shared those same positions in the sky about 2000 years ago. By definition, the tropical zodiac always begins at 0° of Aries, the vernal equinox or the first day of spring, regardless of which constellation of fixed stars 0° of Aries happens to occupy due to the precession of the equinoxes. In contrast, the sidereal zodiac is based on the positions of the planets relative to the backdrop of fixed stars. The tropical and sidereal zodiacs are distinct but related ways of measuring the positions of planets, much as Fahrenheit and Celsius are different but related techniques for measuring temperature. As mentioned previously, this text will focus on the use of the tropical zodiac in delineating Solar Returns.

•   *Volguine used the modern rulers of the signs of the zodiac.* Volguine used Uranus as the modern ruler of Aquarius, Neptune for Pisces, and Pluto for Scorpio. In Morin's time these modern planets had not yet been discovered. My own practice is to use primarily the traditional rulers of the zodiacal signs as rulers of house cusps but also to consider the modern planets as co-rulers. I have found this practice useful, and several charts will be presented to illustrate this point so that the reader can decide. Recall that in classical astrology Saturn rules Aquarius; Jupiter, Pisces; and Mars, Scorpio. The noted astrologer Rob Hand, who at one time was an advocate of Koch houses, now uses only the traditional rulers of house cusps and prefers the method of Whole Sign houses, which Morin also used as a supplement to the information he gained from Regiomontanus houses.

•   *Volguine did not adjust the chart for precession of the equinoxes.* According to Ellie Crystal, "precession is like a star clock that helps us date the rotations of earth in our solar system through our galaxy."[6] As the earth spins on its axis, it acts like a rotating toy top. About every 26,000 years the tilt of the earth's axis makes a complete circle in a direction opposite to the spin of the earth. As a result, each point on the ecliptic (the path of the sun), when measured against the backdrop of fixed stars, appears to move backward in the zodiac at a rate of one degree every 72 years. Thus at age 72 a person's Solar Return, corrected for precession, will not occur until the Sun reaches a point on the ecliptic an entire degree past its natal position. Many modern authors have found that that adjusting for precession produces meaningful Solar Returns, but neither Volguine nor Morin made use of this precessional adjustment. My own experience suggests that both the precessed and the non-precessed Solar Return charts give valuable information, each chart having its own point of view. The non-precessed chart seems to be more psychological and inner-directed whereas the precessed chart appears more event-oriented and outwardly directed. Often the key events of a year will "jump out" at you though the angular prominence of planets in the precessed Solar Return chart.

•   *Volguine cast the Solar Return chart for the actual location of the individual at the moment that the Sun returns to its natal position.* In today's world a person can be almost anywhere on the globe at the time of the Solar Return. To use the methods of Volguine or Morin, the astrologer must ascertain the person's actual whereabouts at the time of the Sun's return. The idea is that you can only be where you are, that is, you can only celebrate your astrological birthday in the place where you are at the time of the Sun's return. In doing research on notable people who travel a great deal, it may be difficult to discover where they actually spent their Solar Return. Sometimes when studying celebrities we must resort to other potentially meaningful charts at the time of the Sun's return. These alternative charts are basically relocated Solar Return charts cast for the birth place, the place of residence, the place of a major event during the year, and so on. As relocated charts, these alternative Solar Returns will be meaningful but will not be as informative as the actual Solar Return, could its true location be verified. Some astrologers have utilized the ideas of Volguine and Morin to advise a client where to travel for a Solar Return to assure a favorable year and minimize any adverse factors in the chart. This idea of altering your fate by freely choosing the location of your Solar Return appears to have originated in the teachings of Morin de Villefranche. We will study Morin's aphorisms regarding Solar Returns in a later chapter.

•   *Never interpret the Solar Return in isolation.* The Solar Return chart can only be interpreted in the context of other considerations, most importantly with regard to the promise of the natal chart, but also with reference to the current progressions, directions, lunar and other returns, eclipses, transits, and with reference to the prior and subsequent Solar Returns. Jean-Baptiste Morin[7] repeatedly emphasized the importance of interpreting the Solar Return (or solar revolution, as he called it) in the context of the natal chart. Attempts to read a Solar Return without reference to these other factors can cause significant errors in judgment because, for a given individual, the planets, regardless of their general nature or status in a return, also always mean what they signify in the birth chart. Some modern astrologers have given up on Solar Returns because they have tried to interpret returns as stand-alone charts without reference to the promise of the nativity or to the natal progressions and directions in effect during the current year. *If something is not already promised in the natal chart, it cannot be delivered by a solar revolution.* As mentioned previously, the Solar Return is a key that unlocks potentials of the birth chart, according to its similarity to natal factors. In judging a solar revolution, it is important to consider the following questions: Where was a planet in the birth chart and where did it move to in the return? What role did a planet play in the natal chart and what role does it play in the return? How similar, different, or contradictory are the roles played by the same planet in each chart?

•   *Always interpret the Solar Return chart in the context of the birth chart.* A full understanding of the Solar Return depends on the superimposition of the Solar Return and natal charts. Nothing significant happens in a person's life that is not already promised in the birth chart. The return chart acts to release certain natal potentials so that they are able to manifest in the current year. In many ways the interpretation of the Solar Return is a study of the synastry between the birth horoscope and the chart of the current astrological birthday. Throughout one's life the planets always carry with them their individualized birth meanings derived from the natal houses that they occupy or rule in the natal chart. At the end of this chapter we will consider the chart of a minister whose natal Saturn rules her Capricorn Midheaven (honors, career, accomplishments). She assumed greater responsibility in the church during a year in which her annual Saturn appeared in the Solar Return 9th house of religious matters.

•   *Volguine used the Moon to time Solar Returns in a way similar to that of secondary progressions, namely, by the formula "a day for a year."* A key premise of Solar Returns is that the 24 hours following the Sun's return to its birth position can be mapped proportionally onto the coming year. Thus the first two hours following the Sun's return correspond roughly to the first month after the birthday, the second two hours to the second month, and so on. The projection of a solar day following the Solar Return onto the year ahead allows the astrologer to progress the Solar Return chart and discover when events are likely to unfold.

Volguine also timed events from the Solar Return by advancing the chart with the formula: one year = 360 degrees around the wheel. This idea derives from the writings of the old Arabic astrologers like Al-Qabisi (Alcabitius) who timed events from the Solar Return by equating the year of 365 days and 6 hours to the 360 degrees of the Equator. Morin was critical of this technique for timing because it did not take into account the latitude of the Solar Return.[8] Morin advanced the Solar Return on the basis of the formula that the mean daily motion of the Sun is the measure of each day of the year. For directing charts Morin used the mathematically rigorous system of primary directions, which many modern astrologers tend to avoid because of the arduous calculations involved.[9]

•   *The Solar Return Ascendant acts like a weathervane, showing which way the astrological wind will blow in the coming year.* The Solar Return Ascendant – and in fact, the entire annual ascending sign – indicates, by what it highlights in the birth chart, the central themes for the year ahead. To use a naval analogy, the annual Ascendant points to the kinds of waters (which parts of the birth chart) the native will be navigating in the year ahead. Or, to use our lock and key analogy, the Solar Return Ascendant is the blade of the key that inserts into the lock, which is the birth chart. When comparing the Solar Return with the birth chart, the natal house containing the Solar Return Ascendant, and the natal houses containing the zodiacal sign of the Solar Return Ascendant, reveal the most significant events and conditions currently facing the individual. The planetary ruler of the annual Ascendant and its dispositor are also quite significant. The placement of the natal Ascendant in the Solar Return chart is also important.

• *If the Solar Return Ascendant conjoins the natal Ascendant (within 5 degrees), the year will be one of major importance – a year when the potential of the birth chart can most easily manifest because the angles of the birth chart are being repeated in the current year.* A useful metaphor may be to view the birth chart and its potentials as akin to a loaded gun and the repetition of natal factors in the Solar Return as equivalent to pulling the trigger. A conjunction of the annual Ascendant with any angle of the natal chart is important because the angles are especially powerful. If the annual Ascendant falls on one of the other angles of the natal chart (cusps of the 4th house – home, family, endings, the grave; the 7th house – marriage, partnerships, rivalries, dealings with the public; or the 10th house – career, reputation, honors, authority figures), then events related to the natal houses highlighted by the Solar Return Ascendant will become prominent. The Solar Return house and sign position of the planet ruling the annual Ascendant give further indications of major themes for the year ahead. Affairs of the natal houses containing the planet ruling the Solar Return Ascendant and its dispositor will also be emphasized.

• *Solar Return planets that occupy the Solar Return 1st house show the nature of the individual's activity and psychological reactions during the coming year.* According to Volguine, if a 1st house planet lies close to the annual Ascendant, the individual tends to have more personal control over the action. First house planets lying farther away from the annual Ascendant suggest that the individual has less personal control and is more at the mercy of the forces symbolized by those planets. I'm not sure how valid this principle of Volguine is in actual practice.[10] The reader may want to test this idea against case examples with 1st house planets later in this text. For example, in the Solar Return for the year of a miscarriage, the Sun and Saturn appear toward the end of the first house of the return chart (see Sara's baby below).

• *Volguine advocated the interpretation of house cusp placements in the superimposed Solar Return and natal charts.* Following Morin's teachings about house cusps as the power points of each house, Volguine delineated all the combinations of natal house cusps falling within the houses of the Solar Return chart, and vice versa. For example, in Richard Nixon's 1974 Solar Return for Washington, DC, his Solar Return Leo Ascendant falls in the 12th house of his natal chart. Volguine would have told Nixon that this Solar Return 1st house cusp placement in the natal 12th house is "a dangerous position indicating a year of ordeal," possibly involving "secret enemies…calumnies and snares of all kinds, gossip…lawsuits…the health always suffers…psychological collapse…[11]" We will look at Nixon's chart in more detail in a later chapter.

Sara's Baby Revisited

Readers of my 1991 book on horary astrology will recall the horary question asked by my friend Sara, "Is the baby healthy?" Sara, who was pregnant in the summer of 1987, was worried about the health of the fetus. At that time I was still a novice at horary astrology; and when Sara and I tried to analyze the horary chart, the answer seemed overwhelmingly negative. Doubting my own abilities as a horary astrologer, I tried to reassure Sara that the baby would be fine. Nonetheless, a few days later (on August 12, 1987) the ultrasound confirmed that the fetus had died. I was so shocked by the accuracy of the horary methods that I went on to research and write a book on the topic.

Recently I was talking with Sara about this book on Solar Returns, which I was in the midst of writing. She suggested looking at her returns for the time of the miscarriage in 1987 and also for the birth of her son a year later, in July of 1988. Back in the 1980s I had experimented with Solar Returns but found them confusing and difficult to fathom because I had no systematic method to follow (my natal Sun lies in Virgo). Only in the past decade, after becoming familiar with the writings of Volguine and Morin, do I feel more confident in analyzing solar revolutions.

Sara resides in New York City where she was born on November 28, 1949 "a little after 6 AM." Over the years I have found that a birth time of 6:05 AM works well for the events in her life (Figure 1). In fact, if she were born at precisely 6:05:22 AM, her primary directed Midheaven (at one degree per year in right ascension) would have exactly semi-squared her natal Saturn on August 12, 1987, the day of her depressing ultrasound. In Sara's birth chart Mars rules the Aries 5th house of children. Natal Mars conjoins natal Saturn and opposes the natal Moon, a natural signifier of children, in the 4th house of home and family. There are clear indications in the natal chart of a potential for deprivation or hardship with regard to pregnancy and children. Fortunately natal Mars, the ruler of the natal 5th of children, also trines benefic natal Venus, so the possibility of a successful pregnancy also exists in the nativity.

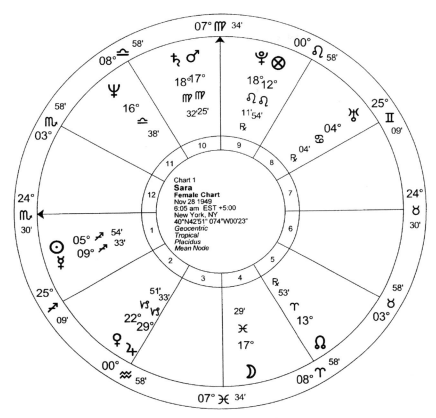

Figure 1: Sara Natal Chart

The angles of Sara's 1986 Solar Return (Figure 2) are almost identical with those of her birth chart, indicating that 1986 will be a highly significant and memorable year. The more closely the return chart resembles the nativity, the more powerfully it acts to manifest the natal potential in a given year. The Solar Return Ascendant occupies the natal 12th house of loss and sorrow, so that 12th house issues (sorrow) will come to the fore during this Solar Return year (birthday 1986 to birthday 1987). The most angular planet in the Solar Return is annual Mars on the return IC (family, home, endings). Mars happens to rule Sara's 5th house of pregnancy and children as well as her Ascendant (her body and vitality) in both the annual and the birth charts. Hence issues related to children and her physical well-being will be prominent. The Sun occupies the return 1st house (her body) where it conjoins annual Saturn (deprivation). This annual Sun/Saturn conjunction in the return 1st house squares both annual Mars and annual Jupiter in the return 4th house of family

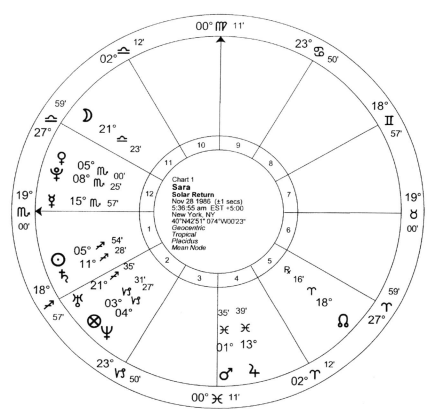

Figure 2: Sara 1986 Solar Return prior to miscarriage

and endings, a house which Jupiter also rules. Finally the natal 12th house cusp conjoins Solar Return Venus, ruler of the annual 12th of sorrow. The annual chart clearly presages sadness, health issues, endings, domestic concerns, and difficulties involving children.

Sara's 1987 Solar Return (Figure 3) paints a very different picture. Aquarius rises in the annual chart, making Saturn and Uranus the rulers of the Solar Return. Annual Saturn and Uranus conjoin at the beginning of her annual 11th house of hopes, wishes, and good fortune. The 1987 annual Saturn/ Uranus conjunction also aligns with the "lesser benefic" annual Venus (in the annual 11th) and receives a trine from the "greater benefic" annual Jupiter, which falls in the natal 5th house of children. The Sun (vitality) is strong in the return 10th house where it conjoins the Midheaven; in fact, the Sun is the only truly angular planet in her 1987 Solar Return. Sara's son was born in late July 1988 with his Sun in the early degrees of Leo, ruled by the Sun. Annual

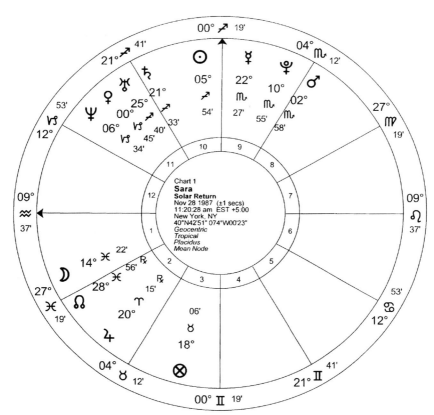

Figure 3: Sara 1987 Solar Return prior to birth of son

Mercury rules the annual 5th house of pregnancy and conjoins the natal Ascendant, making children's issues prominent. Furthermore the Solar Return Ascendant is almost exactly sextile natal Mercury. Things look favorable for her health and the birth of a child during her 1987-88 Solar Return year.

A Minister Advances Her Career
Let us now consider the chart of another friend of mine, a minister born May 31, 1951 at 2:30 AM EDT in Brooklyn, New York (Figure 4). In 2004 she achieved a position of greater responsibility and prominence within her church. Her birth chart reveals a strong interest in the ministry as evidenced by the following natal factors:

•   Jupiter, ruler of the spiritual signs Sagittarius and Pisces, occupies the natal first house.

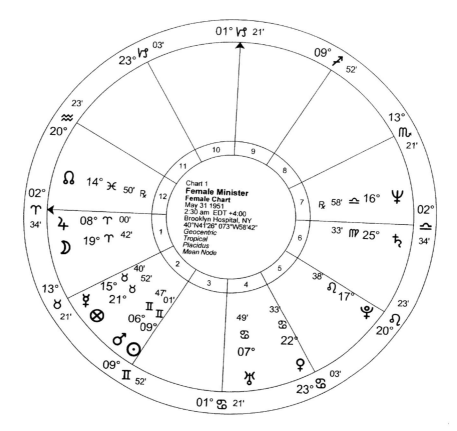

Figure 4: Natal Chart of Female Minister

- Jupiter rules her natal 9th house of philosophy and religion.
- Jupiter conjoins her Ascendant, indicating that Jupiter-ruled matters will be especially important in her life.
- Jupiter trines her Placidus 9th house cusp of church matters.
- Natal Sun, which is conjunct the natal Placidus 3rd house cusp (communication), closely opposes the natal 9th house cusp (the ministry). Morin taught that each house also partakes of the significance of the house opposite.
- Natal Saturn rules her 10th house of vocation and occupies Virgo, a sign of service, in the natal 6th house of ministering to the needs of others.

In the summer of 2004 she received a significant promotion within her church. The data for her Solar Return are May 29, 2004 at 10:07 PM EDT in Fairfield, Connecticut (Figure 5). If we superimpose her natal chart upon the Solar Return chart, we find that the natal Midheaven closely conjoins the Solar Return Ascendant, highlighting this as an important year for career, honors, and public standing. Recall that the Solar Return Ascendant points to that part of the natal chart that will be emphasized or in ascendancy during the year ahead.

Her natal Saturn (ruler of her natal 10th house of career and 11th house of hopes and wishes) exactly conjoins the Solar Return 9th house cusp of religious affairs. Volguine repeatedly observed that planets closely conjunct house cusps in the superimposed natal and return charts are extremely important. Saturn is especially prominent in 2004 because it rules her Solar Return Ascendant. Saturn also rules her natal Midheaven (career). In the

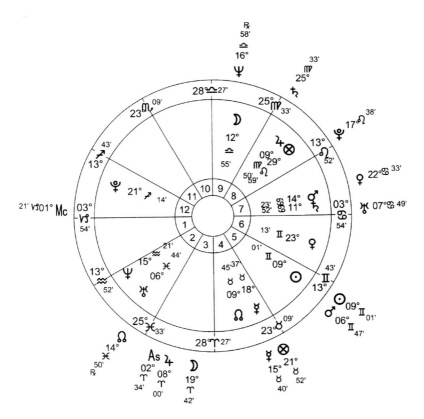

Figure 5: Minister's Natal Chart Superimposed on Solar Return

superimposed charts natal Saturn exactly aligns with the annual 9ᵗʰ house cusp (church matters). In addition, annual Saturn is disposed by the annual Moon, which occupies the 9ᵗʰ house of religion in the return chart; and the annual 9ᵗʰ house Moon, in turn, trines the Solar Return Sun.

Finally, annual Venus – the ruler of the Solar Return Libra 10ᵗʰ house of career – trines the annual Midheaven and also trines natal Neptune, a co-ruler of the natal 12ᵗʰ house (spirituality).

To summarize, the following close connections between the natal and Solar Return charts enable us to pinpoint the emphasis in the year ahead:

- Solar Return Ascendant, which occupies the natal 10ᵗʰ house of career, conjoins the natal Midheaven signaling an important year for professional achievement and public status.
- Natal Saturn (ruling natal 10ᵗʰ house of vocation and public standing) conjoins the Solar Return 9ᵗʰ house cusp, highlighting career-related church matters.
- Natal Neptune, a natural ruler of spirituality, occupies the Solar Return 9ᵗʰ house of church affairs and closely trines Solar Return Neptune, which lies on the Solar Return 2ⁿᵈ house cusp of income.
- The annual Moon, which occupies the Solar Return 9ᵗʰ house of religion, trines the Sun.
- Annual Midheaven-ruler Venus trines natal Neptune (ruler of the natal 12ᵗʰ) in the Solar Return 9ᵗʰ house.

NOTES

1. Astronomers have noted that the mean tropical year appears to be slowing down. According to *wikipedia.com*, "the mean tropical year, measured in SI days, is getting shorter. It was 365.2423 SI days at about AD 200, and is currently near 365.2422 SI days. SI refers to the International System of Units (abbreviated SI from the French *Le Système international d'unitiés*)" See: http://en.wikipedia.org/wiki/Solar_year.
2. http://www.skyscript.co.uk/ezra.html.
3. According to *AstroDataBank*: In Volguine's book, *Ruler of the Nativities*, he cites a rectified time of 5:45:13 AM LMT, with a recorded time of 5:45, on March 3, 1903, in Novaya Pragan, Ukraine, 48N33; 32E54. Rated A.
4. Gavin Kent McClung, 'A SALUTE TO OUR HERITAGE: What Makes A True Astrologer? *Dell Horoscope*, June 2000, pp. 66-77.

5.   The following is quoted with permission from a description of Rob Hand's book on Whole Sign Houses at http://www.johnhayes.biz/store/view_product.php? product=WHOEVABX4:

> "After several years of research into the oldest texts of our astrological tradition we now know what the earliest house system was. And in a way it was not a house system at all as we understand house systems. Rather, it was the signs of the zodiac, themselves, used as a house system. In this system the rising degree of the zodiac marks the sign it is located in as the 1st house. The rising sign itself thus becomes the 1st house, as we would refer to it, from its very beginning to its end, regardless of where in the sign the rising degree may fall. The next sign to rise after the rising sign becomes the 2nd house and so forth. It is not that the signs were used as houses so much as there were no houses at all, merely the signs of the zodiac used as we would use houses, with no second, separate, twelve-fold division of the chart at all. Whole Sign Houses describes this oldest way of dealing with houses, and shows how effective it can be in modern astrology, so effective in fact that the author (as well as many other students of traditional astrology) has completely given up on modern house systems."

6.   http://www.crystalinks.com/precession.html.

7.   Jean-Baptiste Morin, *Astrologia Gallica: Book Twenty-Two Directions*, translated by James H. Holden, AFA, Tempe, Arizona, 1994, Selections from Book Twenty-Three, pages 257-270.

8.   Morin, *Book 23*, translated by James Holden, AFA, 2003, p. 106.

9.   I highly recommend Bob Makransky's book on Primary Directions, available at this website: http://www.dearbrutus.com/

10.   For example astrologer Marc Penfield (personal communication) was involved in a freak accident in 2004. A truck crashed through the window of a café where he was having his morning tea. He was nearly killed and had little control over what happened (except that he tried to dive out of the way of the oncoming vehicle). The 1st house of his Solar Return for that year had Neptune close to the Ascendant with Uranus and Mars far from the Ascendant toward the end of the 1st house. Certainly he had little control over the accident symbolized by Uranus/Mars late in the return 1st house. Perhaps his attempt to take control by diving out of the path of the out-of-control vehicle is symbolized by Neptune near the Ascendant.

11.   Alexandre Volguine, *The Technique of Solar Returns*, ASI Publishers, New York, 1978, p. 25.

3

The Annual Ascendant and Midheaven, the Superimposition of Houses, and the Dignities of the Planets

Morin and Volguine stressed the importance of the Ascendant and Midheaven – and their corresponding 1st and 10th houses – as the most powerful regions of the chart. The angular 1st and 10th houses are followed in strength by their opposite 7th and 4th houses. In any given year these powerful angular regions of the Solar Return chart will activate certain potentials of the natal chart. Because of the overarching power of the Ascendant, which represents and uniquely locates the individual at the moment of the Solar Return, the Ascendant/1st house is a logical staring point for the interpretation of the annual chart.

The "annual" Ascendant of the Solar Return chart acts like a supercharged point of energy that activates whatever it touches by location, conjunction, or aspect in the natal or return charts. A planet conjunct the Solar Return Ascendant often denotes major events related to the nature of the planet or the houses that the planet rules in the natal or return charts. For example, if the 7th house-ruler conjoins the annual Ascendant, it may indicate the year that one marries or divorces. Uranus conjunct the annual Ascendant (or prominent within the annual 1st house) can signify an accident, a period of disruption, or a sudden event caused by the actions of the individual.

The entire sign ascending in the Solar Return is activated by virtue of its containment of the annual Ascendant. The annual rising sign acts like a concentrated beam of light that illuminates and energizes a key 30-degree segment of the birth chart when the natal and annual figures are superimposed. Any house cusps ruled by the annual ascending sign become especially prominent because they reveal which natal houses are "rising" or coming into ascendancy in the year ahead. The planetary ruler of the annual Ascendant becomes highly charged, as does the dispositor of the Ascendant-ruler, that is, the planet ruling the sign that the Ascendant-ruler occupies.

To summarize, a study of the annual Ascendant reveals which features of the natal chart are activated or "rising" and thus likely to manifest. Various factors in the Solar Return serve to stimulate potentials in the natal chart and spur them on to fruition. Morin emphasized the importance of the annual Ascendant and also identified the notion of similarity as a primary activating principle, stating that *"the revolution either brings forth or inhibits the effect of the nativity, and it can only bring it forth from a similarity of figures..."*[1] The more the Solar Return resembles or repeats the configurations of the birth chart, the more those natal potentials are likely to be triggered into action during the coming year. Similarity breeds manifestation.

Volguine's Delineation of the Solar Return Ascendant Superimposed on the Natal Houses

To give the reader a flavor of Volguine's approach to interpreting the superimposition of the houses of the annual and natal charts, I will summarize some of his findings. Below is a synopsis of Volguine's keywords for delineating the Solar Return Ascendant when superimposed on the natal houses. Volguine is referring not only to the natal house occupied by the Solar Return Ascendant but also to the natal houses that have the annual Ascendant sign on their cusps. The natal house containing the annual Ascendant, however, is most important. Also significant are aspects that the annual Ascendant forms with natal planets and house cusps. Both Volguine and Morin used a 5-degree orb for aspects involving house cusps, and Volguine extended that orb to 8 or 9 degrees for the angular houses (1, 4, 7, and 10).

The list below is intended to convey an overview of Volguine's ideas about house superimpositions, and it follows the traditionally understood meanings of the houses. Volguine stressed that the Ascendant refers to actions undertaken with the free will of the native and also to the consequences of those actions. The natal house position highlighted by the superimposed annual Ascendant and its corresponding 1st house usually identifies the major themes for the year. Morin pointed out that each house accidentally takes on the meanings of the one opposite. Thus, for example, the annual Ascendant falling in the natal 2nd house will also highlight 8th house issues.

Themes highlighted by the superimposition of the annual Ascendant (and its corresponding 1st house) onto the natal chart:
- Annual Ascendant superimposed *on the Natal 1st house*: freedom of choice, new enterprises, one's body and health, personal projects, the ability to fulfill the promise of the birth chart.
- Annual Ascendant superimposed *on the Natal 2nd house*: income, finances, movable goods, possessions, acquisitions, bills, expenses, money lent, business accomplishments.

- Annual Ascendant superimposed *on the Natal 3rd house*: siblings, relatives, one's associations, people close at hand, travel, short trips, vehicles, mental work, communication, writing, speaking, literary work, editing.
- Annual Ascendant superimposed *on the Natal 4th house*: home, residence, relocation, the parents, family matters, domestic concerns, foundations, establishment, desire for stability, significant endings, the completion of a project, the end of life.
- Annual Ascendant superimposed *on the Natal 5th house*: love, romance, fun, getting engaged, matters related to children, pregnancy, the birth of a child, creative projects, offspring of the body or the mind, the arts, speculation, gambling, risk taking, technical instruction. Volguine often found that the annual Ascendant and Uranus both fell in the natal 5th house of women who suffered miscarriages during the year.
- Annual Ascendant superimposed *on the Natal 6th house*: duties, obligations, tedious work, domestic problems, health concerns, sickness, lack of energy, weariness, worry, exhaustion.
- Annual Ascendant superimposed *on the Natal 7th house*: marriage, partnership, one's spouse, the health of a partner, lawsuits, problems caused by a partner, public activity, coming before the public, lack of success in social life, separation, divorce. Because the Ascendant symbolizes the body, Volguine found that when the annual Ascendant opposed the natal Ascendant, the individual often suffered illness, injury, accidents, operations, or health problems. In other words, planets conjunct the annual Descendant are opposite the annual Ascendant and often suggest concerns about health and bodily integrity.
- Annual Ascendant superimposed *on the Natal 8th house*: according to Volguine, there may be a death within the native's family or circle of acquaintances; worries about health, life-threatening injury or illness, death of the native, fatigue, depression, the need for medical or surgical treatments; financial returns, inheritance, life insurance, income from investments; an interest in the occult or the afterlife. Morin, in contrast, felt that the 8th house only referred to the death of the native as opposed to someone else's demise.
- Annual Ascendant superimposed *on the Natal 9th house*: an important journey, foreign travel, those at or from a distance, philosophy, religion, the law, the church, the clergy, a religious ceremony, higher education, publishing, intellectual development, dealings with judges and lawyers.
- Annual Ascendant superimposed *on the Natal 10th house*: personal action related to career, promotion at work, honors, changes in career or public standing, professional opportunities, assumption of work-related responsibilities, vocational success or failure caused by the actions of the native.

• Annual Ascendant superimposed *on the Natal 11th house:* friends, help from friends, new friendships, realization of one's hopes and wishes, difficulties caused by friends, loss of friends.

• Annual Ascendant superimposed *on the Natal 12th house:* ordeals, opposition from secret enemies, calumny, gossip, troublesome lawsuits, illness, limitation, resignation, confinement, psychological distress, grief, worry, anxiety, self-undoing.

Volguine's Delineation of the Annual Midheaven Superimposed on the Natal Houses

Next is a summary of Volguine's delineations of the annual Midheaven and 10th house superimposed upon the natal houses. Most important is the placement of the Solar Return Midheaven in one of the natal houses. Volguine also considered the aspects formed by the annual Midheaven with the planets and house cusps of the natal chart. Whatever the Solar Return Midheaven contacts in the natal chart can release the natal potential for 10th house matters, especially with regard to vocation and profession.

Themes highlighted by the superimposition of the annual Midheaven (and its corresponding 10th house) onto the natal chart:

• Annual Midheaven superimposed *on the Natal 1st house:* the ability to influence one's destiny and choose one's vocation; career opportunities, benefits come through patronage.

• Annual Midheaven superimposed *on the Natal 2nd house:* income from career will be an important theme for the year.

• Annual Midheaven superimposed *on the Natal 3rd house:* social position connected with travel or writing; worldly status is affected by a trip or a document.

• Annual Midheaven superimposed *on the Natal 4th house:* home, residence, land, parents, retirement, important endings, and completion of a longstanding project. Volguine noted that a loss of position or public status may occur if the Solar Return Midheaven opposes the natal Midheaven.

• Annual Midheaven superimposed *on the Natal 5th house:* a position in the arts, the success of children, accomplishment through children, devotion to children, public standing improved by an engagement, important examinations (for students), worldly pleasures. Volguine notes that if the annual Midheaven opposes the natal 11th cusp, there is a risk of failed hopes and wishes.

- Annual Midheaven superimposed *on the Natal 6th house:* a subordinate or dependent position, the effect that poor health has on one's career, workaholic tendencies, restricted freedom of choice in professional matters.
- Annual Midheaven superimposed *on the Natal 7th house:* a promotion through marriage, a partnership or a business contract; professional changes related to divorce, breakup of a partnership, lawsuits.
- Annual Midheaven superimposed *on the Natal 8th house:* debts, financial returns, inheritance, settling of accounts, a death that affects career, problems with financial obligations.
- Annual Midheaven superimposed *on the Natal 9th house:* a journey related to one's career, business with foreigners or faraway places, success coming from a distance, professional matters related to foreign languages.
- Annual Midheaven superimposed *on the Natal 10th house:* the natal promise regarding career, reputation, and honors readily manifests; a highly important year for career.
- Annual Midheaven superimposed *on the Natal 11th house:* friends and connections help or hinder career; ability to achieve one's hopes and wishes; ability to work toward future goals.
- Annual Midheaven superimposed *on the Natal 12th house:* a year of ordeal with regard to career matters; problems finding or keeping a job; possibility of libel or slander; discontent with one's professional life.

Volguine's Delineation of the Remaining Solar Return Houses Superimposed on the Natal Houses

Volguine described the impact of the superimposition of each of the twelve annual houses when superimposed upon the natal chart. The reader is referred to Volguine's text for his detailed delineations. His basic premise, confirmed by observation, is that the superimposition of the annual and natal houses combines the meanings of the houses in each of the charts. For example, if the annual 5th house (love, pleasure, children) falls on the natal 3rd house (short trips, close kin, correspondence), one can expect brief trips for pleasure or sex, literary creativity, the engagement of siblings or close relatives, the birth of nieces or nephews, and so on. Especially important are the houses that contain annual planets because the planetary occupants energize such houses. A room with a guest gets more use.

The list that follows summarizes some keywords that Volguine and Morin used to delineate the houses, supplemented by my own experience, my study of the work of Deborah Houlding[2] on the meanings of the houses in traditional astrology, and the research of R.C. Davison[3] on the houses in secondary progressed charts. Readers should, of course, compare these findings with their own experience and knowledge of the astrological houses. According to Morin, each house participates accidentally in the meaning of the one opposite; and a planet in one house often triggers – through opposition – events related to the house directly across the wheel. For example, significant activity in the natal 11th house may refer to events in the lives of 5th house children in addition to 11th house friends. The late New York astrologer Zoltan Mason referred to Morin's idea of the shared significations of opposing houses as the principle of "ricochet."

Keywords for the Houses:
1st House: symbolizes the rising of the Sun; hence, the native's life, health, physical body, vitality, personality, and spirit; the self, temperament, personal appearance, head and face, character, habits, social identity, mental ability, individual self-expression, freedom of choice, initiative, enterprise, self-assertion, personal projects, original ideas, personal freedom, approach to the world, mannerisms, self-interest, personal actions – especially those of an active or pioneering nature. According to Morin, the Ascendant rules the life of the native, and any planets occupying or ruling the 1st, 8th, or 12th houses have special significance in connection with matters of health or life.[4]

2nd House: income, assets, resources, substance, estate, wealth, profit, moveable goods, money earned (as opposed to the 8th house of money not earned), financial affairs, possessions, personal goods, ownership, budgeting, earning capacity, money loaned to others, financial investments, practical security, business interests, values, talents, assistance from others, the neck. According to Deborah Houlding, "succedent houses generally show the resources and support given to the preceding angle, i.e., the 5th will show the financial status and assistance of the father, the 8th will show the wealth of the partner and the enemy's resources and supporters, and the 11th will show the friends and supporters of whoever is in power and the profit to be made from the business."[5] Morin regarded the 2nd house as potentially unfortunate because it lies opposite the 8th house of death.

3rd House: news, near kin, communication, day-to-day travel, the immediate environment, commuting, movement, short trips, mobility, transit, the system of transport, roads, vehicles, transportation, travel accidents, mental powers, study, learning, primary education, the press, magazines, gossip, messages, messengers, postal service, telephones, communication devices, reports, written research, ideas, the mind, writing, phone calls, errands, opinions, letters, paperwork, manuscripts, correspondence, written documents (including written deeds and contracts), declarations, brothers and sisters, cousins, neighbors, salesmen, reporters, teachers, lecturers, booksellers; the shoulders, arms, hands, fingers. Volguine found that the annual 3rd in the natal 4th often heralds a change of residence. William Lilly in the 17th century had also noted that the 3rd house often denotes "removing from one place to another." Volguine added that if the cusp of the annual 3rd house falls in a fixed sign (Taurus, Leo, Aquarius), there was little likelihood of travel, especially if the Moon and ruler of the 3rd also fell in fixed signs.

4th House: symbolizes the darkest point of the Sun's journey as it passes deep beneath the earth to begin a new ascent toward dawn; hence, the end of anything, roots, foundations, completions, settlements, the culmination of an enterprise, the end of life, the grave, the accumulation of past experience, domestic concerns, family life, parents, fathers, grandparents, paternity, the past, ancestry, tradition, history, old people, one's home, base of operations, inherited property, lands, houses, tenements, place of residence, personal and family secrets, domestic matters, remodeling or decorating the home, landed property, savings, frozen assets, hidden things, root causes, mines, assets buried in the ground, resources in the earth, harvests, crops, buildings, land, farming, agriculture, real estate; the breasts and lungs. Volguine found that in female charts the annual 4th in the natal 5th often occurred during the year of conception of a child and the annual 4th in the natal 8th, during the year of menopause. The annual 8th in the natal 4th may indicate a death in the family, or the sale or loss of real estate. Morin regarded the 4th house as potentially unfortunate because it symbolizes the end of life and one's burial in the earth.

5th House: creative self-expression, offspring, the state of a woman with child, the health or sickness of children, events in the life of a child, procreation, pregnancy, birth, medical problems with childbearing, lovemaking, love affairs and breakups, gift giving, courtship, romance, amorous interests, pleasure, fun, merriment, enjoyment, luxuries, indulgences, emotional attachments, betrothal (getting engaged to marry), sensuality, recreational sex, entertainment, hobbies, games, recreation, competitions, sports, parties, holidays, vacations, creative pursuits, artistic or theatrical endeavors, drama, show business, jewelry, finery, decorating, making things beautiful, ostentatious display, attracting attention to oneself, schools, exams, childhood education, technical instruction, organizing ability, activities with children, coaching a sports team, expansion, amusement, luck, lotteries, gambling, betting, risk taking, games of chance, matters whose outcome depends mainly on chance; the stomach, liver, heart, sides, and back. Volguine found that the annual 5th in the natal 3rd often heralds a new love affair and the annual 5th in the natal 8th house, significant gifts given or received.

6th House: sickness – its quality and cause, decreased freedom, social inferiors, labor, obligatory or tedious work, service rendered to others, jobs, duties, subordination, subordinate positions, submission to another's will, employees, tenants, co-workers, servants, maids, caretakers, day laborers, public employees, uncles, aunts, kin of the father, pets, domestic animals, ministering to the needs of others, apprenticeship, diligent practice, attention to details, routines, techniques, tools, the ordering and utilization of resources, diet, farmers, crops, food reserves, exercise regimens, attempts to improve or perfect something, employment, hindrance, adjustments, restriction, obstacles, difficulties, disease, accidents, matters related to health; feelings of anxiety, inadequacy, or inferiority. According to William Lilly, the 6th "rules the inferior part of the Belly, and intestines even to the Arse." Volguine points out that when the annual 6th falls in the natal 1st house, the native has little freedom of choice and finds it difficult to accomplish independent projects. Morin regarded the 6th house as potentially unfortunate because it lies opposite the 12th house of illness, sorrow, confinement, and undoing.

7th House: partners, significant others, sweethearts, the spouse, marriage, open enemies, opponents, adversaries, thieves, competitors, conflicts, struggles, one-to-one relationships, counselors, advisors, consultants, binding contracts, agreements, cooperation in business, public relations, dealings with the public, collaborations, negotiations, trials, disputes, lawsuits, open breaches, legal proceedings, the lower courts, strife, competition, rivalry, battles, war, fugitives, runaways, couples issues, divorce, sunset; the haunches and the area from the navel to the buttocks. Planets conjunct the 7th cusp (Descendant) are opposite the Ascendant (the body) and can indicate health concerns. Because the Descendant symbolizes the setting of the Sun, it has had a traditional signification of death. Volguine found that the annual 7th house (the spouse) in the natal 3rd house (contacts in the local environment) often occurred in years when the native or the spouse had an extramarital love affair. He regarded Gemini, the 3rd sign, as a flirtatious sign of sexual polarity and sexual attraction.

8th House: resources or money of a spouse or partner, money owed to others, death and all matters related to death, personal vulnerability, life-threatening illness or injury, danger to life, fear and anguish of mind, anxiety, loss, near-death experiences, the severing of ties, separations or endings that feel like a death, bereavement, wills, debts, financial obligations, the resources of others, taxes, alimony, insurance, inheritance, trusts, loss of a valued possession or relationship, rejection, shared property, the power to transmute resources, money from legal proceedings, transformation, crisis, regeneration, decay, destruction, forced renunciation, necessary letting go, poison, garbage, extremes, intense feelings, endings that pave the way for new beginnings, waste removal, surgery, the need for healing or repair, therapy, invasive medical procedures, research, investigation, intense probing, occult studies, matters affecting health or life, one's bladder and private parts. Morin regarded the 8th house as unfortunate because it symbolizes life-threatening danger and death.

9th House: journeys, exploration, voyages, long-distance travel, flights, cruises, foreign lands, distant places, the larger world, justice, the Law, higher courts, the legal profession, judicial rulings, legal issues, appeals to a higher court, the practice of law, affairs at a distance, foreign matters, advanced learning, books, scholarships, higher education, promotion of ideas, advertising, publishing, dissemination of knowledge, philosophy, the search for meaning, preaching, spiritual seeking, belief systems, inspired thoughts, dreams, visions, academics, intellectual activity, politics, science, literature, religion, church matters, religious ceremonies and activities, university students, lawyers, publishers, authors, clergy, in-laws, travelers, pilgrims, explorers, divination, the forecasting of future trends, the area from the buttocks to the hips and thighs.

10th House: symbolizes high noon of the blazing Sun; hence, dignity, honors, preferment, distinctions, being in the public eye, career, profession, vocation, one's calling in life, the mother or partner of the 4th house father, undertakings, the result of public actions, community standing, taking on new responsibilities, ambition, status, social position, leadership, power, prime officers, reputation, conscious striving to reach a goal, desire to be the ultimate authority, success, fame, celebrity, advancement, public standing, awards, promotions, distinctions, formalities, official matters, kings, princes, royalty, heads of state, powerful people, those in authority, judges, those who enforce the law, the powers that be, employers, the boss, the chief, being in charge, government, respected people, the administration of an organization, desire for a positive public image, ascension, public recognition, events in the life of one's parents, one's knees and hams. Morin says the 10th is primarily the house of the "native's actions and undertakings."[6]

11th House: traditionally called the "House of Good Fortune," the 11th symbolizes one's circle of friends, associates, supporters, patrons, benefactors, succor, help or hindrance from friends, counsel, clubs and group activities, social connections, aspirations, beneficial fate, ambitions, hopes and wishes, confidence, praise and dispraise, optimism, plans and goals for the future, comfort, trust, safe harbor, personal freedom, relief from suffering, making friends, networking, social consciousness, activities based on friendship, income from professional projects, finances of the mother, the government's money, matters related to electricity and modern science, the legs from the knees to the ankles; also, the children, speculative risks, and love affairs of a spouse or partner (the 11th house is the 5th of the 7th). In Morin's time the 11th house represented the favorite of the king. Volguine found that the annual 7th (marriage, conflicts) in the natal 11th (friends, hopes and wishes) commonly manifested as struggling to achieve one's ambitions, changes in relations with friends, or participation in a friend's wedding as bridesmaid or best man.

12th House: illness, sorrow, imprisonment, solitude, hospitalization, confinement, private enemies, informers, sadness, loss, trials and tribulations, illusion, privacy, secrecy, hidden matters, restriction, seclusion, isolation, limited freedom, secret enemies, those who undermine our interests, conspiracies, activities that require solitude or secrecy, places of retreat, behind-the-scenes activities, clandestine relationships, spirituality, study of the occult, introspection, the subconscious mind, secret societies, using circuitous means to achieve one's goals, privacy, complications, fraud, deception, scandal, skeletons in the closet, unpleasantness, chronic troubles, personal fears, falling short, sacrifice, selfless service, escapism, evasion, exhaustion, self-undoing, failure, defeat, faulty adjustment to life, one's own Achilles heel, character flaws, worry, discontent, grief, personal limitations, anxiety, ordeal, tedium, fatigue, intrigue, moral lapses, cloistered environments, convalescence, matters of health or life, exile, retreat, resignation, large animals, mother's siblings, those less fortunate than oneself, those who care for the sick, the feet. Volguine noticed that the annual 12th in the natal 4th often corresponded to falls and stomach troubles. He also found that the annual 12th (tribulations) in the natal 9th house (legal affairs), together with many planets in the annual 12th house, heralded such things as infractions against laws and ordinances, involvement with police, and disputes with tax officials. Morin regarded the 12th house as unfortunate because it symbolizes illness, frustration, limitation, and undoing. Deborah Houlding states that traditionally the 12th house "is a wholly unfortunate house, associated with sad events, sorrow, anguish of mind, tribulation, captivity, imprisonment, persecution, hard labour, all manner of affliction and self-undoing."[7]

Dignities and Debilities of the Planets

To understand the potential of the natal chart, it is important to consider the dignities and debilities of the natal planets. Essential dignity refers to the strength a planet has due to its location in a compatible region of the zodiac. The ancients noticed that each of the seven visible planets tended to act more effectively in some places of the zodiac than in others.

The greatest dignity a planet can have is to occupy its home sign or domicile: *domal dignity*. A planet opposite its home sign is debilitated and said to be in *detriment* or in *exile*. Next in strength comes dignity by *exaltation*. Each planet has a sign in which it is exalted and can act according to its nature without impediment. The exaltations of the planets are places of great strength and integrity, probably derived from the ancient Babylonian assignments of planets as rulers of the zodiacal signs. A planet occupying the sign opposite its exaltation is debilitated and said to be in the sign of its *fall*. Debilitation brings out the negative traits of a planet. For example, in Connecticut Governor Jodi Rell's natal chart (Figure 4), which we will consider in greater detail later in this chapter, the Moon in Capricorn is debilitated because it occupies the sign of its detriment. This debilitated Moon in Rell's natal 8th house is one indicator of the natal potential for surgery and danger to life involving the breasts.

Yet another type of dignity has to do with a planet occupying one of the signs of its *triplicity*. There are various systems of assigning planets to triplicities of zodiacal signs. Finally there are two minor forms of dignity having to do with terms (or bounds) of planets and with faces (or decans) occupied by planets. For our purposes we will consider only dignity by home sign (domicile) and by exaltation and their corresponding debilities of detriment and fall. The following table summarizes the dignities used in this text.

Table: Dignities and Debilities of the Planets

Planet	Dignity: Domicile or Home Sign	Dignity: Exaltation	Debility: Detriment	Debility: Fall
Sun	Leo	Aries	Aquarius	Libra
Moon	Cancer	Taurus	Capricorn	Scorpio
Mercury	Gemini & Virgo	Virgo	Sagittarius & Pisces	Pisces
Venus	Taurus & Libra	Pisces	Scorpio	Virgo & Aries
Mars	Aries & Scorpio	Capricorn	Libra & Taurus	Cancer
Jupiter	Sagittarius & Pisces	Cancer	Gemini	Capricorn & Virgo
Saturn	Capricorn & Aquarius	Libra	Cancer	Aries & Leo

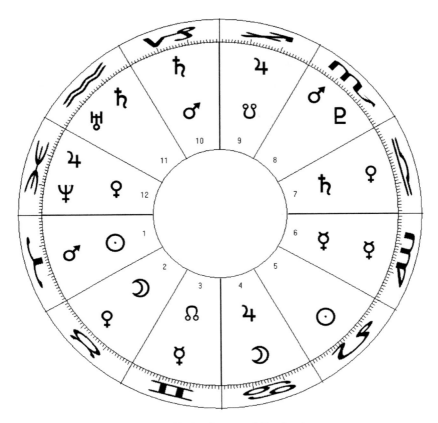

Figure 1: Rulerships and Exaltations:
Rulerships in outer position, Exaltations inside

An Example from Morin of the Annual Ascendant Conjunct the Natal Midheaven

Jean-Baptiste Morin, in his book on solar revolutions, delineates the 1616 solar revolution of Louis Tronson, whom King Louis XIII of France retained in his service and honored in 1616. Based on the charts provided by Morin, I deduced that Louis Tronson was born in Paris on September 1, 1576 (NS) at about 9:18:27 AM LMT (Figure 2) and spent his 1616 Solar Return in Nancy, France (Figure 3). According to Morin, Louis Tronson's good fortune, dignities, and elevation by the king are shown by numerous factors, including:

- The Solar Return Ascendant closely conjoins the natal Midheaven.
- The Sun and Moon rule the natal 10th house (royalty, honors) and also rule the 1st house of the Solar Return.

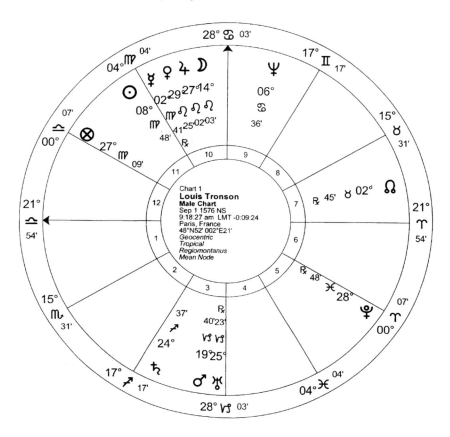

Figure 2: Louis Tronson Natal Chart

- The Sun and the annual Moon trine each other in the solar revolution.
- The Sun is powerful because it is exalted in Aries, the sign on the annual Midheaven.
- The Moon, ruler of the annual Ascendant, is exalted in Taurus in the annual 10th house.
- Benefic annual Venus disposes the annual Ascendant-ruler Moon and conjoins the Sun.
- The primary directed natal Sun conjoins the natal Midheaven on December 8, 1616 (calculated with *Solar Fire* at a rate of one year per degree on the Midheaven).
- Annual Mercury, which disposes the Sun and rules the natal 11th house of good fortune, conjoins the natal Venus/Jupiter conjunction in the natal

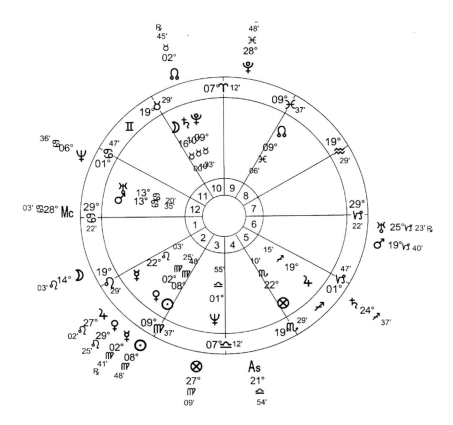

Figure 3: Tronson Natal Chart on 1616 Solar Return

10th and receives a trine from annual Jupiter. Also there is a favorable mutual reception between annual Mercury in Leo and the Sun in Virgo.

•   Annual Venus conjoins natal Mercury at the cusp of the natal 11th house of the favorite of the king.

•   Their respective favorable aspects to their dispositors in the Solar Return diminished the malefic potential of annual Mars and annual Saturn. Annual Mars, though in its fall in Cancer in the annual 12th, sextiles the annual Moon, ruler of Cancer. Annual Saturn in Taurus receives a trine from annual Venus, its dispositor, and also a trine from the Sun. According to Morin, without these favorable aspects to their dispositors, the noxious effects of annual Mars and annual Saturn would not have been dissipated and poor Tronson would have fallen victim to 8th and 12th house maleficence.

The 2004 Superimposition of Houses of Connecticut Governor Jodi Rell
The year 2004 was one of the most eventful in the life of Connecticut's
Lieutenant Governor Jodi Rell, who was sworn in as governor of Connecticut
on July 1, 2004, after her boss and predecessor, Governor John Rowland, was
forced to resign because of corruption charges. Mr. Rowland went on to spend
time in federal prison. According to the *Hartford Courant*, Jodi Rell was born
in Norfolk, Virginia, on June 16, 1946, at 4:16 AM EDT (Figure 4). At the
time of her 2004 Solar Return (Figure 5) she had been living in Brookfield,
Connecticut, for many years. During a routine mammogram just before
Christmas 2004 she was diagnosed with breast cancer. On December 27, 2004,
she underwent a mastectomy and reconstructive surgery.

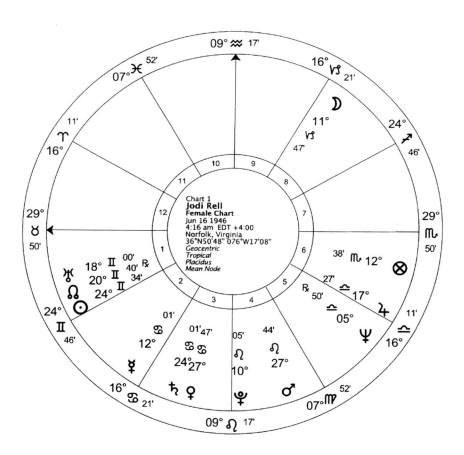

Figure 4: Jodi Rell Natal Chart

In her natal chart, Rell has Taurus rising, making Venus the ruler of her Ascendant (her body). Venus also rules her 6th house of health issues. Natal Ascendant-ruler Venus conjoins Saturn, which is debilitated in Cancer, the sign of its detriment. The Ascendant-ruler Venus conjunct Saturn in Cancer (breasts) is one indication of a potential for health problems involving the breasts.

The natal Moon, which also symbolizes the breasts, is debilitated in Capricorn, the sign of its detriment, and occupies the 8th house of surgery, invasive medical procedures, and radical transformation. The natal Moon forms a stressful quincunx (150 degrees) with natal Pluto (crisis, dramatic change). Furthermore, the Moon, which is exalted in Taurus, rules her Ascendant (her

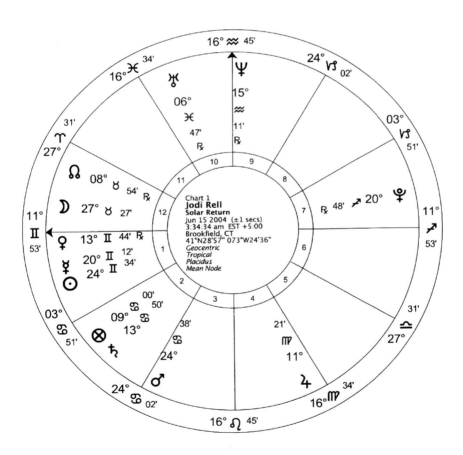

Figure 5: Jodi Rell 2004 Solar Return

body) by exaltation. The natal 8th house Moon squares natal 8th ruler Jupiter, which conjoins the natal 6th house cusp of health concerns and opposes the natal 12th cusp of hospitalization. The potential for breast cancer and reconstructive surgery is clearly indicated in the natal chart.

By primary direction (at her natal solar rate, calculated with *Solar Fire*)[8] on September 18, 2004, the natal Ascendant-ruler/6th-house-ruler Venus conjoined her natal Ascendant and simultaneously squared her natal Midheaven. The year 2004 would thus be important for personal, health, and career matters. Furthermore, the annual Ascendant fell in her natal 1st house, and the annual Midheaven occupied her natal 10th house (Figure 6). This marks a year when the natal potential for 1st house matters (the body, individual action) and 10th house affairs (career) can readily manifest.

The annual Ascendant at 11° Gemini 53' forms a trine with her natal Midheaven at 9° Aquarius 17' suggesting favorable career changes. This positive career aspect is reinforced by a primary direction (at the natal solar rate) of her natal Sun to sextile the natal Midheaven in January of 2004 and a primary direction (also at the natal solar rate) of the natal Sun to sextile its own birth position in April of 2004.

The stress of assuming the governorship under the shadow of the scandal involving her boss is reflected in the primary direction (at the rate of one degree per year) of her natal Midheaven to square natal Mars on August 22 and to oppose natal Uranus on August 24, 2004. Annual Neptune conjunct annual Midheaven most likely refers to the scandal that led to her being appointed governor. In addition, in both the annual and the natal charts, Neptune co-rules the 11th house of friends, groups, legislatures, networking organizations, hopes and wishes – maybe she had a dream of becoming governor some day.

Annual Venus (ruling the 6th house of health matters) on the Solar Return Ascendant suggests concerns about illness during the year. The Solar Return Moon in the annual 12th closely conjoins the natal Ascendant, highlighting the significance of the debilitated 8th house Moon in her natal chart. Since the natal Moon (in the natal 8th and quincunx to natal Pluto) is an indicator of breast cancer and mastectomy, this is a year in which this potential can easily manifest. Annual Saturn opposes her natal Moon in the 8th House. Her primary directed Mars (at a rate of one year per degree) semi-squares her natal Ascendant on December 13 and her primary directed 8th house Moon (at a rate of one year per degree) squares her natal Ascendant-ruler Venus on December 28, 2004 – one day after her breast surgery.

The fact that the annual Moon is exalted in Taurus in the annual 12th house correlates with the timely discovery and rapid treatment of the breast cancer. The Solar Return Ascendant-ruler Mercury (her body) opposes annual Pluto and the natal 8th house cusp, suggesting a need for intensive medical treatment. Annual Pluto also opposes her Sun and conjoins the cusp of the natal 8th of surgery. Annual Mercury conjoins her natal Moon's North Node, suggesting a fateful year in which she would fulfill her destiny. Annual Uranus conjoins her natal 11th cusp (friends, associates) and opposes 11th-ruler Jupiter in the Solar Return, reflecting her separation from Governor Rowland for whom she had served as Lieutenant Governor.

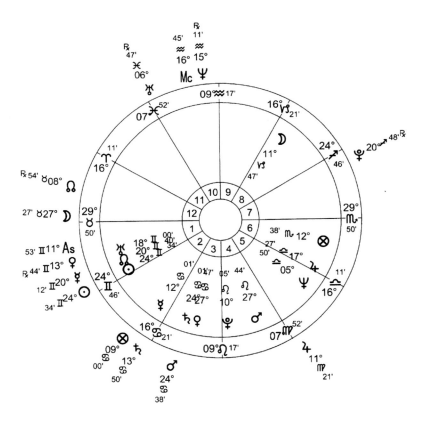

Figure.6: Rell's Solar Return Superimposed on Natal Chart

NOTES

1.   Morin, *Book 23*, translated by James Holden, AFA, 2003, p.130.
2.   Deborah Houlding, *The Houses – Temples of the Sky*, The Wessex Astrologer, April 2006. Excerpts can be found online at http://www.skyscript.co.uk/temples/h1.html.
3.   R.C. Davison, *The Technique of Prediction*, L. N. Fowler & Co., 1971, pp 27-35.
4.   Morin, *Book 23*, translated by James Holden, AFA, 2003, p.139.
5.   Deborah Houlding at http://www.skyscript.co.uk/temples/h2.html.
6.   Morin, *Book 22, Astrologia Gallica*, translated by James Holden, AFA, 1994, p.98.
7.   Deborah Houlding at http://www.skyscript.co.uk/temples/h12.html.
8.   Unless otherwise noted, all the primary directions used in this text were calculated using Solar Fire Delux version 6.0.32.

4

A Look at the Holy See, the Precessed Solar Return, and a Crisis in the Life of Salvador Dali

In 2005 the College of Cardinals at the Vatican elected a new Pope just three days after his 78th birthday. This event offers an illuminating case study on Solar Returns. On April 19, 2005, at about 5:50 PM local time, Cardinal Joseph Ratzinger[1] was elected Pope and assumed the name of Benedict XVI. His conservative views and his work as Prefect of the Congregation for the Doctrine of Faith had earned him the nickname of "the Enforcer." His supporters viewed him as a charming and brilliant guardian of orthodoxy. According to astrological theory, Cardinal Ratzinger's elevation to the papacy should be reflected in his 2005 Solar Return. His papal role should also be "promised" in his birth chart and should be visible in his progressions, directions, revolutions, and transits of 2005.

Cardinal Ratzinger's Natal Promise
The astute reader will notice the similarities between the chart of Pope Benedict XVI and that of the female minister we discussed in Chapter Two.

The new Pope was born with benefic Jupiter rising in the 1st house in Pisces (Figure 1). Ecclesiastical Jupiter traditionally rules spiritual Pisces and philosophical Sagittarius – the sign on the cusp of his 9th (religion, higher education) and 10th houses (career, public standing). The ruler of his 10th house conjoins his natal Ascendant, suggesting a prominent career. Conservative Saturn in Sagittarius (beliefs) on the cusp of his 9th house (religious doctrine) reflects his orthodoxy. The conjunction of natal Jupiter, Mercury, and Uranus in the 1st house suggests a razor-sharp mind. Natal Mars in Gemini shows a man in hot pursuit of ideas, and Mars square his Jupiter-Mercury-Uranus conjunction reveals a person willing to fight for his beliefs, a true enforcer. Mars sextile the Sun gives courage, competitiveness, and a love of challenge. At the same time, the natal Moon in Libra in the 7th house grants charm and tact in dealing with others.

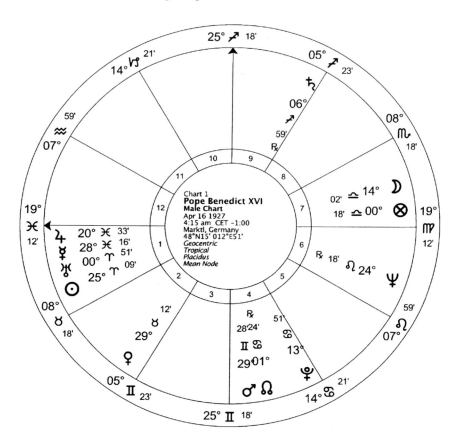

Figure 1: Cardinal Ratzinger's Natal Chart

Ratzinger's natal Sun (leaders, authority figures) is exalted in Aries, sign of the warrior. His natal Sun is trine the Sagittarius Midheaven, promising a prominent and successful career. The grand trine of the Sun, Neptune, and the Midheaven suggests a career connected to illusion or spirituality. His natal Sun also lies on the midpoint of Venus and Jupiter, the two most benefic planets in astrology. In turn, his natal Midheaven (career) lies on the midpoint of benefic Jupiter and the Part of Fortune, another promise of career success.

The Pope's Significant Secondary Progressions in 2005

If we secondarily progress[2] the new Pope's natal chart for his birthplace to April 2005 (Figure 2), we find the secondary progressed Sun exactly on the progressed Ascendant (suggesting prominence and recognition) and also applying to trine the secondary progressed Midheaven. With his natal Sun almost exactly trine his natal Midheaven, this 2005 applying progressed trine helps to trigger the natal Sun/Midheaven trine into manifestation during the coming year or two. In addition, the secondary progressed Venus conjoins secondary progressed Neptune, and these progressed planets trine his natal Sun and natal Midheaven. The stage is set for favorable changes in his career and worldly status in 2005.

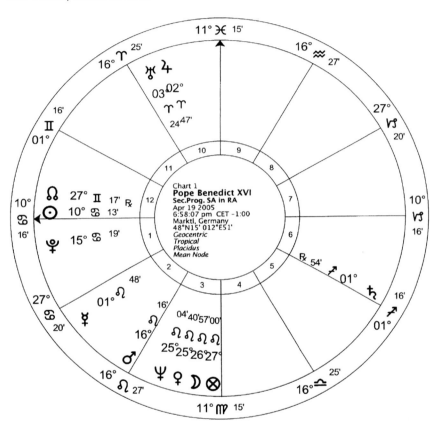

Figure 2: Ratzinger's Secondary Progressed Chart for April 2005

The 2005 Non-precessed Solar Return of Cardinal Ratzinger

Cardinal Ratzinger's non-precessed Solar Return chart for 2005 (Figure 3) has Capricorn rising with the annual Ascendant-ruler Saturn prominent on the western horizon. Return planets that conjoin any of the four angles (ASC, DSC, MC, or IC) are highly significant. This will be a Saturnian year in which he assumes much responsibility and adopts an attitude of conservatism, discipline, authority, and respect for tradition.

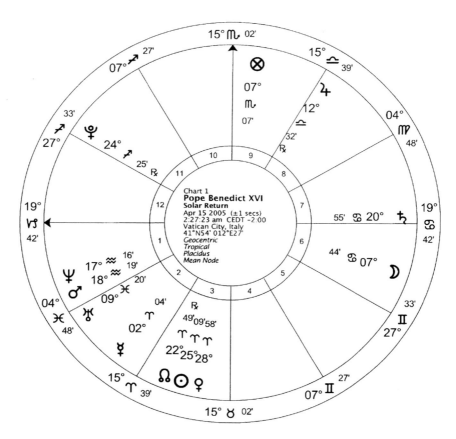

Figure 3: Ratzinger's 2005 Solar Return at the Vatican

Annual Saturn trine the annual Midheaven promises an important and favorable period for professional matters. Symbolically Saturn, Capricorn, and the Midheaven relate to honor, prestige, status, reputation, and authority. Annual Saturn trine the return Midheaven implies well-deserved public recognition for dedication, perseverance, and a job well done. According to Merriman's text on Solar Returns, Saturn favorably aspecting the Midheaven of the return chart indicates "respect and prestige in one's work or community… enhances the native's image as an authority…and he/she may feel as if he/she has finally 'arrived'… realizing one's 'calling in life'…"[3]

Annual Saturn (ruler of the Solar Return Ascendant) lies in Cancer and is thus disposed by the Moon, also in Cancer which it rules (domal dignity). Morin taught that the dispositors of the rulers of houses play powerful roles in determining the effects of those house rulers in any given chart.[4] The annual

Moon, which rules return Saturn, closely trines the annual Part of Fortune residing in the ecclesiastical 9th house of the Solar Return. Furthermore, annual Jupiter conjoins the annual 9th house cusp. All these factors promise an important and favorable year for church-related matters. It is also noteworthy that annual Saturn disposes annual Midheaven-ruler Mars in Aquarius, again highlighting career issues during this Solar Return year.

The message of annual Saturn is further reinforced by the fact that annual Mars, ruler of the annual career-related Midheaven, makes a close parallel of declination with Sirius, the Dog Star, a harbinger of fame and positions of honor and influence. Perhaps he will become Pope or be bitten by a dog in 2005.[5] Annual Saturn squares his natal Sun (Figure 4), making this a stressful year that could take a toll on his health. After the election, Ratzinger's brother was quoted in the press as saying, "I'm scared my brother's health is too fragile for the papacy." Return Venus, however, favorably conjoins his natal Sun and serves a protective function, suggesting that his health would be okay and that he would avoid the dog bite suggested by Sirius. The transiting Sun exactly conjoined annual Venus – ruler of the Solar Return 9th house of church matters – late in the day on April 18th, less than 24 hours before he was elected Pope.

With Saturn prominent in the Solar Return, we should also consider the meaning that Saturn carries from the birth chart. The Pope's natal Saturn lies in Sagittarius on the cusp of his natal 9th house of religious affairs, higher education, and long distance travel. Natal Saturn rules his natal 11th house of hopes, wishes, and dealings with groups of like-minded individuals, such as the College of Cardinals. Natal Saturn is also the ruler of his natal 12th house of self-sacrifice, behind-the-scenes matters, cloisters, places of confinement, and spiritual retreats. Themes related to these significations of natal Saturn are likely to be prominent this year

The Sun in the Solar Return chart, by definition, occupies the same zodiacal position as in the birth chart. The closest aspect to the Sun is a trine from annual Pluto, which turned stationary retrograde at 24° Sagittarius 31' on March 28, 2005, in very close conjunction with his natal Midheaven. The stations of transiting outer planets have a powerful influence extending over a long period of time. The fact that transiting Pluto made its station close to its position in the Solar Revolution reinforces the importance of its aspects. Annual Pluto trine the Sun and conjunct the natal Midheaven suggests major, often life-transforming events related to public standing and vocation. Such events tend to divide one's life into "before and after." Pluto is a planet of power, intensity, and transformation. It is fitting that Solar Return Pluto would occupy the natal Midheaven and also harmoniously trine the natal Sun of the man to assume ultimate authority in the Roman Catholic Church. To quote Merriman, annual Pluto favorably aspecting the Solar Return Midheaven suggests "a position of great influence...the power to change things – to improve things – for the better."[6]

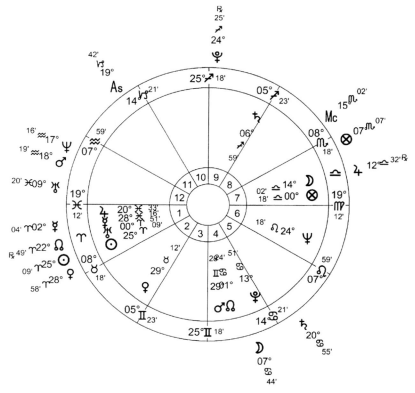

Figure 4: 2005 Solar Return Superimposed Upon the Natal Chart

The Precessed Solar Return of Cardinal Ratzinger for 2005

Although Volguine did not adjust for precession, it is striking to consider the precessed Solar Return of Cardinal Ratzinger for 2005 (Figure 5). The angles of the precessed return are almost identical to those of the birth chart. The repetition of natal angles in a Solar Return always indicates a highly important year in the life of the individual – a year in which the natal potential is free to manifest. The more the Solar Return resembles the birth chart, the more efficacious it is likely to be. Similarity breeds manifestation.

The Ascendant of the precessed Solar Return conjoins the natal Ascendant and also natal Jupiter, which is the planetary ruler of the natal 9th

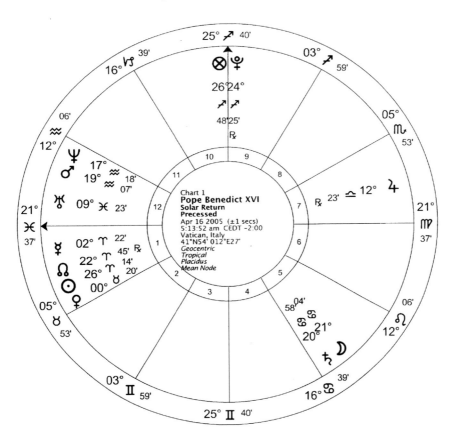

Figure 5: Precessed Solar Return of Cardinal Ratzinger for 2005

of church matters and natal 10th of professional achievement. In addition, the Solar Return Midheaven, which is almost identical to the natal Midheaven, closely conjoins both return Pluto (radical transformation) and the return Part of Fortune (an extremely fortunate influence). The precessed Solar Return Sun is also closely trine the conjoined annual Part of Fortune, annual Midheaven, and annual Pluto. We see in Cardinal Ratzinger's 2005 Solar Return charts, precessed and non-precessed, two distinct but informative figures, each reflecting in their own way the major events in his life.

Let us now turn our attention to the precessed and non-precessed Solar Returns of the painter Salvador Dali for 1984, a year of major personal and professional crisis.

A Crisis in the Life of Salvador Dali

By all accounts 1984 was a stressful year for the surrealist painter Salvador Dali, born May 11, 1904 at 8:45 AM GMT in Figueras, Spain (Figure 6). When his beloved wife Gala died two years earlier (on June 10, 1982), the grieving Dali went into a prolonged seclusion. Reportedly he lost much of his will to live and apparently starved and dehydrated himself. On June 7, 1984, thieves tunneled into the Signature Gallery and stole over a half-million dollars worth of Dali's paintings, spoiling a display that was to honor his 80th birthday. On August 30, 1984 a fire, attributed to a short circuit in the electrical system, broke out in Dali's bedroom at Púbol Castle, nearly killing him in his sleep. The severely malnourished Dali was hospitalized and required skin graft surgery for burns to his upper legs and groin. Some observers speculated whether the fire was a suicide attempt. Dali eventually died of heart failure on January 23, 1989.

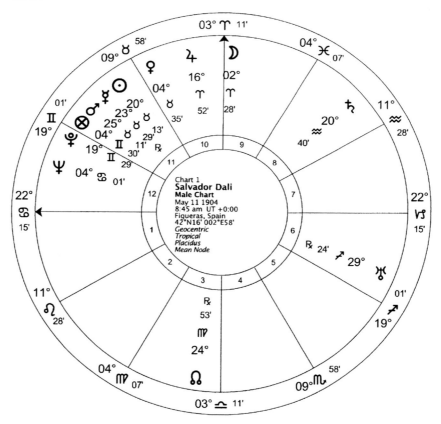

Figure 6: Salvador Dali Natal Chart

Dali's natal chart shows the risk of accidental injury in an electrical fire as symbolized by the following:

• Saturn in Aquarius (electricity) in the natal Aquarius 8th house of life-threatening illness or injury.
• Saturn in the 8th squares the Sun, Mercury, and Mars (fire) in the 11th. The natal Saturn/Sun square is almost exact and probably signifies his demise from heart disease.
• Uranus (accidents, electricity) in Sagittarius (a fire sign) in the natal 6th house of sickness opposite Neptune (carelessness) in the natal 12th house of hospitalization.
• The Moon ruling the natal Ascendant (his body) in Aries (a fire sign)

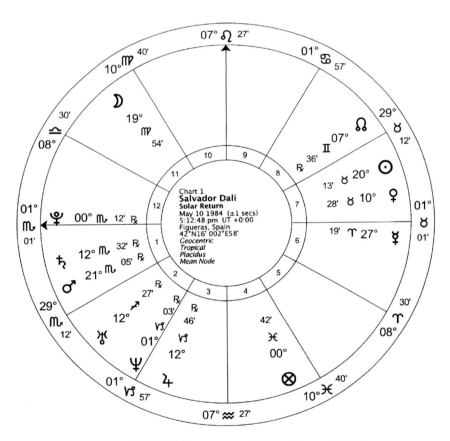

Figure 7: Dali Non-precessed Solar Return 1984

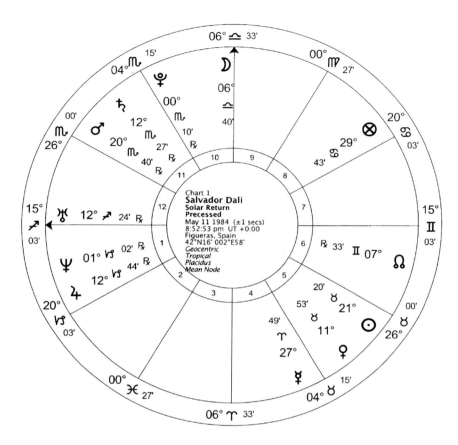

Figure 8: Dali Precessed Solar Return 1984

in a T-Square configuration with the Uranus/Neptune 6th/12th house opposition.

•   Mars (fire) conjunct Mercury, the ruler of the natal 12th house.

Dali's non-precessed 1984 Solar Return (Figure 7) has an angular Pluto (crisis, surgery) in the 12th house (hospitalization) closely conjunct the annual Scorpio Ascendant. Pluto on an angle denotes a year of dramatic change. Annual Ascendant-ruler Pluto opposes annual Mercury in Aries in the 6th house of sickness, and annual Mercury rules the annual 8th house of danger to life (Gemini intercepted in the 8th). The malefics, Mars and Saturn, occupy the annual 1st house. Annual Ascendant-ruler Mars (his body) closely opposes the Sun, and annual Saturn opposes annual Venus, which rules the Solar Return 12th house (hospitalization). Annual Uranus (accidents, unexpected events) is tightly sesqui-square annual 8th ruler Mercury. The annual Moon, ruler of the natal Ascendant (the body) closely squares natal Pluto at the cusp of the unfortunate 12th house. Clearly 1984 would be a difficult crisis-prone year that would take a toll on his health.

The precessed 1984 Solar Return (Figure 8) emphasizes the possibility of surprising adverse happenings with Uranus (accidents) in the 12th (confinement) conjunct the Ascendant (his body). The precessed annual Moon, which rules the natal Ascendant (his vitality) and also governs the precessed annual 8th of danger, forms a paran-square with Uranus (electricity). The precessed annual 8th ruler Moon squares precessed annual Neptune (carelessness) in the 1st house and also semi-squares Mars. The Sun co-rules the precessed annual 8th (Leo intercepted) and closely opposes a retrograde Mars (fire), suggesting problems caused by heat or unregulated energy.

The first Solar Eclipse of the Solar Return year on May 30, 1984, at 9° Gemini 25', opposed annual Uranus, thus supercharging the planet of accidents and disruption. This solar eclipse fell in the 8th house of the non-precessed annual chart and in the 7th house of the precessed return chart conjunct the Descendant. As was the case with the Pope, we again see the utility of both the precessed and non-precessed Solar Return in identifying major themes of the year ahead from differing perspectives. We will explore this topic further in the next chapter.

NOTES

1. *AstroDataBank* gives his birth data as: Ratzinger, Joseph; Apr 16, 1927, 04:15 (4:15 AM) MET (-1:00), Marktl, Germany, 48 N 15 / 12 E 51, AA / Quoted BC/BR.

2. This secondary progressed chart is calculated using the rate of true solar arc in right ascension, that is, the right ascension of the Midheaven is progressed by the same right ascension arc as the Sun. Generally in secondary progressed charts the Midheaven is calculated at a prescribed rate and the other progressed angles are derived from the progressed Midheaven. There are several methods for calculating the Midheaven of secondary progressed charts, including the common technique of progressing the Midheaven's longitude by the same arc of longitude as the Sun. In a subsequent chapter we will see the usefulness for timing events by progressing the Solar Return Midheaven at the "mean quotidian" rate of approximately 361 degrees per day. Secondary progression at the mean quotidian rate is also called the method of "daily houses."

3.   Raymond A. Merriman, *The New Solar Return Book of Prediction*, 1998, Seek It Publications, W. Bloomfield, MI, pp. 77-78.
4.   The dispositor is sometimes referred to as the "secondary ruler." In this 2005 Solar Return, Saturn rules the Ascendant. Saturn happens to lie in Cancer, so that Saturn is ruled by the Moon, which becomes the "secondary ruler" of the Solar Return Ascendant. According to Morin, the influences of both Saturn and the Moon as "rulers" of the Ascendant will be highly significant for Pope Benedict during this Solar Return year.
5.   I didn't really think he would be bitten by a dog, but the older astrology literature makes this association with the star Sirius (for example, see http://users.winshop.com.au/annew/Sirius.html)
6.   Merriman, ibid, pp. 80-81.

5

To Precess or Not To Precess –
That is the Question

As mentioned previously, there exists a controversy among astrologers about whether to adjust the Solar Return chart for precession. Neither Volguine nor Morin precessed their charts, yet some modern authors believe that precession is the only way to calculate an annual chart and that tropical non-precessed Solar Returns are simply invalid. As we saw in the charts of Pope Benedict XVI and surrealist painter Salvador Dali, both types of annual charts are worth considering because they shed different types of light on the Solar Return. The difficulty that some modern astrologers encounter with tropical non-precessed Solar Returns may be due simply to their unfamiliarity with the techniques of Volguine and Morin de Villefranche.

Woman Burned in a Fire

Noted astrologer Marc Penfield in his book *Solar Returns in Your Face*[1] strongly advocates the use of precession when calculating Solar Returns. He comments that for years he had used non-precessed charts with minimal success but that once he started using a precessional factor, "events" that he had personally experienced "were sticking out like sore thumbs." To test the hypothesis, Penfield collected charts for an extended period of time and studied both their precessed and non-precessed Solar Returns. He then judged which types of return charts more accurately matched the events that actually took place and found that the precessed chart were significantly more accurate. Unlike Morin, Penfield always calculated the Solar Return for the current place of residence, regardless of the actual location of the person at the time of the return.

Although I have great respect for Penfield's work and agree with him that precessed returns are event-oriented, my own experience has shown that the techniques of Volguine and Morin produce equally significant results with non-precessed tropical Solar Returns. To check Penfield's assertion about precession I recalculated several of his precessed Solar Returns and found that, in each instance, the non-precessed Solar Return chart was as informative as the precessed one, if not more so. Both the precessed and non-precessed Solar Returns appear to provide valuable information, albeit from differing perspectives.

Let's consider a specific Solar Return from Penfield's book but in its non-precessed format. On page 22 of Penfield's text he describes the precessed return of a woman who was severely burned in a fire at Christmastime 1984. She was born October 12, 1950 at 10:30 AM EST at coordinates 40N41, 80W17 (Figure 1). In her natal chart the fire sign Sagittarius is rising and fiery Mars, close to the Ascendant in Sagittarius, occupies her 1st house (the physical body). This birth configuration suggests a fiery, outgoing, energetic personality, especially with Mars in Sagittarius sextile her stellium of the Sun, Neptune, Venus, and Mercury in Libra.

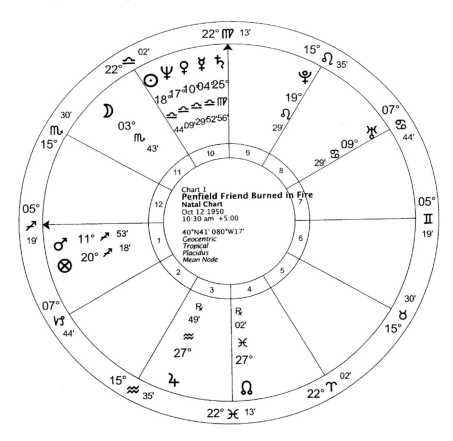

Figure 1: Woman Burned in Fire Natal Chart

Her natal Mars rules the Placidus 12th house of hospitalization and is stressfully configured by both a quincunx and a contraparallel to Uranus, a significator of electricity and accidents. Uranus conjoins the cusp of the Placidus 8th house, suggesting a sudden need for medical or surgical treatment at some time in her life. Because Uranus occupies her natal 8th house, it becomes a significator of 8th house issues, including life-threatening injury or illness. Jupiter rules her natal Ascendant and signifies her body. Natal Jupiter is quincunx Saturn and sesqui-square Venus – the ruler of her 6th house of health concerns. Natal Venus (6th house health matters) is square natal 8th house Uranus (accidents). The birth chart clearly carries the potential for a life-threatening accident (Uranus in the 8th) involving fire (Mars).

From the precessed Solar Return in Penfield's book, I reconstructed that her non-precessed 1984 return took place on October 11, 1984 at 2:26:29 PM MST at coordinates 31N10, 113W30 (Figure 2). In the non-precessed Solar Return, Aquarius is rising, raising the possibility of usual or unexpected events involving modern inventions, electricity, or electrical wiring. Uranus, the ruler of Aquarius, is associated with both electricity and accidents. In this case the fire started as a result of an electrical short circuit in a lamp in her home. Her natal Moon – ruler of the natal 8th of danger to life – occupies the natal 11th house, which astrologer R.C. Davison's research found to be linked to "the use of power in all forms – particularly the use of electrical power."[2]

Uranus, the modern ruler of Aquarius, co-rules the annual Ascendant and signifies her body. Solar Return Uranus (electricity) conjoins her natal Mars (fire) in the 1st house of the natal chart and also forms a quincunx with her natal Uranus at the cusp of her natal 8th house of surgery, death, and life-threatening illness. The non-precessed Solar Return Aquarius Ascendant squares her natal Moon, which rules her natal 8th house. Annual Saturn (the traditional ruler of the Aquarius Solar Return Ascendant) lies on the cusp of the natal Placidus 12th house of hospitalization. In addition, annual Venus, which rules her natal 6th house of health concerns, prominently conjoins the Solar Return Midheaven. Finally, a stellium – consisting of the natal Midheaven, Saturn, Mercury, Venus and Neptune – occupies the Solar Return 8th house, making 8th house matters especially prominent in 1984. In the final chapter of this book we will see a similar stellium of natal planets in the 8th house of the Solar Return of my friend Don who needed to undergo experimental chemotherapy for colon cancer. Any astrologer studying this burn victim's non-precessed return chart would see the potential for an accident involving electricity and fire as well as the need for surgical treatment in a hospital during the 1984 Solar Return year.

The Total Solar Eclipse Prior to the Fire

Solar Returns do not exist in a vacuum; rather, they are part and parcel of the astrological tapestry enveloping the life of the native. Morin recommended studying three Solar Returns in succession – the one for the current year plus the returns for the years immediately preceding and following the current return – to get a view of the flow of the native's life during a consecutive three-year period. He also considered the current directions of the natal chart, eclipses, fixed star contacts, Lunar Returns for the current year, and the current transits. Eclipses are an important feature of the astrological landscape; and I have found that the first solar eclipse of the Solar Return year, when superimposed on the annual chart, highlights the key issues for the year ahead.

On November 22, 1984 a total solar eclipse (Figure 2) occurred in the first degree of Sagittarius in the native's natal 12th house close to her natal Ascendant. This eclipse took place near the Solar Return Lunar South Node, which was opposite the fixed star Alcyone of the Pleiades (the "weeping sisters"

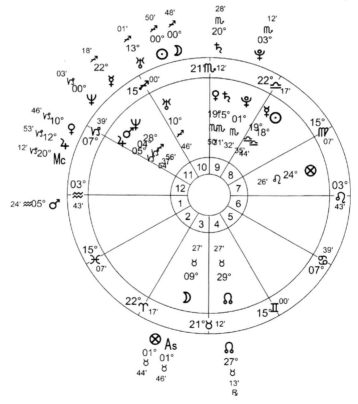

Figure 2: 'Burned in Fire' – Solar Eclipse on Solar Return

at 29° Taurus 46') – often an indicator of some sadness entering one's life. The Ascendant of the eclipse chart was Taurus, making Venus the eclipse's Ascendant-ruler. Note that in this technique the eclipse chart is cast for the same location as the Solar Return. Eclipse Venus falls in the annual 12ᵗʰ house (hospitalization) conjunct the 12ᵗʰ house cusp. Eclipse Jupiter, dispositor of the Sagittarius solar eclipse itself, also occupies the annual 12ᵗʰ house, as does the eclipse Midheaven.

Eclipse Pluto in Scorpio stressfully squares Mars in the eclipse chart and also squares the non-precessed Solar Return Ascendant. Pluto/Mars squares affecting the annual Ascendant are often harbingers of intense and potentially violent circumstances. Eclipse Mars in Aquarius (electrical fires) stands out prominently conjunct the annual Aquarius Ascendant. Eclipse Saturn in Scorpio closely conjoins the annual Midheaven, forming a paran-square with eclipse Mars in the Solar Return chart. Because the malefics of the eclipse chart so strikingly conjoin the angles of this non-precessed Solar Return, because eclipse Pluto squares eclipse Mars which is conjunct the annual Ascendant, and because the planetary dispositors of the eclipse and its Ascendant fall in the annual 12ᵗʰ house, the astrologer can reasonably forecast that this will be a difficult year with the possibility of hospitalization or confinement.[3]

Timing Events by Progressing the Moon and Angles of the Solar Return
As for timing, Penfield does not give the exact date of the fire but does say that his friend did not meet him as planned for Christmas in 1984. He called her only to discover that she had been burned in a house fire, which prevented her from traveling on Christmas day. Judging from Penfield's comments, it appears that the fire took place on Christmas Eve (December 24, 1984).

In general we use the secondary progressed Solar Return Moon and the secondary progressed angles of the return chart for timing. In this case the Moon is especially important because it rules her natal 8ᵗʰ house of surgery and life-threatening illness. There are several approaches we can take to progress the Solar Return Moon. These include using the average daily motion of the Moon on the day of the Solar Return, using the Conversion Table in the Appendix of this book, or simply calculating the secondary progressions of the Solar Return Moon with the aid of a computer program. For illustrative purposes we will briefly consider each of these methods in the following paragraphs.

On the day of her 1984 Solar Return the annual Moon was traveling at a rate of 12 degrees per day. The non-precessed Solar Return Moon lies at 9° Taurus 27' and is applying to quincunx natal Mars at 11° Sagittarius 53'. This annual Moon quincunx natal Mars aspect will perfect in 2 degrees and 26 minutes. Each degree of the Moon's motion is equivalent to about a month; thus, 2 degrees 26 minutes – the distance to perfect the quincunx to Mars – is equivalent to about 74 days after the Solar Return of October 11, 1984. Hence the quincunx perfects by progression of the annual Moon on December 24, 1984, making Christmas Eve 1984 the most likely time for the triggering of natal Mars, which astrologers associate with fires.

We could also use the Conversion Table in the Appendix of this book to progress the Solar Return chart to December 24, 1984 (Figure 3). Seventy-four calendar days is equivalent to advancing the Solar Return chart by 4 hours 50 minutes 58 seconds. Since the Solar Return occurred at 2:26:29 PM on October 11, 1984, the Solar Return chart progressed to December 24th should be cast for 7:17:27 PM on October 11, 1984.

An advantage of using the Conversion Table is that it not only progresses the annual Moon and all the annual planets but also meaningfully progresses the angles of the Solar Return (the angles progress through a complete 360 degree circle in the course of a year). This method is sometimes called the "mean quotidian progression of the Midheaven" or the "method of daily houses."[4] If you have an astrological computer program that does mean quotidian secondary progressions of the Midheaven, you will not need to use the Conversion Table provided in this text.

According to the Conversion Table, the annual Ascendant progresses to 14° Taurus 44' on Christmas Eve and to 16° Taurus 00' on Christmas Day. In fact, just after midnight on Christmas Eve of 1984 the progressed annual Ascendant exactly opposed both her natal 12th house cusp of hospitalization and her annual Saturn, which rules the Solar Return Ascendant as well as the Solar Return 12th house.

An alternative way to find the progressed annual Moon's position for any date during the Solar Return year is simply to secondarily progress the annual chart and read the position of the secondary progressed Moon. Most astrology software programs offer secondary progression as an easy option. By secondary progression, the annual Moon advances to quincunx natal Mars at 11° Sagittarius 53' at 7 PM on Christmas Eve, 1984.

On Christmas day 1984 the transiting Sun (at 4°-5° of Capricorn) exactly conjoined Solar Return Mars. At the same time the progressed Solar Return Ascendant conjoined the natal 6th house cusp opposite Solar Return Saturn. Hence the two traditional malefics, Mars and Saturn, were highly active in this woman's Solar Return on Christmas day 1984. Fortunately she survived the fire, despite burns over a large part of her body, and ultimately received a large insurance settlement.

Summary of Penfield's Method

Before looking at more examples of precessed and non-precessed returns, let us summarize Penfield's approach:

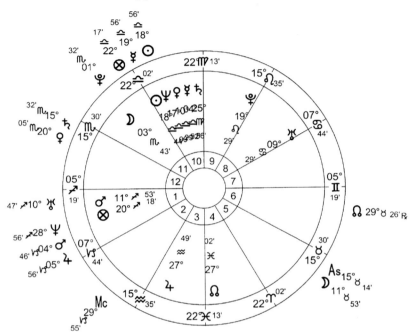

Figure 3: 'Burned in Fire' Progressed Solar Return Superimposed on Natal
Chart

•   Penfield calculates the *precessed* tropical Solar Return chart. This amounts to an increment in the return position of the Sun of one degree for every 72 years of life, or about 50 additional seconds of arc for each year.
•   He uses the Porphyry system of houses.
•   He is "firmly convinced that you should calculate the return chart for the place where you live, your regular address, the place where you pay rent and receive your mail."[5] This is at variance with Morin and Volguine who use the person's actual location at the time of the return.
•   He finds most compelling the aspects made by the angles of the Solar Return chart with any annual or natal planets or points.
•   He looks for chart patterns in the annual chart, especially any that involve the angles. These include T-squares, grand squares, grand trines, and planetary distributions such as the bowl, bucket, bundle, or locomotive.

•   He notes which house of the natal chart is rising in the return. Volguine and Morin also relied heavily on this factor.

•   Borrowing from horary astrology, Penfield pays special attention to whether the final three degrees of a sign are on the precessed annual Ascendant or Midheaven. He finds that late degrees on the Ascendant or Midheaven refer to endings or to changes in career or residence. "If the final degrees fall on the Ascendant, this is often a potent warning regarding one's health or time left on this planet."[6]

•   Penfield believes that people can feel the effect of a Solar Return up to three months before their birthday, and he finds that the return continues to work for about six months after the birthday. Then for the remaining six months of the year or until the person begins to sense the next Solar Return, the individual feels in limbo, "waiting to wrap things up before it is possible to start a new cycle."[7]

•   As for timing, Penfield uses the transits of the planets Mars through Pluto as they aspect the angles of the precessed return chart. He finds that the transits of Mars and Uranus are the most accurate timing devices.

What Happened in Los Angeles?

The next example grew out of an email correspondence I had with an astrologer who was a staunch proponent of using only the precessed Solar Return. After reading some comments I made about tropical non-precessed Solar Returns at the *AstroDataBank* Internet site (http://astrodatabank.com), he sent an email challenging my assertion that non-precessed charts could yield accurate predictive information. To test the validity of the non-precessed technique, he challenged me to interpret the non-precessed Solar Return of someone who had an eventful year in Los Angeles. I accepted the challenge and he sent the birth data, defying me to discover what happened to the unknown native in Los Angeles, California, in January of 1997. The individual in question was born on July 12, 1937 in Philadelphia at 0:30 AM EDT (Figure 5).

Armed only with the birth data, I calculated the 1996 Solar Return in effect for this native in January 1997 (Figure 4). Since the email did not specify otherwise, I assumed that the individual spent his Solar Return in Los Angeles. The resulting non-precessed annual chart appears below.

Annual Mars (force) is prominent in the 12th house (loss, sorrow) almost exactly conjunct the Solar Return Gemini Ascendant. I have repeatedly found in Solar Returns that a malefic planet appearing toward the end of the 12th house conjunct the Solar Return Ascendant correlates with a disquieting and sometimes tragic year.

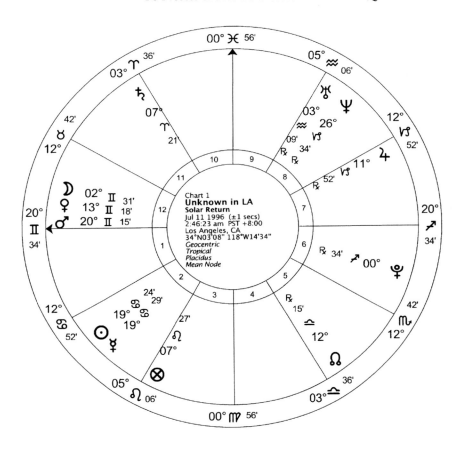

Figure 4: 'What happened in LA' 1996 Solar Return

I speculated that with such a prominent angular Mars, the event could relate to a young man (Mars) in his life. Mars also has to do with energy, impulse, aggression, fire, heat, and violence. The annual Moon (emotions) in the unfortunate 12th house supported the idea of some type of sadness, especially as the annual Moon (ruler of the Taurus 12th by exaltation) opposed annual Pluto in the 6th house. Pluto is associated with crises, intense emotional states, and the coercive use of force. I also noticed that natal Uranus at 13° Taurus 05' closely conjoined the annual 12th house cusp, suggesting a sudden disruptive event that triggered a sense of sorrow. It seemed likely that this individual had been exposed to some type of violence, perhaps involving a young man and resulting in a sense of loss, grief, or sorrow.

I emailed these observations to my astrological colleague who then told me that the natal data belonged to Bill Cosby whose son was murdered in

Los Angeles on January 16, 1997. He agreed that my comments were on target, but added that my accuracy must have been a fluke because he knew from his experience that non-precessed charts simply do not work. At the time I had not yet read Morin's *Book 22 on Directions* in which he observed that "a malefic in the 12th house of the native's figure portends death to his children... for the ruler of the native's 12th is the 8th with respect to the 5th... of his children..."[8]

In any case, my curiosity was aroused. From a search of news reports, I could not determine where Bill Cosby actually spent his 1996 Solar Return preceding his son's death. He may have been in Los Angeles on business or visiting his son around the time of his birthday. He could also have been in Manhattan where he was residing at the time. The Solar Return relocated to New York City, his place of residence, was less dramatic but also informative as relocated Solar Returns typically are. In other words, the relocation of a Solar Return chart to the place of a significant event affecting the individual is informative, even if the person has not spent time at that location.

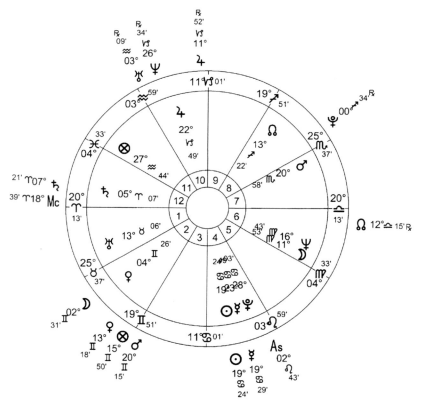

Figure 5: 'What Happened in LA' 1996 SR in NYC on Natal Chart

Superimposing the New York (residence) Solar Return on his natal chart, we see several conjunctions to house cusps (Figure 5). The annual Midheaven conjoins his natal Ascendant, marking this as an especially important and memorable year with regard to career and public standing. Annual Jupiter conjoins his natal Midheaven, highlighting his increased publicity and ongoing professional success. Solar Return Mars in Gemini conjoins his natal 3rd house cusp, suggesting stressful conditions related to travel and people at a distance.

The Solar Return Leo Ascendant for New York conjoins his natal 5th house cusp (creativity, children, love affairs) and simultaneously opposes annual Uranus (sudden upsetting disruptive events). This annual Uranus/Ascendant opposition became exact by secondary progression in the winter of 1997 around the time of his son's death.

The rising sign Leo shares many significations with the 5th house. Recall that Volguine regarded the annual Ascendant as a kind of weathervane pointing to the most important issues in the year ahead. The stress on 5th house matters was certainly accurate in 1997. During this period Cosby was very creative professionally. It was also the time when his son died and when a young woman named Autumn Jackson allegedly tried to extort money from Bill Cosby by claiming to be his out-of-wedlock daughter (another 5th house issue).

The Disappearance of Jimmy Hoffa

The mystery of the disappearance of labor leader James Riddle Hoffa remains unsolved. On July 30, 1975, Jimmy Hoffa was waiting outside the Machus Red Fox Restaurant in Bloomfield Township, Michigan and anxiously called his wife to say he had been stood up. Hoffa was scheduled for a 2 PM meeting with the mob, presumably to discuss running again for president of the Teamsters. His wife never heard from him again. One theory is that the mob assassinated him to thwart his leadership aspirations. At the time of this writing Hoffa's body still has not been found.[9]

According to *AstroDataBank*, Jimmy Hoffa was born on February 14, 1913 in Brazil, Indiana, just after sunrise at 6:52 AM CST (Figure 6). His leadership potential is shown by the natal Sun closely conjunct the Ascendant in trine to natal Pluto in the 4th house. With four planets occupying the natal 12th house, behind-the-scenes activities will be important in his life. The Sun, which rules his 7th house of partners and open enemies, occupies the 12th house of secret enemies – consistent with his mob alliances.

Natal Saturn, by exaltation, rules Hoffa's Libra 8th house of death and squares natal Sun, ruler of the 7th of alliances in the 12th of secret enemies. Natal Mars (violence, aggression) conjoins the natal 12th house cusp (secret enemies, hidden matters), is quincunx to natal Pluto (potential for exposure to violence), and opposes natal Neptune (deception), which is conjunct the 6th house cusp (health matters). These aspects of Mars and Saturn set the stage for a possible murder and secret disposal by the mob.

Hoffa's Solar Return for 1975 should have indications of his disappearance on July 30th of that year. At the time of his death Hoffa was living near Detroit in Lake Orion, Michigan. His non-precessed Solar Return (Figure 7) has an angular Moon/Pluto opposition across the horizon. The annual Moon in the 12th house closely conjoins the Solar Return Ascendant,

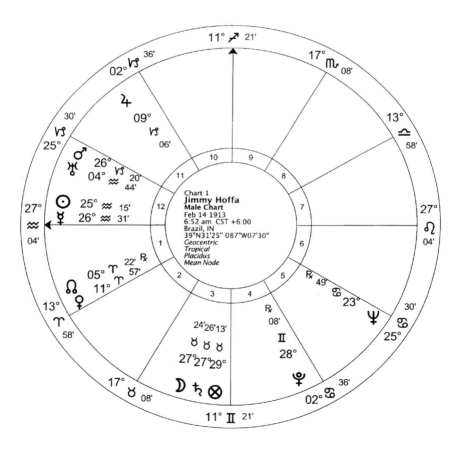

Figure 6: Jimmy Hoffa Natal Chart

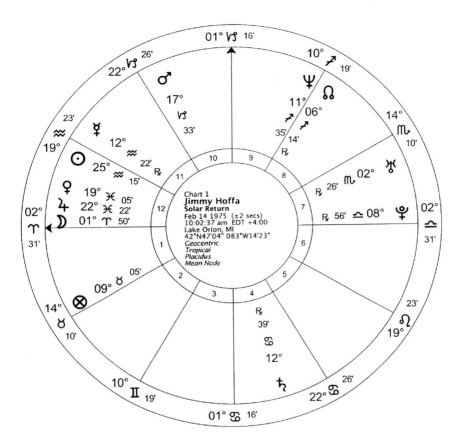

Figure 7: Hoffa 1975 Non-Precessed Solar Return

suggesting many changes during the year. The annual Moon also rules the return 4th house of endings. Annual Pluto (the underworld) in the 7th house of open enemies conjoins the Solar Return Descendant. Annual Pluto also rules the annual Scorpio 8th house of death. In addition, Hoffa's natal Pluto conjoins the Solar Return 4th house cusp (end of life). The annual Sun occupies the Solar Return 12th house of secret enemies along with three other planets (Venus, Jupiter, Moon), placing a heavy emphasis on 12th house issues in 1975.

The precessed Solar Return for 1975 (Figure 8) has even clearer suggestions of violence, with annual Mars (aggression, firearms) toward the end of the 12th house almost exactly conjunct the annual Ascendant, just as in Bill Cosby's Los Angeles return for the year his son was shot. The annual 12th house Mars opposes annual Saturn in the 6th house – a troublesome aspect between two malefic planets in unfortunate houses. Again we see how the

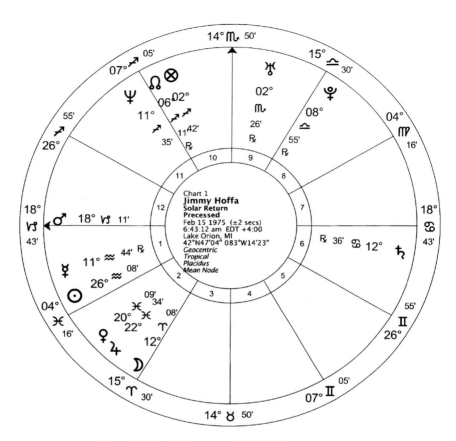

Figure 8: Hoffa Precessed 1975 Solar Return

precessed and non-precessed Solar Returns offer different slants on the same underlying information.

Precession and the Death of Nicole Brown Simpson

The trial of O.J. Simpson (nicknamed "The Juice") for the murder of Nicole Brown captivated national attention. According to her birth certificate, Nicole was born on May 19, 1959 at 2 AM MET in Frankfurt am Main, Germany (Figure 9). She married O.J. Simpson[10] in 1985 and they divorced in 1992, though they remained in contact after the divorce. On June 12, 1994 Nicole and her friend Ronald Goldman (born July 2, 1968) were found dead, having been brutally murdered; both were slashed and stabbed in Nicole's Brentwood, California, home. Her former husband O.J. Simpson was accused but was subsequently acquitted of the killings on October 3, 1995.

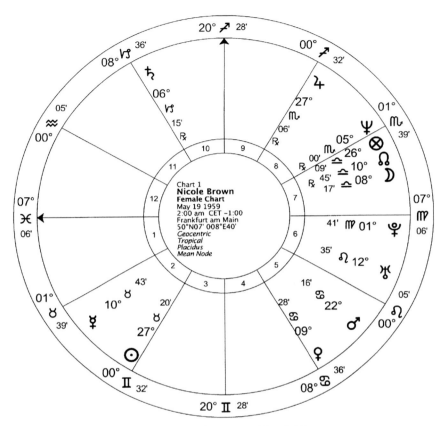

Figure 9: Nicole Brown Natal Chart

Nicole's natal chart has Pluto (domination, jealously, violence) conjunct the Gemini Descendant (marriage, the spouse). Mercury rules her natal 7th house cusp and symbolizes her marriage partner. Natal Mercury opposes Neptune (illusion, infatuation) and squares Uranus (sudden or explosive disruption). These astrological factors suggest that she is drawn to seductive (Neptune), volatile (Uranus) and intensely emotional, potentially violent (Pluto) men as partners. An angular Pluto is common in the natal charts of persons who suffer abuse, trauma, or domestic violence at some time in their lives.

Nicole's non-precessed Solar Return for the year of her death (Figure 10) has annual Uranus as the most angular planet, prominently conjunct the Midheaven. This year will be one of sudden changes and disruptions affecting her public and domestic life (the meridian axis). The annual Ascendant ruler

Venus is stressfully quincunx both annual Uranus on the Midheaven and annual Pluto in the 7th house of partnerships. There is a troubling, almost exact square to annual Uranus from annual Mars (aggression) in the 12th house (misfortune, sorrow). Recall Bill Cosby's Solar Return for Los Angeles in which Mars occupied the annual 12th house for the year of his son's death and Jimmy Hoffa's precessed Solar Return in which annual Mars also occupied the annual 12th house. Unlike Cosby and Hoffa, Nicole's Solar Return Mars does not conjoin the annual Ascendant; however, it does form a powerful square to the annual Midheaven, which is joined closely to the return Uranus, making the 12th house Mars square Uranus aspect the most outstanding feature of her 1994 Solar Return. In other words, the sudden assertion of force (Mars square Uranus) is the keynote of Nicole's 1994 year.

Nicole's Sun is powerfully placed in the annual 1st house opposite annual Pluto in the Solar Return 7th house, suggesting that her personal integrity

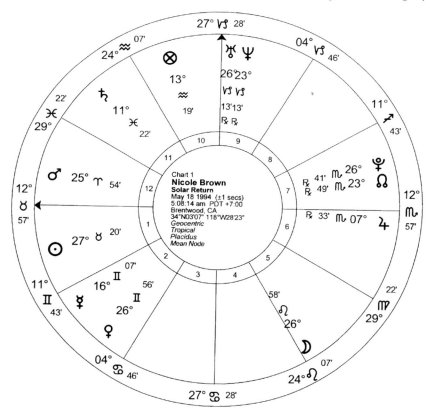

Figure 10: Nicole Brown 1994 Non-precessed Solar Return

(the Sun) may be threatened by a powerful partner (Pluto). The annual Moon (ruler of the natal 5th house) on the cusp of the Solar Return 5th house (love affairs) forms part of a T-square with the annual Sun/Pluto opposition, suggesting that a jealous partner (Pluto in the 7th) may be upset (opposition) with her (Sun in 1st) regarding a love affair (Moon in 5th).

Nicole's precessed 1994 Solar Return (Figure 11) is even more striking in describing the major events during this Solar Return year. Annual Uranus (unexpected or explosive events) is angular as it conjoins the annual IC (endings). Annual Mars (force, aggression, knives) is also angular as it conjoins the Descendant (her partner). As mentioned above, annual Mars and annual Uranus form a close zodiacal square. The Sun lies almost exactly on the cusp of the precessed Solar Return 8th house of death, opposed by annual Pluto (domination, jealousy). Annual Mercury, which rules her husband in the natal chart with its Gemini Descendant, conjoins Emerson's Point of Death

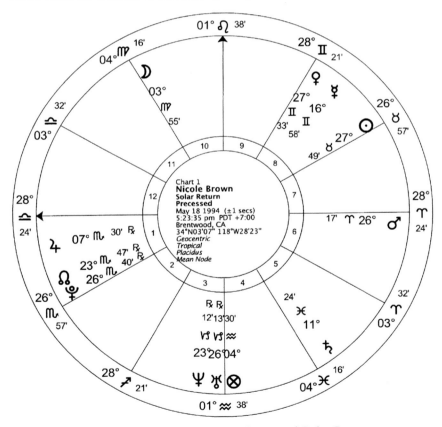

Figure 11: Nicole Brown 1994 Precessed Solar Return

(Midheaven + Saturn – Mars) at 16° Gemini 45' in the precessed annual 8th house. More will be said about Emerson's Death Point in a later chapter.

Finally, the reader may wish to review O.J. Simpson's Solar Return (Figure 12 cast for Los Angeles) in effect at the time of the murders. His annual Mercury at 26° Cancer 23' rules the Solar Return Ascendant, Midheaven, and 12th house. Strikingly, the Juice's annual Mercury conjoins Nicole's annual 4th house cusp (endings), almost exactly opposes her annual Uranus at the Midheaven, and closely squares her annual Mars in her Solar Return 12th house. Thus, O.J.'s Solar Return is intimately tied to Nicole's annual Mars/Uranus square, which is the most prominent feature of her Solar Return for the year of her death. If we secondarily progress O.J.'s Solar Return to the date of the murder using the Mean Quotidian method described previously (Figure 12), we find the progressed annual Ascendant at 9° Virgo

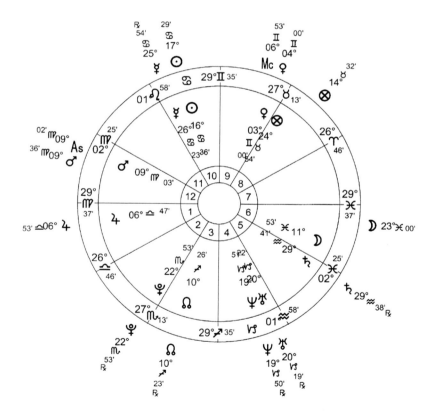

Figure 12: O.J. Simpson Progressed SR for June 12,1994 on Solar Return in LA

02' almost exactly conjunct his Solar Return Mars at 9° Virgo 03'. In addition, the Midheaven of his annual return progressed to June 12, 1994 has a Midheaven in the 7th degree of Gemini conjunct his natal Mars.

NOTES

1. Marc Penfield, *Solar Returns in Your Face*, American Federation of Astrologers, Tempe, AZ, 1996.
2. R.C. Davison, *The Technique of Prediction*, op.cit., p.33.
3. I say "possibility" advisedly. The astrologer can be fairly certain of general trends for the year ahead from the Solar Return, but it is difficult to say specifically how that difficulty will play out because of the myriad possibilities contained in astrological symbolism and chart configurations.
4. The chart calculation program *Solar Fire Deluxe* offers this method as one of its options for progressing the angles of a secondary progressed chart.
5. Mark Penfield, *Solar Returns in Your Face*, AFA, 1996, p.3.
6. Mark Penfield, ibid, p.3.
7. Mark Penfield, ibid, p.3.
8. Morin, *Book 22*, op. cit., p.124.
9. The source of data for Hoffa's disappearance is http://www.crimelibrary.com/notorious_murders/famous/jimmy_hoffa/1.html.
10. O.J. Simpson was born July 9, 1947, 8:08 AM PST in San Francisco, CA (Sun Cancer 16°36', ASC Leo 24°37').

6

The Importance of the Ascendant – A Personal Example

Volguine regarded the Solar Return Ascendant as a key factor in his method of interpretation. Cardinal Ratzinger's 2005 Solar Return demonstrated the importance of the Solar Return Ascendant in Capricorn (organizational responsibilities) as an indicator of the major themes for the year ahead. The zodiacal sign Capricorn is associated with tradition, authority, dogma, organization, status, business, and the structure of society. The following personal example further illustrates the significance of the Solar Return Ascendant.

My Mother's Untimely Death

The most significant event of my childhood was the untimely death of my mother a few days before my 8th birthday in 1953. She had contracted rheumatic fever as a young adult and had suffered damage to a heart valve as a result. She died of her heart condition in the early morning hours of Sunday August 30, 1953. The funeral took place on the day of my eighth birthday.

When I began to study astrology in my teens, my mother was deceased and my father could not remember the hour of my birth. He knew, however, that I was born on Labor Day morning, September 3, 1945. My father recalled that the sun was shining, and he was reasonably sure that I was born before 10 or 11 in the morning. Using my mother's death to rectify my birth time, I experimented with a number of morning charts and decided that 9:04 AM EWT was a likely time of birth. I discovered that a chart for around 9:04 AM had the primary directed Saturn conjoining my natal Midheaven around the date of my mother's death.

For years I continued to use 9:04 AM as my rectified birth time without any proof that this time was indeed accurate. It produced a chart that appeared astrologically valid and matched the events of my life. Then in the late 1980s when my father and stepmother were selling their home I helped them clean out their attic. To my delight I discovered a notebook in which my father had recorded the birth data for each of his children. There in my father's handwriting I read: "Anthony, September 3, 1945, 9:09 AM Waterbury Hospital." I was a bit stunned that the rectified time I had used for so long differed by only five minutes from the birth time recorded by my father. This discovery appeared to be a validation of the truth of astrological teachings. I have continued to use a rectified birth time but over the years have adjusted it to 9:05:36 AM based on other events in my life (Figure 1).

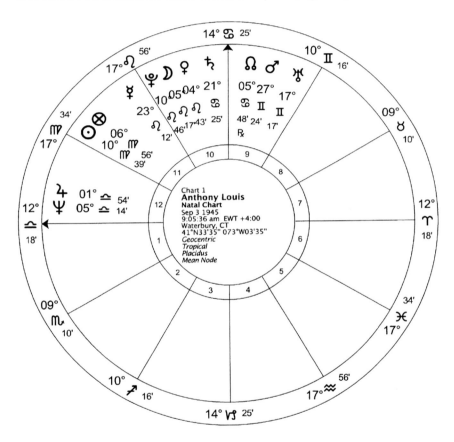

Figure 1: Author's Natal Chart

The Author's 1952 Solar Return

According to Volguine's system, my mother's death occurred before my 1953 Solar Return and should therefore be indicated in the 1952 Solar Return (Figure 2). The return chart for 1952 has Cancer rising with the Solar Return

Ascendant ruler Moon in late Aquarius in the 9th house. The sign Cancer relates to home, family, nurturing, the mother, and early childhood; these should be major themes for the year ahead.

Solar Return Uranus rules the annual Aquarius 8th house of death and rises in Cancer in the return 1st house, just 4 degrees from the annual Cancer Ascendant. Annual Uranus also squares both annual Saturn and annual Neptune, which conjoin the natal Ascendant in the Solar Return 4th house of home, parents, and final endings. The 1952 Solar Return Ascendant in Cancer closely squares both the natal Ascendant and annual Saturn in Libra. These factors indicate a difficult year involving sudden loss and sadness. The Solar Return Moon conjoins the return 9th house cusp (long journeys). As a result of my mother's death, my brother and I were sent to stay temporarily with relatives in a neighboring state – a long-distance trip for a child.

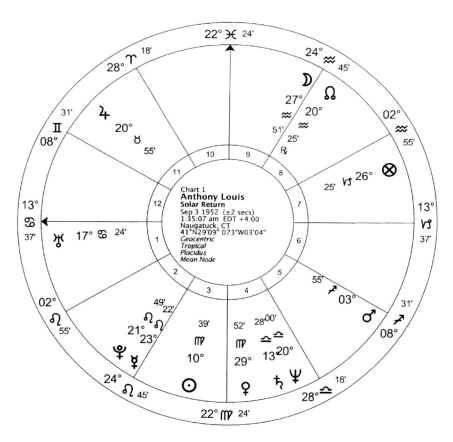

Figure 2: Author's Solar Return for 1952

Superimposition of the 1952 Solar Return onto the Natal Chart

When we superimpose the Solar Return on the natal chart (Figure 3), we find that the 1952 Solar Return Ascendant lies in the 9th house of long-distance travel and conjoins the Midheaven. Recall that in the minister's chart the Solar Return Ascendant also conjoined the natal Midheaven in a year when she experienced a significant professional achievement. For a child of 8 years old, the Solar Return Ascendant conjoining the natal Midheaven is more likely to be reflected in the lives of the parents, who are also signified by the meridian axis.

Solar Return Uranus in the natal 10th house conjoins both the natal Midheaven and natal Saturn, suggesting some type of sudden disruption or loss in the lives of the parents. This interpretation is reinforced by the appearance of both Solar Return Saturn and Solar Return Neptune in the natal 1st house, conjoining the natal Ascendant. In addition, Solar Return

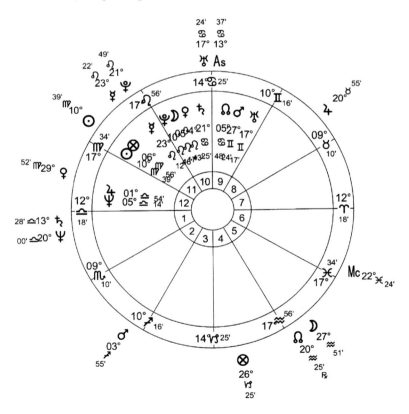

Figure 3: Author's 1952 Solar Return Superimposed on Natal Chart

Pluto, a natural signifier of death, conjoins both natal and Solar Return Mercury (it happens also to be the time of a Mercury return), with Mercury ruling the natal 12th house of grief and sorrow.

The 1952 Eclipses and Mother's Death

The eclipses of 1952 also point to the potential for loss of a parent in 1952. If we take the natal 10th house to represent the mother, then the planets occupying or ruling the 10th are all related to the mother. These include the natal 10th ruler, the Moon, as well as natal Saturn, Venus, and Pluto – all of which were activated by the eclipses of that year. In addition, the Solar Return Moon, which rules the natal 10th of the mother and also rules the annual Ascendant, falls in the natal 5th house, which is the derived 8th house of death of the natal 10th house mother. This Solar Return Moon at 27° Aquarius 51' – representing both the mother and her death – is activated by a close conjunction with the first (and usually the most significant) solar eclipse (at 25° Aquarius 02') after the Solar Return. The following table lists all the eclipses that occurred in the Solar Return year during which my mother died. The reader may wish to consider how these eclipses interacted with my Solar Return for 1952-53.

Solar and Lunar Eclipses during 1952 Solar Return Year

Date	Type	Position
Jan 29, 1953	Lunar Total	9° Leo 49'
Feb 14, 1953	Solar Partial	25° Aquarius 02'
Jul 11, 1953	Solar Partial	18° Cancer 30'
Jul 26, 1953	Lunar Total	3° Aquarius 12'
Aug 9, 1953	Solar Partial	16° Leo 44'

The Author's 1953 Solar Return

My mother's funeral took place on my 8th birthday just a few hours after my 1953 Solar Return (Figure 4). The annual 1953 Virgo Ascendant occupies the natal 12th of bereavement and conjoins the natal 12th house cusp within 4 degrees. The 1953 annual Midheaven, on the "family and career" meridian axis, conjoins natal Uranus, suggesting an unexpected separation from a parental figure. Annual Uranus, ruler of the natal 5th, which is the derived 8th of death of the mother, conjoins natal Saturn in the natal 10th house. An annual Neptune/Saturn conjunction in the natal 1st house squares the annual Uranus/natal Saturn conjunction in the natal 10th. A powerful annual Mars/ Pluto conjunction conjoins natal Mercury, ruler of the natal 12th of sorrow and also of the Solar Return Ascendant. Annual Mercury, ruler of the annual Ascendant, occupies the Solar Return 12th house of sorrow. Annual Venus, ruler of the natal 8th of death, almost exactly conjoins the natal Moon in the natal 10th, representing the mother. This annual Venus/natal Moon conjunction occurs close to the degree sensitized by the total lunar eclipse of July 26, 1953 about a month before her death.

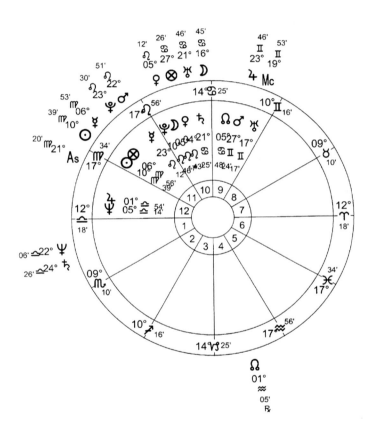

Figure 4: 1953 Solar Return (Mother's Funeral) on Natal Chart

Issues Related to the Sign Rising in the Solar Return

Following are brief descriptions of issues that may become important, depending on which sign of the zodiac is ascending in the Solar Return. The planets ruling each sign are listed together with any planet exalted in that sign. Morin considered each house to be governed by those planets whose domiciles or exaltations were any signs contained even partially within the house. For example, if the 1st house were to extend from 24° Aries to 18° Taurus, then the final six degrees of Aries (Mars ruler, Sun exalted) and the first eighteen degrees of Taurus (Venus ruler, Moon exalted) would occupy the 1st house; and there would be four 1st house rulers – Mars, the Sun, Venus and the Moon. In this example, only Mars and the Sun rule the Aries Ascendant.

The ruler of the annual Ascendant is especially important according to its placement and aspects in the Solar Return. The meanings of each zodiacal sign are quite general and must always be combined with the specific role that the rising sign, together with its planetary occupants and rulers, plays in the natal and annual charts.

Keywords for the Solar Return Ascendant:

• *Aries Annual Ascendant* (ruled by Mars; exaltation of the Sun): Initiative, new beginnings, efforts to get ahead, personal desires, courage, leadership, competition, force of will, pioneering spirit, independence, autonomy, egocentricity, self-assertion, innovation, taking charge, self-reliance, impulsiveness, rash action, boldness, impatience, physical exertion, mechanical devices, automobiles, anger, arguments, risk taking, self-discovery, forging one's own identity, promoting change, how you present yourself to others, self-absorption. Because Aries represents such a masculine energy, a significant male may figure prominently in your life. Affairs of the *natal* house(s) containing Aries, especially any natal house with Aries on the cusp, will be highly emphasized. In addition, any natal or annual house containing Mars or the Sun will be a focus of attention in the year ahead.

• *Taurus Annual Ascendant* (ruled by Venus; exaltation of the Moon): Patience, self-worth, dependability, steady progress, sensuality, money, financial responsibility, building wealth, values, resources, beauty, material comforts, gift giving, physical pleasures, self-indulgence, materialism, accumulating possessions, enjoyment of nature, persistence, determination, taking care of your body, an attractive appearance, reluctance to change, stagnation, laziness, stubbornness, conspicuous consumption. Affairs of the *natal* house(s) containing Taurus, especially any natal house with Taurus on the cusp, will be highly emphasized. In addition, any natal or annual house containing Venus or the Moon will be a focus of attention in the year ahead.

• *Gemini Annual Ascendant* (ruled by Mercury; exaltation of the Lunar North Node): Mental activity, movement, travel, transit, means of transport, motor vehicles, local travel, the roads, news, communication, learning, teaching, quick thinking, decision making, listening, speaking, phone calls, new studies, education, curiosity, variety, androgyny, adaptability, restlessness, ingenuity, logic, wit, siblings, neighbors, kin, young people, being very busy or on-the-go, nervous energy, scattering of interests, having too many irons in the fire. Affairs of the *natal* house(s) containing Gemini, especially any natal house with Gemini on the cusp, will be highly emphasized. In addition, any natal or annual house containing Mercury or the Lunar North Node will be a focus of attention in the year ahead.

• *Cancer Annual Ascendant* (ruled by the Moon; exaltation of Jupiter): Nurturing, emotional security, mothering, maternal instincts, cooking, feeding, caretaking, intimacy, sensitivity to others, home, family, the affairs of a parent, history, tradition, domestic life, landed property, hospitality, child rearing, women's issues, emotions, empathy, fluctuating moods, vulnerability, financial savvy, valuing personal feelings, being overly protective. Affairs of the *natal* house(s) containing Cancer, especially any natal house with Cancer on the cusp, will be highly emphasized. In addition, any natal or annual house containing the Moon or Jupiter will be a focus of attention in the year ahead.

• *Leo Annual Ascendant* (ruled by the Sun): Creativity, pride, self-confidence, royalty, arrogance, hubris, center of attention, showing off, leadership, pleasure, fun, playfulness, games, romance, making love, drama, recreational risk taking, sporting events, parties, entertainment, vacations, generosity, dignity, honor, approval, gifts, the affairs of children, coaching, speculation, artistic projects, assuming control, self-actualization. Affairs of the *natal* house(s) containing Leo, especially any natal house with Leo on the cusp, will be highly emphasized. In addition, any natal or annual house containing the Sun will be a focus of attention in the year ahead.

• *Virgo Annual Ascendant* (ruled by Mercury; exaltation of Mercury): Physical and emotional health, altruism, healing, therapeutics, medications, diagnostics, health consciousness, diet, exercise, service, humility, modesty, routine, daily work, errands, service repair persons, co-workers, dependents, tenants, pets, small animals, aunts and uncles, logic, critical analysis, efficiency, reliability, quality assurance, attending to details, organization, information management, categorization, critical thought, self-improvement, perfectionism, precise use of language, worry, nervous tension. Affairs of the *natal* house(s) containing Virgo, especially any natal house with Virgo on the cusp, will be highly emphasized. In addition, any natal or annual house containing Mercury will be a focus of attention in the year ahead.

•   *Libra Annual Ascendant* (ruled by Venus; exaltation of Saturn): Partnerships, agreements, conflicts, litigation, lawsuits, engagements, marriage, contracts, mediation, dialogue, collaboration, alliances, public relations, dealing with large organizations, establishing effective relationships, counseling, teamwork, networking, negotiation, open enemies, dealings with the public, socializing, being attractive to others, elegance, music, harmony, beauty, art, tact, refinement, diplomacy, luxury, balance, justice, seeing both sides of an issue, indecision. Affairs of the *natal* house(s) containing Libra, especially any natal house with Libra on the cusp, will be highly emphasized. In addition, any natal or annual house containing Venus or Saturn will be a focus of attention in the year ahead.

•   *Scorpio Annual Ascendant* (ruled by Mars and Pluto): Transformation, personal changes, metamorphosis, renovation, major shifts, crises, uprooting, elimination, psychological issues, crises, penetrating insight, healing ability, digging below the surface, occult matters, investigation, determination, resourcefulness, secrets, power struggles, passion, jealousy, vindictiveness, paranoia, compulsions, intense experiences, sexuality, taboos, magic, matters related to death and dying, reincarnation, mortality, deep emotional connections, financial matters, joint finances, insurance, inheritance, investments, loans, taxes, surgery, invasive medical therapy, discovery, revealing what was previously hidden. Affairs of the *natal* house(s) containing Scorpio, especially any natal house with Scorpio on the cusp, will be highly emphasized. In addition, any natal or annual house containing Mars or Pluto will be a focus of attention in the year ahead.

•   *Sagittarius Annual Ascendant* (ruled by Jupiter; exaltation of the Lunar South Node): Philosophy, religion, faith, church services, inspiration, legal matters, court proceedings, formal ceremonies, adventure, enthusiasm, eagerness, exuberance, taking up a sport, boundless optimism, bold action, risk taking, travel, wanderlust, long journeys of the body or the mind, dealings with strangers or foreigners, exploration, enjoying the outdoors, expanding one's horizons, seeing the big picture, higher learning, languages, foreign interests, matters at a distance, searching after truth, positive thinking, seeing the glass half-full, communication on a large scale, respecting one's intuition, difficulty making a commitment. Affairs of the *natal* house(s) containing Sagittarius, especially any natal house with Sagittarius on the cusp, will be highly emphasized. In addition, any natal or annual house containing Jupiter or the Lunar South Node will be a focus of attention in the year ahead.

• *Capricorn Annual Ascendant* (ruled by Saturn; exaltation of Mars): Tradition, authority, government, patronage, responsibility, seriousness, self-criticism, practicality, perseverance, conservatism, maturity, wisdom, discipline, realism, seeing the glass half-empty, ambition, hard work, career matters, honors, recognition, status, public image, achievement, being in control, establishing solid foundations, problem solving, inflexibility, dogmatism, goal orientation, assuming a new role, moving up the ladder in an organization, all work and no play. Affairs of the *natal* house(s) containing Capricorn, especially any natal house with Capricorn on the cusp, will be highly emphasized. In addition, any natal or annual house containing Saturn or Mars will be a focus of attention in the year ahead.

• *Aquarius Annual Ascendant* (ruled by Saturn and Uranus): Originality, innovation, iconoclasm, independence, rebelliousness, the desire to do something new and different, erratic behavior, breaking the mold, analytical thinking, inventiveness, novel techniques, surprises, unexpected events, unusual occurrences, New Age interests, astrology, unconventional ideas, experimental or high tech approaches, electricity, broadcasting, quirkiness, humanitarianism, detachment, objectivity, aloofness, eccentricity, involvement with friends and groups, clubs, fraternal organizations, dealings with like-minded individuals, marching to the beat of your own drummer; matters connected with technology, electrical wiring, electronics, or modern science. Affairs of the *natal* house(s) containing Aquarius, especially any natal house with Aquarius on the cusp, will be highly emphasized. In addition, any natal or annual house containing Saturn or Uranus will be a focus of attention in the year ahead.

• *Pisces Annual Ascendant* (ruled by Jupiter and Neptune; exaltation of Venus): Spirituality, otherworldliness, escapism, sacrifice, imaginative activities, music, poetry, illusion, ill-formed ideas, wishful thinking, sensitivity, intuition, compassion, caring for those less fortunate, large animals, solitude, seclusion, surrender, the need to retreat and regroup, contemplation, meditation, self-reflection, quiet time, withdrawal, secrecy, hospitalization, deception, self-pity, limitations, disappointment, clandestine relationships, altered states of consciousness, psychic experiences, trusting in a higher power. Affairs of the *natal* house(s) containing Pisces, especially any natal house with Pisces on the cusp, will be highly emphasized. In addition, any natal or annual house containing Jupiter, Neptune, or Venus will be a focus of attention in the year ahead.

7

Issues of Timing and Emerson's Point of Death

The murder of 6-year-old JonBenet Ramsey on the day after Christmas of 1996 became one of the most celebrated detective cases of the 1990s. An event of this magnitude should show up clearly in her Solar Return.

Known as America's Tiny Little Miss, JonBenet behaved publicly like a little beauty queen. Her sexual molestation and murder in the basement of her home in Boulder, Colorado during the early morning hours of December 26, 1996, caught national attention. Images of little blonde JonBenet in her beauty pageant outfit or cowgirl attire flooded the media. The local police apparently botched the investigation. Although the crime lab found unidentified DNA under JonBenet's fingernails and in her underwear, the comments by police and the press raised suspicion that the parents were complicit in the crime. Many observers felt that the police had missed their opportunity to capture the real intruder.

JonBenet's Natal Promise
JonBenet Ramsey was born at 1:36 AM EDT on August 6, 1990 in Atlanta, Georgia.[1] She has Gemini rising and her Ascendant-ruler Mercury trines Neptune, indicating personal charm and attractiveness. Ascendant-ruler Mercury also conjoins the cusp of the 5th house of theater and creative pursuits.

A striking feature of her chart is an uncommon configuration, namely, a grand square involving a natal Sun/Moon opposition at a 90-degree angle to a natal Mars/Pluto opposition. Prominent hard aspects between Mars and Pluto are indicators of potential exposure to violence (as victim or perpetrator) during one's lifetime, especially if connected to significant personal points such as the Sun or the Moon. In JonBenet's chart, the Sun, Moon, Mars, and Pluto occupy the four corners of a square. Whenever any one of them is activated by transit, direction or progression, the entire grand square is activated.

Natal Mars (aggressive young men) in her natal 12th house of secret enemies exactly opposes Pluto (violence, dominance, criminal behavior) in the 6th. Thus the natal Mars/Pluto opposition falls across the 12th and 6th houses, considered unfortunate in traditional astrology because, among other things, these houses are linked to illness, undoing, sorrow, confinement, and secret enemies. Furthermore, the natal Mars/Pluto opposition squares the MC/IC axis, which has to do with public recognition, parental figures, and final endings.

This potential for violence (Mars opposite Pluto from the 12th to the 6th houses) is most likely to manifest when natal directions, secondary progressions, or major transits to the natal chart trigger this natal Mars/Pluto aspect. On the date of her death, secondary progressed Mars at 19° Taurus 43' was closely square her secondary progressed Sun at 19° Leo 39'. In addition, the secondary progressed Midheaven at 17° Aquarius 45' was almost precisely square the midpoint of natal Mars and secondary progressed Mars, which lay

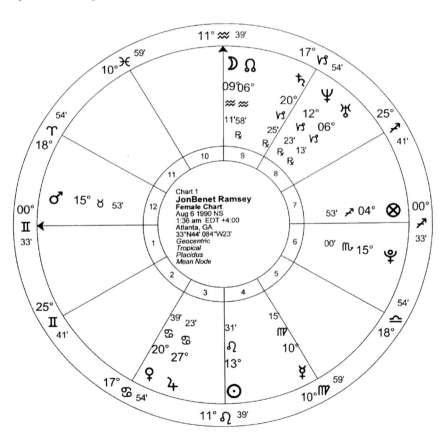

Figure 1: JonBenet Ramsey Natal Chart

at 17° Taurus 48'. Her secondary progressions clearly warned of potential violence in 1996.

Ramsey's 1996 Solar Return

JonBenet's 1996 Solar Return has several striking features. Most notably she has a T-square of annual Mars opposing annual Jupiter and squaring annual Saturn. Furthermore, this T-square falls on the angles of the Solar Return chart, making it both a zodiacal and a paran-T-square, which underscores its overwhelming importance in 1996. In her birth chart Mars rules her natal 12th house of secret enemies and Jupiter governs her natal 8th house of death. In addition, annual Pluto at 0° Sagittarius 20' and retrograde conjoins her natal Descendant (her personal sunset), closely opposing her natal Ascendant at 0° Gemini 33'. The strong emphasis on Mars and Pluto in the Solar Return

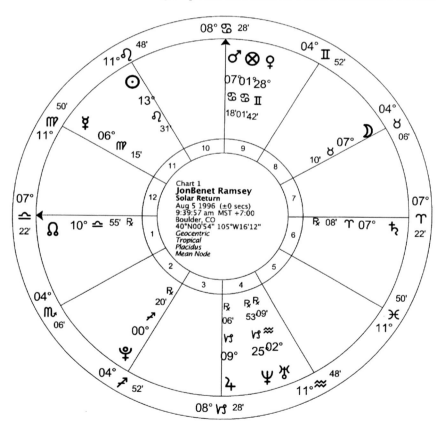

Figure 2: JonBenet Ramsey 1996 Solar Return

acts to trigger the potential of her natal Mars/Pluto opposition. The natal Ascendant falls in the Solar Return 8th house of death. Her natal Ascendant-ruler Mercury conjoins the return 12th house of sorrow and secret enemies. Finally, natal Uranus conjoins the return IC (final endings) and opposes return Mars (unexpected aggression).

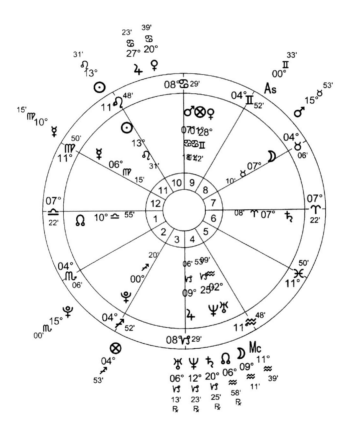

Figure 3: Ramsey Natal Chart Superimposed on 1996 Solar Return

Emerson's Point of Death

$$\boxed{\begin{array}{c} \text{Emerson's Death Point} = \\ \text{MC} + \text{Saturn} - \text{Mars} \end{array}}$$

Whenever death is an issue, it is useful to calculate Emerson's Point of Death in a chart. Charles Emerson (1923-1992) was a prominent New York astrologer and one of the founders of the NCGR. He did significant original work in Uranian, medical, and mundane astrology. One of his findings was that a particular horoscopic point is often prominent in charts involving death. Emerson's Point of Death has the formula: MC + *Saturn* – *Mars*. In JonBenet's Solar Return, Emerson's Death Point lies at 8° Aries 18', and it makes crucial contacts with other points in the chart.

Using a one-degree orb, we see that the annual Point of Death opposes the Solar Return Ascendant, squares the return MC/IC axis, and also squares the annual Mars/Jupiter opposition. Unpacking this symbolism, we might say that the annual Death Point opposite the annual Ascendant (the body) raises the possibility of death. The annual Death Point squaring the annual MC (public standing) and IC (final endings) has obvious symbolism. The annual Death Point square annual Jupiter (ruler of the natal 8th house of death) suggests a possible demise. The annual Death Point square annual Mars (aggression, ruler of the natal 12th of undoing) is also foreboding. With natal Uranus and Neptune in her 8th house at birth, there is a clear potential for an unusual death (Uranus in the 8th) under mysterious circumstances (Neptune).

Progressing the Solar Return Chart

It is possible to progress a Solar Return symbolically by the method of secondary progression, which equates a day with a year. In other words, the day following the return of the Sun to its exact natal position is projected onto the year ahead. In this divinatory system, the 24 hours following the precise time of the Solar Return is mapped onto the roughly 365 days until the next Solar Return. The first two hours after the sun's return are roughly equivalent to the first month, the second two hours to the second month, and so on, so that the final two hours of the 24-hour period after the Solar Return are equivalent to the month preceding the next Solar Return.

This may all sound very simple, but in astronomy there are various types of days and years, each slightly different in length from the other. After experimenting with these various factors, I have come to prefer the following formula:

The time it takes for the earth to spin on its axis in a complete circle (360 degrees) following the Solar Return EQUALS the coming Solar Return year (the number of days between the current and the next Solar Return). In this formula, one complete daily cycle of the Sun equals one complete annual cycle of the Sun.

For astronomy buffs, the time it takes the earth to spin 360 degrees in its rotation is called an apparent sidereal day and has a length of 86,164.09 seconds, which is 23 hours, 56 minutes, 4.091 seconds. We have already seen that the length of the tropical year (the time from one Solar Return to the next) is 365.2422 solar days.

The above formula equates one complete rotation of the earth after the Solar Return to the year ahead. Using the above figures, one can calculate the following formula:

Each day of the Solar Return year corresponds to 3.93182 minutes of the Solar Return day. Thus, to progress a Solar Return chart for any day in the coming year, you would count the number of days that have transpired since the Solar Return and multiply that number of days by 3.93182 minutes to find the amount of time that has elapsed since the exact moment of the Solar Return.

Using JonBenet Ramsey's chart, we see that her 1996 Solar Return took place on August 5, 1996 at 10:39:56 AM MDT in Denver and her death occurred on December 26, 1996. There are 143 days between August 5th and December 26th. Days between dates can easily be calculated in a spreadsheet or with a dedicated "days between dates" computer program. Several such programs are available free on the Internet.

To find out how far the Solar Return chart has progressed in 143 days, we must multiply 143 days by 3.93182 minutes for each day elapsed since the Solar Return.

Multiplying 143 x 3.93182, we get 562.2503 minutes.

Dividing 562.2503 minutes by 60 minutes per hour, we find that the Solar Return has progressed by 9.3708 hours (or 9 hours 22 min 16 sec) by the day of her death. Doing the conversion, we find that we need to advance the Solar Return chart by 9 hours, 22 minutes, 16 seconds to find its progression to the day of the murder.

Her 1996 Solar Return occurred at 10:39:56 AM MDT in Denver, Colorado. To this time we must add 9 hours, 22 minutes, 16 seconds:

10 hours 39 minutes 56 seconds AM MDT of Solar Return
+ 9 hours 22 minutes 16 seconds of progression to Dec 26, 1996

---

19 hours 61 minutes 72 seconds totals =

20 hours 2 minutes 12 seconds MDT = progression to Dec 26, 1996.

We see in the Solar Return chart progressed to December 26, 1996 that the return Ascendant has progressed to 13° Aquarius 25', which places her natal Sun on the Descendant of the progressed Solar Return chart. In other words, on December 26, 1996, the sunset of her life, her natal Sun at 13° Aquarius 31' is setting in the progressed Solar Return chart. The angular

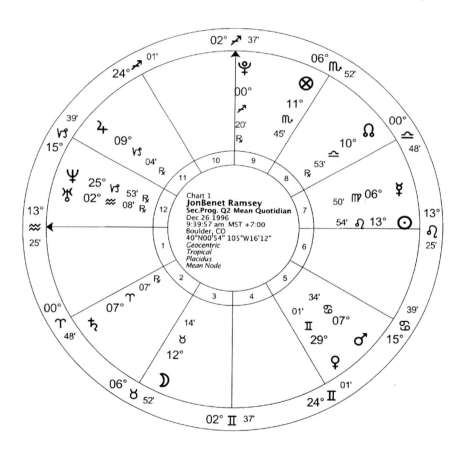

Figure 4: JonBenet's Solar Return Progressed to December 26, 1996

position of the natal Sun in the progressed Solar Return chart triggers the natal grand square and sets off the natal Mars/Pluto opposition, which indicates potential violence.

This chapter contains a convenient table for converting the number of days during the Solar Return year that are equivalent by progression to the corresponding number of hours, minutes, and seconds that have elapsed since the time of the Solar Return. For every five days of calendar time after the Solar Return, you can progress the Solar Return by 19 minutes 40 seconds to calculate the corresponding progressed Solar Return chart. To find a specific day within that five-day interval, recall that each day corresponds to just under 4 minutes of progression of the Solar Return chart. This technique is often called the *mean quotidian method of secondary progression*, and computer programs like *Solar Fire Deluxe* offer this calculation as an option – which will save the reader from using the Table and doing the calculations by hand.

Converting Days after the Solar Return into Hours, Minutes, and Seconds to Progress the Solar Return Chart
(Mean Quotidian Secondary Progression of the Solar Return)
(An extended daily version of this table appears in the Appendix.)

Number of CalendarDAYS after SR	Is Equivalent to Minutes after SR =	Or this many hours after the SR, which is	HOURS	MINUTES	SECONDS
1	3.9318	0.0655	0	03	56
5	19.6591	0.3277	0	19	40
10	39.3182	0.6553	0	39	20
15	58.9773	0.9830	0	58	59
20	78.6364	1.3106	1	18	39
25	98.2955	1.6383	1	38	18
30	117.9546	1.9659	1	57	58
40	157.2728	2.6212	2	37	17
50	196.5910	3.2765	3	16	36
60	235.9092	3.9318	3	55	55
90	353.8638	5.8977	5	53	52
120	471.8184	7.8636	7	51	50
150	589.7730	9.8296	9	49	47
180	707.7276	11.7955	11	47	44
210	825.6822	13.7614	13	45	41

240	943.6368	15.7273	15	43	39
270	1061.5914	17.6932	17	41	36
300	1179.5460	19.6591	19	39	33
330	1297.5006	21.6250	21	37	31
360	1415.4552	23.5909	23	35	28
365.2422	1436.0666	23.9344	23	56	04

More Examples Illustrating Emerson's Death Point

As I was working on this chapter, there were two prominent deaths in the news: newscaster Peter Jennings and Supreme Court Justice William Rehnquist. It seemed as if the universe were providing additional data by which to test Emerson's Death Point in the Solar Return. Let's take a look.

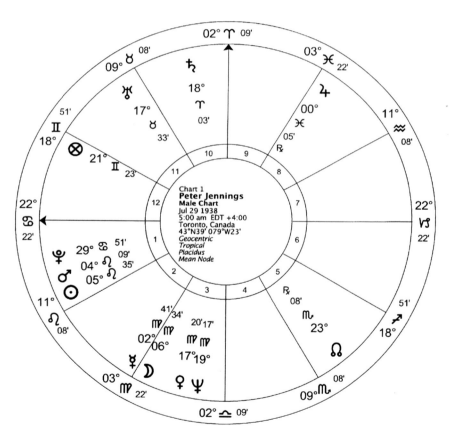

Figure 5: Peter Jennings Natal Chart

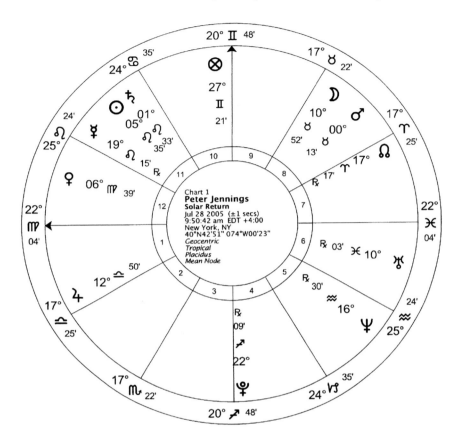

Figure 6: Peter Jennings 2005 Solar Return

Peter Jennings

Peter Jennings, by his own report, was born at 5 AM on July 29, 1938 in Toronto, Canada. He died of lung cancer in New York City on Sunday August 7, 2005. Jennings' Solar Return for 2005 has annual Pluto (a natural significator of death) angular in the 4th house of endings conjunct the IC (endings). Emerson's Point of Death in the Solar Return chart lies at 22° Virgo 09', almost exactly conjunct the annual Ascendant at 22° Virgo 04'.

Justice William Rehnquist

According to *AstroDataBank*, William Hubbs Rehnquist, the 16th Chief Justice of the United States, was born at 11:32 AM CST in Milwaukee, Wisconsin, on October 1, 1924. He died at the age of 80 on Saturday evening September 3, 2005, at his home in Arlington, Virginia. In his natal chart Jupiter (legal

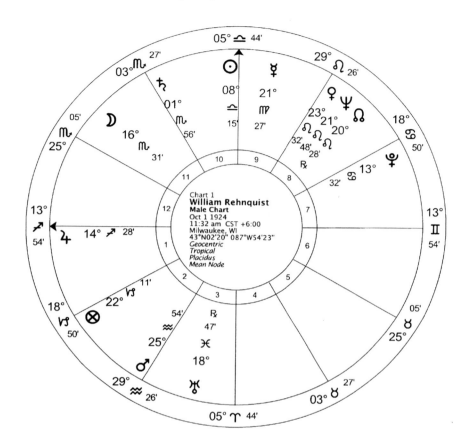

Figure 7: William Rehnquist Natal Chart

matters) rises and conjoins the natal Ascendant. The 10th house Sun rules his 9th house of jurisprudence and conjoins his natal Midheaven, suggesting prominence in the field of law.

Rehnquist's 2004 Solar Return, which was in effect at the time of his death, has several significant configurations. Annual Pluto (death) conjoins the annual Descendant (his personal sunset) in opposition to the Solar Return Ascendant. Annual Venus, which rules the Solar Return 12th house of hospitalization and the natal 6th house of sickness and which occupies the natal 6th house of death, conjoins the annual IC (endings, the grave). In fact, annual Venus is very close to its natal position in Leo in the 8th house of death. This similarity of the annual and birth charts unleashes the natal potential of Venus during this Solar Return year.

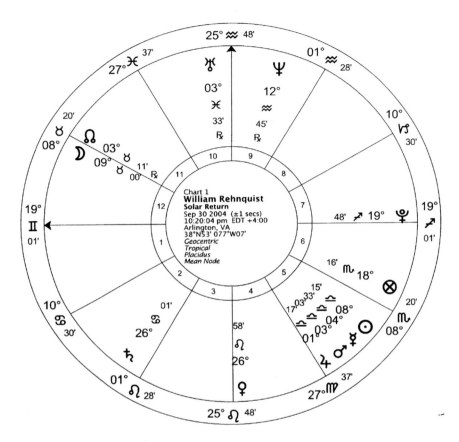

Figure 8: William Rehnquist 2004 Solar Return

The Solar Return Moon, which rules his natal 8th house of death, closely conjoins his annual 12th house cusp. Emerson's Part of Death in the annual chart lies at 18° Sagittarius 47' and conjoins annual Pluto as well as the annual Descendant. The annual Midheaven almost exactly conjoins natal Mars, which rules his natal 12th house of hospitalization as well as the Solar Return 6th house of sickness.

Lady Diana Frances Spencer

Lady Diana Frances Spencer[2] was born on July 1, 1961, at 7:45 PM BST in Sandringham, England. What factors in Diana's natal chart indicate the potential for an untimely and tragic death in a motor vehicle accident?

Looking to her 8th house, we see that Uranus, Mars, and Pluto all occupy the house of death. Uranus in the natal 8th suggests a sudden death. Mars and

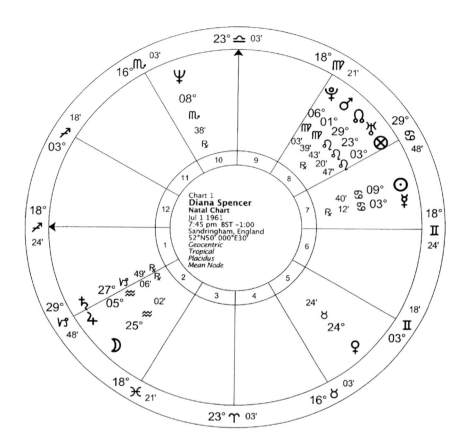

Figure 9: Lady Diana Frances Spencer Natal Chart

Pluto in that house show a potential for a violent death. Natal Jupiter rules her Sagittarius Ascendant (the body) as well as the Pisces 3rd house (transport, motor vehicles). Ascendant-ruler Jupiter is quincunx Pluto in the 8th. Finally, Emerson's Point of Death in her birth chart lies at 19° Pisces 13', closely conjunct her Placidus 3rd house cusp of local travel.

At the time of her death on August 31, 1997, Lady Diana had two stressful secondary progressed aspects involving her 8th house planets. Secondary progressed Neptune was semi-square progressed Mars in the 8th, and secondary progressed Saturn was quincunx progressed Uranus. In addition, the secondary progressed Moon in Gemini (transport) was quincunx to progressed Saturn and sextile to progressed Uranus, forming the so-called "finger of fate" configuration.

The transits on the date of her death are also quite striking. According to news reports, Diana was taken to a trauma ward after her car crashed in a Paris tunnel about a half hour after midnight. Doctors were unable to revive her, and she was pronounced dead around 3:50 AM Paris time, as the transiting Moon, Sun, and Mercury all occupied the natal 8th house of death. Transiting Neptune closely conjoined natal Saturn, and transiting Uranus closely conjoined natal Jupiter, ruler of her natal Ascendant and 3rd house of short-distance travel.

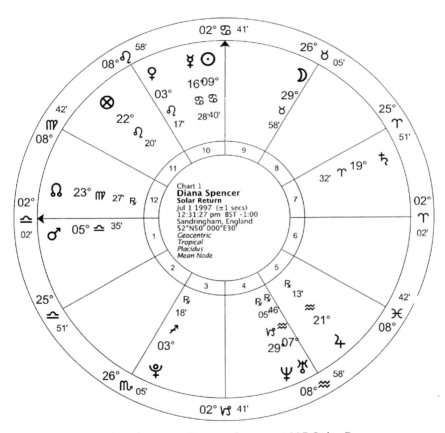

Figure 10: Lady Diana Frances Spencer 1997 Solar Return

The Solar Return of the Year of Diana's Death

Diana's Solar Return cast for her birthplace[3] has 2° Libra 02' rising with Ascendant-ruler Venus at 3° Leo 17', conjoining the cusp of her natal Placidus 8th house of death. Annual Mars, which rules the annual 3rd of local travel and

8th of death, rises early in Libra near the return Ascendant. Annual Pluto (a natural significator of death) forms an exact conjunction with the cusp of the natal 12th house (sorrow, undoing, grief, hospitalization) – this is often a portent of an illness or accident that will require hospital care.

The Solar Return Midheaven closely conjoins natal Mercury (vehicles, travel), highlighting Mercurial themes for the year. Emerson's Point of Death in the Solar Return lies at 16° Capricorn 38' opposite annual Mercury, raising the possibility of death related to travel. Diana's Solar Return Moon at 29° Taurus 58' (conjunct the fixed star Alcyone of the Pleiades associated by Ptolemy with violent death) occupies the natal 5th house of love affairs and squares her natal Moon's North Node, which lies in the 8th house of death. Finally, the cusp of the annual 9th house (foreign travel) at 26° Taurus 05' closely conjoins the malefic fixed star Caput Algol at 26° Taurus 07', a star associated with misfortune, violence, sudden death, and decapitation.

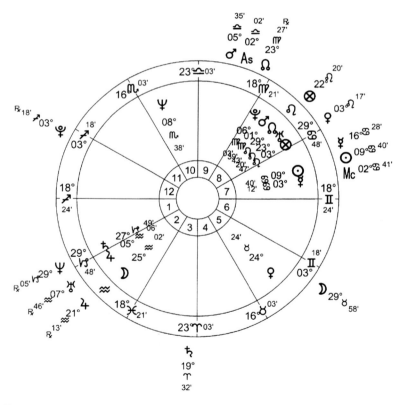

Figure 11: Diana's 1997 Solar Return Superimposed on her Natal Chart

Activist Rachel Corrie

Rachel Corrie died at the youthful age of 23 when she was still a senior at Evergreen State College in Olympia, Washington, where she was a student of community organizing. An activist and a talented writer, she was a member of the International Solidarity Movement, a group that opposed the Israeli occupation of the West Bank and Gaza Strip. Prompted by a strong sense of social justice, she traveled to Palestine in January 2003 as part of an independent study program. At about 5 PM on March 16, 2003, while trying to act as a human shield to protect Palestinian homes in Rafah, an Israeli military bulldozer ran her over and she was pronounced dead in the hospital at 6:30 PM. A dispute about her death ensued. The Israeli Army labeled it a regrettable accident, but her fellow protesters claimed that the bulldozer had

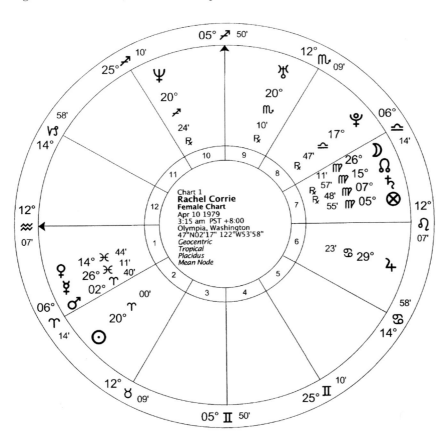

Figure 12: Rachel Corrie Natal Chart

deliberately run her over more than one time. Since the time of her death at least three theatrical plays have appeared commemorating her beliefs and experiences in the Middle East.

According to *AstroDataBank*, Rachel Corrie was born on April 10, 1979 at 3:15 AM PST in Olympia, Washington (47°N02'/122°W53') – the city where she also attended college. Her sense of social justice is reflected in the Aquarius Ascendant with its co-ruler, freedom-loving Uranus, occupying her 9th house of beliefs and foreign lands. Her activism is also related to the Sun in independent Aries with the Sun's dispositor Mars, also in Aries, occupying the natal 1st house. Planets that rule or occupy the 8th house signify her death. Pluto in the 8th raises the possibility of death through violence or overwhelming force. Venus rules the 8th and occupies the 1st (personal actions) in Pisces (concern for the underdog). Pluto in the 8th opposes the natal Sun, ruler of her 7th of open enemies. The natal chart is consistent with the events and actions that led to her demise. Emerson's Point of Death in the natal chart lies at 10° Taurus 59'. We shall see what role the Point of Death plays in her Solar and Lunar Returns.

Rachel's Solar Return occurred on April 9, 2002 in Olympia, Washington, where she was born and was attending college. Her annual Ascendant falls in Libra, the sign of her natal 8th house of death. Annual Venus (at 10° Taurus 48') rules her natal 8th house and has migrated to the annual 8th house where Venus conjoins the natal Emerson's Point of Death (at 10° Taurus 59').

In other words, the natal ruler of death occupies her annual house of death and simultaneously conjoins Emerson's natal Point of Death in the annual 8th house. Venus also rules the annual 9th house of foreign travel. Annual Mars, which rules the Solar Return 8th of death, conjoins the return 9th house cusp, suggesting death in a foreign land. Annual Mars (ruling the annual 8th of death) closely squares annual Uranus (ruler of the natal Ascendant, signifying her body and life force), suggesting a fatal accident related to a mechanical device or vehicle. The Solar Return Moon, which is always connected with the health of the body, occupies the annual 6th house and forms a T-Square with annual Saturn, her natal Ascendant ruler, and Pluto, which occupies her natal house of death. A similar T-square involving the Moon, Pluto, and Saturn repeats in the Lunar Return that was active at the time of her death.

The Lunar Return in effect at the time of her death is also striking. According to biographical accounts of her activities at the time, Corrie spent her Lunar Return on February 19, 2003 in or near Rafah where she was participating in protests against the Israeli forces. Ascendant-ruler Jupiter at

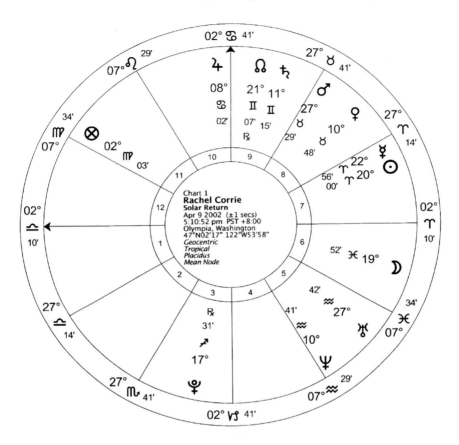

Figure 13: Rachel Corrie 2002 Solar Return

10° Leo 58' lies in the 9th house of the Lunar Return and is square the natal Emerson's Pont of Death at 10° Taurus 59'. Recall that the Ascendant rules her body and her life.

Ascendant-ruler Jupiter lies opposite Neptune, which is one of the rulers of the Lunar Return 4th house of the grave. Lunar Jupiter also forms a semi-square with the Moon, ruler of the Lunar Return 8th house of death. The Moon, in turn, participates in a T-square involving Mars, Pluto, and Saturn. Pluto, which occupies her natal 8th of death, conjoins Mars (violence) in the Lunar Return 1st house where it opposes Saturn, a co-ruler of her natal Ascendant, in the Lunar Return 7th house of open enemies. The Sun in the Lunar Return closely conjoins Uranus (accidents) in the 3rd house of transport and local travel.

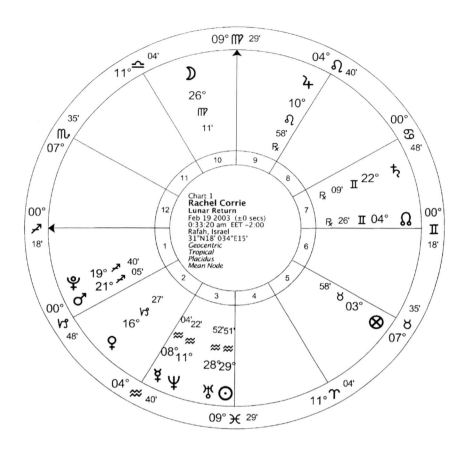

Figure 14: Rachel Corrie Lunar Return February 2003

Enron Founder Kenneth Lay

Kenneth Lay, former CEO of Enron and a friend of President George W. Bush who referred to him as "Kenny Boy," was convicted and awaiting sentence in the conspiracy and accounting scandal when he died unexpectedly of a heart attack on Wednesday July 5, 2006, in Colorado where he was vacationing following the trial. On May 25, 2006 Mr. Lay had been found guilty of ten counts of fraud and corporate conspiracy connected with the collapse of the Houston-based Enron Corporation, the nation's seventh largest energy company before its fall. The collapse of Enron cost 4000 workers their jobs and many of them their life savings. Investors lost billions of dollars.

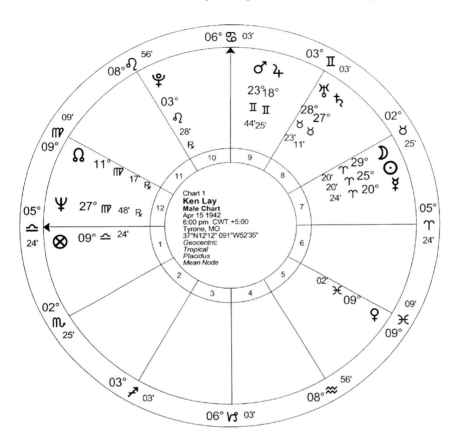

Figure 15: Ken Lay Natal Chart

Lay, whose sentencing was scheduled for October 23, 2006, was facing 25 to 40 years in prison. News reports from the trial had described his demeanor as brash, abrasive, and unwilling to accept responsibility for Enron's demise.

The stress of the trial and the pending prison were thought to have precipitated his coronary collapse. The autopsy confirmed that Lay suffered from severe coronary artery disease and that he had been treated with stents to hold open his blocked arteries and had suffered at least two prior heart attacks. *The DenverPost.com*[4] reported that around 1 AM on July 5, 2006, at his vacation home near Aspen, Colorado, Lay got up to use the bathroom. His wife heard a "thump" and found him unresponsive on the bathroom floor. He was taken to Aspen Valley Hospital where he was pronounced dead at 3:11 AM MDT.

Ken Lay's 2006 Solar Return

Lay's annual chart is cast for Houston, Texas, where he resided and was a participant in the Enron trial at the time of his 2006 solar revolution. Zero degrees of Aries (a cardinal degree) rise, connecting Lay's personal Solar Return with the fate of the larger community. Annual Mercury, which rules Lay's natal 12th house of imprisonment, closely conjoins the Solar Return Ascendant from the annual 12th house of scandal and conspiracy.

The Solar Return Aries Ascendant occupies the natal 6th house of health concerns. The sign Aries also rules the natal 7th house of lawsuits, so that the superimposition of the annual Ascendant sign onto the birth chart highlights matters related to lawsuits, partnerships, and health. Annual Ascendant-ruler

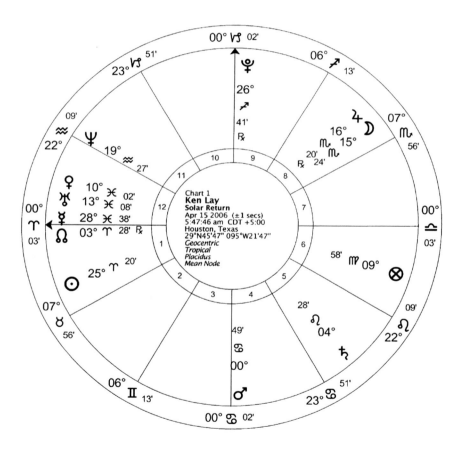

Figure 16: Ken Lay 2006 Solar Return

Mars closely conjoins the annual 4th cusp of final endings, squares the Solar Return Ascendant/Mercury conjunction, and opposes annual Pluto – co-ruler with Mars of the annual 8th of death. In other words, both co-rulers of the Solar Return 8th house of death are angular and in square aspect with the annual Ascendant (his body).

Emerson's Point of Death in the Solar Return is 3° Aquarius 41'. It opposes annual Saturn (blockages) in Leo (the heart) in the Solar Return 5th and also opposes natal Pluto (ruler of the Solar Return 8th of death) in Leo in the natal 10th of professional standing. At the time Lay was pronounced dead (3:11 AM MDT) the transiting Emerson's Point of Death in Aspen, Colorado, was at 3° Aquarius 10' – the same degree it occupies in the 2006 Solar Return, opposite his natal Pluto in the natal 10th house. In other words, Lay was pronounced dead at the very moment that his daily Emerson's Point of Death returned to its zodiacal location in the annual chart.

Also of note is the annual Ascendant/Mercury conjunction joined to Scheat – an unfortunate fixed star at 29° Pisces 27' associated with imprisonment, misfortune, murder, suicide, drowning, and loss of life in catastrophes. In the Lunar Return that was active at the time of his death, the Moon's North Node has moved from its position in Aries in the annual 1st house to conjoin this unlucky fixed star in Pisces (the sign of the North Node's fall) in the unfortunate 12th house of the Solar Return.

Ken Lay's June 2006 Lunar Return

The themes of the solar revolution repeat in the Lunar Return (set for Houston) prior to Lay's demise. The Solar Return 8th house cusp essentially becomes the Ascendant of the lunar revolution that was active at the time he died. Saturn, which rules his natal 4th of endings, lies on the Midheaven of the Lunar Return where it conjoins Mars – ruler of his Lunar Return Ascendant and his Solar Return house of death. Emerson's Point of Death in the Lunar Return at 8° Leo 15' is closely linked to the Saturn/MC/Mars conjunction of the lunar revolution. The planet Venus, ruler of the Ascendant of his nativity and of his natal 8th house of death, lies at 26° Taurus 17' in the Lunar Return, closely aligned with the malefic fixed star Caput Algol at 26° Taurus 15'.

Ken Lay's Progressed Daily Lunar Return for July 4, 2006

After experimenting with various ways to use the Lunar Return for timing, I settled upon a technique that I call the "progressed daily Lunar Return" to generate meaningful progressed angles and house cusps during the month of a Lunar Return. The details of this technique are presented in Chapter Nine.

Ken Lay's Lunar Return took place on June 20, 2006, at 4:13:41 PM CDT in Houston, Texas. He died in the early morning hours of July 5, 2006 –

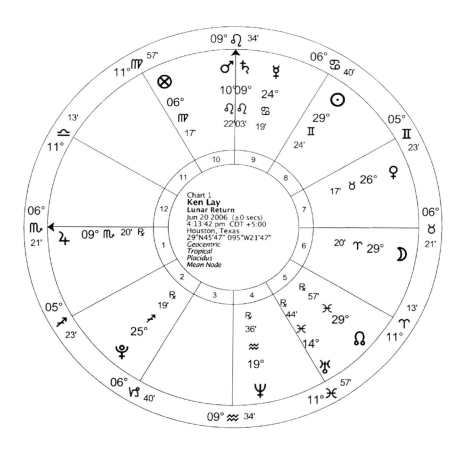

Figure 17: Ken Lay June 2006 Lunar Return

almost 14 ½ days later. The progressed daily Lunar Return chart that was in effect at the time of his death was the one for July 4, 2006. As will be explained, this chart is calculated using the data for the Lunar Return chart but changing the date to July 4th (14 days later) and adding 4 hours 0 minutes 10 seconds (that is, adding 17 minutes 9 seconds for each day elapsed) to the time of the original Lunar Return. This gives a daily progressed Lunar Return time of 8:13:51 PM on July 4, 2006.

This daily progressed Lunar Return in effect the day of his fatal heart attack is striking. The progressed daily Lunar Return Sun and Moon are both angular and form a paran-square. The Sun opposes the Ascendant and rules the 8th of death of the progressed daily lunar chart. The Moon, ruler of the

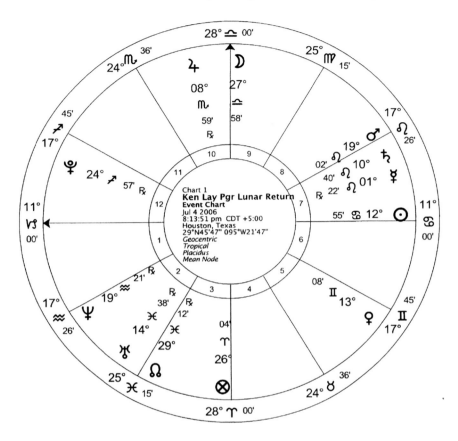

Figure 18: Lay Lunar Return Daily Progressed to July 4 2006

Solar Return 4th cusp of endings, occupies and also rules the annual 8th house of death by exaltation. Mars rules the annual Ascendant and conjoins the annual 4th cusp of endings. Mars in the progressed daily lunar chart conjoins the 8th cusp of death and opposes Neptune, which occupies the natal 12th and rules the Solar Return 12th house of undoing.

NOTES

1.   Source: *AstroDataBank*, http://www.astrodatabank.com/NM/RamseyJon Benet.htm, Rodden Rating B.

2.   For a detailed discussion of the astrology of Lady Diana's death see Garry Heaton's article at http://accessnewage.com/articles/astro/ HEADIANA.HTM.

3.   I do not know Lady Diana's exact location at the time of her 1997 Solar Return, so I chose to erect the Solar Return for her birthplace. The return chart for her residence at Kensington Palace is almost identical to that of her birthplace, with only about ½ degree difference in the angles and house cusps.

4.   The *DenverPost.com* (Article launched: 07/20/2006 01:00:00 AM MDT) at http://www.denverpost.com/business/ci_4071697.

8

The Contributions of Jean-Baptiste Morin

In a revolution, nothing should be predicted – at least nothing significant – unless it is signified by the radix or by its directions at the time of the revolution.[1]

Jean-Baptiste Morin

As mentioned previously, Alexandre Volguine learned and practiced astrology in France, the home of Jean-Baptiste Morin de Villefranche[2] (1583-1656), perhaps the most renowned astrologer of the 17th century. Morin's writings have influenced the practice of astrology in continental Europe and Latin America to this day. He was a man of impressive academic credentials, having studied medicine, philosophy, mathematics, and astrology – interests that he attributed to the almost exact trine of his natal 9th Regiomontanus cusp to his Ascendant. Morin was a contemporary of Rene Descartes ("I think therefore I am") and is said to have debated the famous philosopher in a public forum. He was appointed Royal Mathematician to King Louis XIII, and allegedly was present to time the birth of the future King Louis XIV. Morin's entrenchment in the geocentric astrological worldview got in the way of his acceptance of Galileo's heliocentric ideas, which he opposed throughout his professional life.

With his impressive university education, Morin had a strong rational bent and was fluent in the educated Latin of his time. He devoured the ancient astrological treatises that were preserved by the Arabs and later translated into scholarly Latin. His magnum opus was a 26-volume work on astrology, *Astrologia Gallica*, in which he set out to establish a rational basis for the discipline of astrology. Morin rejected many techniques espoused by the Arabs and Chaldeans as fictitious nonsense, and he only accepted astrological methods that could be empirically demonstrated or deduced from astrological principles. Morin's *Book 21* is regarded as a masterpiece on the significations of the planets in a natal chart. His *Book 23* is a thorough explanation of the 17th century European method of interpretation of Solar Returns (also called Solar Revolutions) stripped of the Arabic fascination with lots (Arabic parts), time lords, terms, decanates, and so on.

As he had foreseen in his own chart, Morin died around 2 AM on November 6, 1656, five years before his encyclopedic work was published. He spent thirty years writing his treatise, but alas during the late 17th century with the rise of modern science, there was diminishing interest in his densely written Latin text on natural philosophy and astrology. Morin's work lay dormant for two centuries and was rediscovered only with the advent of modern astrology. During the late 19th and early 20th centuries several sections of Morin's *Astrologia Gallica* were translated into Spanish, French, and German. Morin's ideas made their way throughout continental Europe and Latin America, strongly influencing the practice of astrology in those regions. It was not until late in the 20th century that Morin's works and the brilliance of his insights became available in English translation.

In Morin's *Book 23* on Solar and Lunar Revolutions he points out that Solar Returns were not in use at the time of Claudius Ptolemy (85-165 CE) when Ptolemy wrote his famous treatise on astrology, the *Tetrabiblos*. Morin notes that Ptolemy "indeed handed down the doctrine of erecting an annual universal revolution of the Sun at the four cardinal points of the zodiac, but not of erecting particular figures for nativities, which in fact he didn't mention."[3] Classical Greek astrology did not have a precise enough method to calculate a chart for the exact moment that the Sun or any other planet returned to its natal location. Techniques for measuring time with enough precision to calculate a Solar Return were not yet available in the Classical Period.

The first mention of Solar Returns in the modern sense occurs in the writings of Paulus Alexandrinus[4] around 378 CE during the Late Classical Period of astrology. As technology advanced and tables of the precise location of the Sun could be calculated, it became possible to erect accurate Solar Return charts. Entire texts on Solar Returns, based on Persian and Arabian traditions (much of which Morin rejected), began to appear in the literature during the medieval period. According to James Holden, the earliest treatises on Solar Returns as we understand them today "are those of the Arabian astrologers, not earlier than the 8th century... they appear to be an invention of the medieval astrologers".[5]

Although Morin discarded much of Arabic and medieval astrology, he embraced the method of Solar Returns. He hypothesized that a planet "returning to its own radical location, renews its own radical force with regard to the native... and it rouses up the seeds of its own influence projected on the one being born, to produce its own effects... by reason of its being *similar* or *dissimilar* to the geniture... [italics mine]".[6] Morin viewed the natal chart as a map of the imprint of the celestial influences bearing upon the native at the precise moment and location of birth. The Solar Return is a map of the native's rebirth for the year ahead, an annual renewal in which current celestial influences are brought to bear upon the native at the precise moment and place where the native is located when the Sun returns to its birth position.

In Morin's view the proper location to cast the annual chart is the exact spot on earth where the native happens to be when the Sun returns to its birth location. The stellar influences at the moment of the Solar Return imprint themselves for the year ahead on the native at the precise time and place that the native occupies when the Sun returns to its birth position. Each location on earth will have a particular configuration of angles and house cusps that, along with the zodiacal positions of the planets, will be imprinted on the native annually at the moment of his or her personal Solar Return. The annual imprint may either clash or harmonize with the birth imprint, thereby impeding or activating the manifestation of natal potentials during that year.

Most significant, in Morin's view, is the precise Ascendant associated with either the natal or the Solar Return charts because the rising degree represents the essential life force and characteristic disposition of the person. Associated with each location on earth is a specific Ascendant, and in Morin's view the logical location to cast an annual chart is the actual location of the native at the time of the return. The late Zoltan Mason, a modern teacher of Morin's methods, taught that the Ascendant is 80% of the horoscope. Robert Corre, a student of Mason and a teacher of Morin's methods, explains in his Forum on Astrology:

> The Ascendant is the most important consideration in the horoscope as it is the body, the physical constitution with its natural predisposition. It is also the psychological organization of the person, the mask of habitual reactions that stand between the outside environment and the internal and subjective private world of a person. ...the Ascendant describes the range of reactions by the person to the environment. A person will respond to and be characterized by the affairs associated with the zodiacal sign on the Ascendant. It will be those affairs that will always be in the back of the person's head.... [7]

Some modern astrologers cast the Solar Return for the birthplace or for the place of residence, regardless of the native's location at the time of the Solar Return. In Morin's system, these other charts are not true Solar Returns because the imprinting of stellar influences can only occur at the very location where the native actually spends the Solar Return. These other charts may be useful, but they are not true Solar Returns. Nonetheless, it is informative to relocate the Solar Return to the birthplace, that is, to cast the Solar Return chart as if the native spent the Solar Return at the birthplace. Essentially, casting the Solar Return for the birthplace gives a progressed chart (at a rate of one day = one year) set for the precise moment of the Solar Return. Such a progressed chart consists of the current transits at the birthplace at the precise moment of the Solar Return and acts like a subsidiary Solar Return. Any progression of the natal chart reveals the unfolding of its potential during the course of the lifetime. A progression occurring at the precise moment of the Solar Return will be especially significant for the year ahead.

In Morin's view the interpretation of the Solar Return always requires a comparison of the natal and the return charts. The astrologer must first determine the natal imprint and only then look to the Solar Return to judge how the natal imprinting will unfold or be impeded during the coming year. The Solar Return cannot produce any effect that is not originally signified by the natal chart. To quote Morin directly:

> "a revolution per se will effect nothing, at least nothing notable, that the genethliacal constitution has not presignified."[8]

The significations of the planets in the natal chart are "fundamental and universal for the entire course of life."[9] If something particular to the native is not indicated in the natal chart, it simply will not occur, regardless of what is happening in the Solar Return. Only those potentials that are imprinted during the nativity are able to manifest later in life.

The meaning of a given planet in a natal chart depends on several factors. Each planet has its own nature, which is universal and independent of a particular nativity. For example, the Moon is always emotional, Mars is rash and impulsive, Saturn is constrictive, and so on. In any given nativity, according to Morin, the significance of a planet depends first on its location in one of the houses, then on the house(s) that the planet rules, and finally on the planet's aspects and antiscion (solstice point) contacts with other planets and significant points, including the house cusps. To quote Morin directly:

> ... the planets are determined by the houses in four ways – by actual location in the houses, or by dignities, aspect, or antiscion in them. The dignities are threefold – that is, they can be in domicile, exaltation or triplicity within a particular house. And again two considerations follow upon the determinations of rulership or location. First, consideration should be given to the analogical meanings of any other planet a planet may be with; for example, if the ruler of the Ascendant were conjunct the Sun it would also refer by this determination to the prestige of the native. Second, consideration should be given to the determination in the horo-

scope of this other planet. So, the ruler of the first house conjunct the Sun ruling the twelfth would foreshadow illness or powerful hidden enemies.[10]

Morin worked within the astrological traditions of his times. He used the tropical zodiac and did not adjust for precession. His preferred house system was Regiomontanus because it produced cusps that he felt best described his personality, his interests, and the circumstances of his life. As mentioned above, Morin noted that only in the Regiomontanus system was his 9th house cusp trine his Ascendant, and he believed that this trine accounted for his abiding interest and success in the fields of philosophy and higher education. His emphasis on the importance of house cusps and of aspects to the house cusps was one of his many contributions to astrology.

To get further information from a chart Morin also used the system of Whole Sign houses in which the degree on the Ascendant is simply the most powerful point within the first house, which is the entire sign ascending, and the second house is the entire next sign, and so on around the wheel. He first looked at the planets locations within the Regiomontanus houses and also often considered their position in the Whole Sign houses. In addition, if only part of a sign occupied a house, Morin often used the ruler of that sign as a co-ruler of the house. If a sign were intercepted in a house, Morin took the ruler of the intercepted sign to be one of the rulers of that house.

Morin also used derived houses to gather information from the client's natal chart about individuals other than the client. For example, to get information about the death of a friend, ruled by the natal 11th house, Morin would look to the 8th house from the natal 11th, which is the natal 6th house. The table shown below lists the twelve natal houses and their associated derived houses.

Table of Derived Houses

Natal House	Its 1st	Its 2nd	Its 3rd	Its 4th	Its 5th	Its 6th	Its 7th	Its 8th	Its 9th	Its 10th	Its 11th	Its 12th
1st	1	2	3	4	5	6	7	8	9	10	11	12
2nd	2	3	4	5	6	7	8	9	10	11	12	1
3rd	3	4	5	6	7	8	9	10	11	12	1	2
4th	4	5	6	7	8	9	10	11	12	1	2	3
5th	5	6	7	8	9	10	11	12	1	2	3	4
6th	6	7	8	9	10	11	12	1	2	3	4	5
7th	7	8	9	10	11	12	1	2	3	4	5	6
8th	8	9	10	11	12	1	2	3	4	5	6	7
9th	9	10	11	12	1	2	3	4	5	6	7	8
10th	10	11	12	1	2	3	4	5	6	7	8	9
11th	11	12	1	2	3	4	5	6	7	8	9	10
12th	12	1	2	3	4	5	6	7	8	9	10	11

To use this table, look in the first column for the natal house that rules the individual (other than the native) under consideration. Then look across the table to find the natal house that represents the derived house of the individual being inquired about. If you want to know about the journey (9th house) of the native's child (5th house), you would study the natal 1st house, which is the derived 9th house of the child in the 5th. If you want to know about the sex life (5th house) of the native's maid (6th house), you would study the 5th from the 6th, which is the 10th house of the natal chart. As you can imagine, the possibilities are endless.

Benefics, Malefics, Good and Bad Houses

In traditional astrology Saturn and Mars are respectively the greater and lesser malefics. Their action is to deny, impede, damage, and to cause hardship and imperfection. Any planet that finds itself in an adverse celestial state (e.g., in detriment or fall, retrograde, slow in motion, unfavorably aspecting a malefic or otherwise debilitated) can act as an accidental malefic. The traditional malefics, Mars and Saturn, in an adverse celestial state are especially nasty and can bring about "disgrace, catastrophe, dishonor, loss of reputation, exile, prison, grave illness, a violent death and similar misfortunes."[11] Such negative outcomes are especially likely when the malefics occupy unfortunate houses such as the 7th (lawsuits, open enemies), 8th (surgery, decay, death), or 12th (prison, sorrow, illness, undoing). The more a planet's nature resonates with the meanings of a house, the more freely that planet is able to express itself, for good or evil, within that house.

Jupiter and Venus are respectively the traditional greater and lesser benefics. Their action is to facilitate, promote, reward, and confer good fortune. Any planet in a good celestial state (e.g., in its own sign or exaltation, direct and rapid in motion, favorably aspecting a benefic, free of hard aspects to a malefic, and so on) can act as an accidental benefic.

The houses other than the 7th, 8th, and 12th houses are considered fortunate because they represent desirable things. The 4th house can indicate the end of life and the grave, and Volguine noted the frequent finding of the Solar Return Ascendant in the natal 4th house for the year of death. In addition, Morin pointed out that each house has a twofold significance: an essential one, such as money for the 2nd house, and an accidental one, such as death for the 2nd house, because each house partakes in the meaning of the one opposite. To quote Morin:

> "...death is an accidental meaning of the 2nd house. Similarly the essential meaning of the 6th house is servants and animals but the

accidental one is illness, prison, and hidden enemies; and so on for the other houses."[12]

Thus, in Morin's view, the 2nd house (opposite the 8th of death) and 6th house (opposite the 12th of illness, grief, and sorrow) can act as accidental unfortunate houses. Zoltan Mason referred to this principle as "ricochet." In Mason's metaphor the influence of each astrological house "ricochets" back and forth across the chart.

To summarize, Morin regarded the following houses as potentially difficult or unfortunate because they often represent undesirable things:

- **8th House** of death, danger of death, and life-threatening injury or illness. According to Morin, planets occupying or ruling the 1st, 8th, or 12th houses are relevant in matters of health and life.
- **12th House** of sorrow, grief, fear, undoing, exile, "secret enemies, imprisonment, sicknesses, and other afflictions of the body."[13]
- **7th House**, potentially unfortunate because it opposes the Ascendant and signifies lawsuits, confrontation, struggles, conflicts, wars, and open enemies. Directed or transiting planets opposite the Ascendant (the body) can indicate illness. In addition, the Descendant symbolizes one's personal sunset and is often activated at the end of one's life.
- **2nd House**, accidentally unfortunate because it partakes of the opposite 8th house of death.
- **6th House**, accidentally unfortunate because it partakes of the opposite 12th house of bodily afflictions, sorrow, fears, confinement, exile, and undoing.
- **4th House**, potentially unfortunate because it can indicate the end of life and the grave.

Malefics and King Gustave of Sweden's Solar Return

Morin discusses the chart of King Gustave Adolphe of Sweden in several sections of his masterwork *Astrologia Gallica*. The Swedish king, a Protestant, also referred to as Gustavus Adolphus or Gustav II Adolf, played an important role in the Thirty Years War. King Gustave was born on December 19, 1594 (NS) around 7:13 AM LMT in Stockholm, Sweden (Figure 1). He died of gunshot wounds on November 16, 1632 (NS) in the battle of Lützen, which he waged against the Catholic general, Wallenstein. King Gustave, ignoring his advisors' admonitions to wear his armor into battle, led a cavalry charge against Wallenstein's forces. A thick fog mixed with gunsmoke made the attack treacherous. A Swedish war journal of the period reported that the soldiers could not see farther than four paces in front of them. King Gustave was fatally shot in the battle and died toward 1 pm.[14] Because of Gustave's defeat,

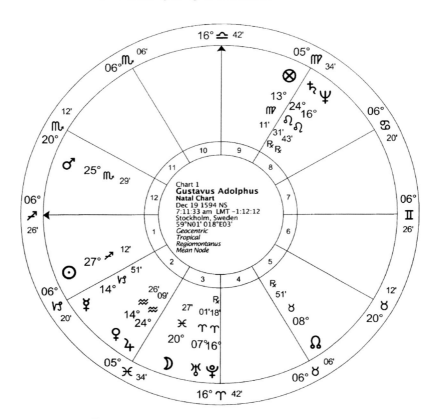

Figure 1: King Gustave Adolphe Natal Chart

"the infamous fog of Lützen has become something of a proverb in Sweden."[15]

Morin's calculations give King Gustave a natal Ascendant of 6° Sagittarius 26' and a Midheaven of 16° Libra 42'. Using a modern computer, I had to adjust the data as follows to get a close approximation to the natal chart Morin used for the king: December 19, 1594 NS, 7:11:33 AM LMT (-1:12:12), 59N01, 18E03. Modern calculations of the planetary positions vary slightly from those given by Morin. The most significant difference is that of Jupiter, which Morin gives as 29° Aquarius 04' versus 24° Aquarius 09' by computer – probably a typo or copyist error in Morin's original text.

Are there indications of the king's violent death in the birth chart? Can his demise be seen in the Solar Return for the year of his death? Morin taught that the unfortunate houses, especially if afflicted by malefics, could indicate a violent death. In King Gustave's chart Mars is strong in Scorpio, which it rules, but Mars occupies the unfortunate 12th house of illness, imprisonment, sorrow, and undoing. Morin notes that the king "had Mars in the twelfth in Scorpio but was not sickly, and was never incarcerated or crushed by hidden enemies,"[16] presumably because Mars is dignified and strong in Scorpio. The king's own rash action (natal Mars square Jupiter), however, led to his self-undoing (12th house) through his refusal to wear armor into battle. Mars frequently appears in the 12th house of the nativity or the annual chart of natives who experience the adverse consequences of violence.

The Greater Malefic, Saturn, occupies the king's natal 8th house of death and is debilitated in Leo, the sign of its detriment (opposite Aquarius which Saturn rules). Malefic Saturn, in an adverse celestial state, occupies the unfortunate 8th house of death, showing the potential of a violent death, especially because Saturn closely squares Mars, the Lesser Malefic, which occupies and rules the unfortunate 12th house. Natal Saturn in the natal 8th house of death also opposes natal Jupiter, ruler of the natal Ascendant (his body). Natal Mars in the 12th squares the natal Saturn/Jupiter opposition, forming a powerful T-square configuration.

A modern astrologer would also note that Neptune (fog) conjoins natal Saturn in the king's 8th of death, thus participating in the ominous Saturn/Mars/Jupiter T-square. In addition, the modern 12th house ruler Pluto (powerful forces) closely conjoins the natal IC (the end of life) and squares natal Mercury, ruler of the natal 7th of open enemies and of the 9th of distance places. Finally, natal Saturn in the 8th closely conjoins the fixed star Regulus (Cor Leonis, the heart of the Lion) at 24° Leo 12' in 1632, which Robson linked to "military honor of short duration with ultimate failure, imprisonment, violent death" (see Chapter One). Thus, there is plenty of evidence in the natal chart of the potential for a violent death in a foreign land.

Morin tells us that King Gustave spent his 1631 Solar Return in Mainz, Germany. Several factors immediately catch our attention in the solar revolution [see Figure 2 next page]. First, the annual Ascendant closely conjoins the natal Ascendant. [Morin's calculations gave a slightly later Solar Return Ascendant of 6° Sagittarius 30' and a Solar Return Midheaven of 4° Libra.] Because of the close alignment of the Ascendants, this is a year when the natal imprinting of stellar influences can easily manifest – a year when the king can "do his own thing" and fulfill the promise of the birth chart. The Solar Return Ascendant at 4° Sagittarius 35' closely conjoins the fixed star Antares (the heart of the Scorpion) at 4° Sagittarius 37', commonly active in the charts of headstrong individuals who are destructive to themselves by their own obstinacy. Morin also noted that Venus, ruler of the natal Midheaven, occupies the annual 1st house together with the violent star Antares (the heart of the scorpion) – the brightest star in the constellation Scorpio.

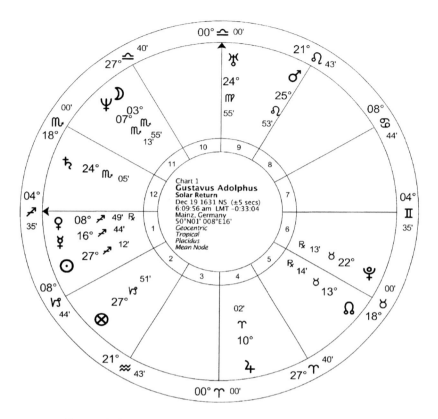

Figure 2: King Gustave Adolphe 1631 Solar Return

According to Morin, annual Venus and the fixed star Cor Scorpionis (Antares) are "joined to Mercury ruler of the seventh [house] of the revolution, also presaging something unfavorable and violent in wars that he would undertake, and in his life."[17] As mentioned above, Vivian Robson – perhaps influenced by Morin's delineation of King Gustave's Solar Return – noted that Cor Scorpionis (Antares) is associated with

> "malevolence, destructiveness, liberality, broad-mindedness, evil presages and danger of fatality and makes its natives rash, ravenous, headstrong and destructive to themselves by their own obstinacy."[18]

Morin tells us that Gustave charged rashly into battle without the recommended protective armor – "a fatal imprudence" – and died as a result of his headstrong decision.

Let's now consider the role of the malefics in Gustave's death. Annual Mars closely aligns with the natal Saturn/Regulus conjunction in the natal 8th house of death; annual Saturn closely conjoins natal Mars in the unfortunate natal 12th house. In the Solar Return, the two malefics – Saturn and Mars – are activating the natal T-square and goading their natal counterparts into action. Saturn, a universal signifier of death, specifically signifies death in the king's nativity through its location in the natal 8th house. Morin taught that a planet's location in a house is a stronger determinant of its signification than its rulership of a house.

If we consider the king's chart from the perspective of Whole Sign houses, Saturn moves from the 8th Regiomontanus house (death) to the 9th Whole Sign house (foreign places). One obvious meaning is the natal potential for death in a foreign land. A modern astrologer would also note in the Solar Return chart the presence of annual Uranus in the 9th conjunct the Solar Return Midheaven (career upset in a foreign land) and the T-square involving annual 12th ruler Pluto in the Solar Return 6th opposite annual Saturn in the Solar Return 12th, both squaring annual Mars in the Solar Return 9th. Also, the annual 8th ruler Moon (death) conjoins annual Neptune (fog) in Scorpio.

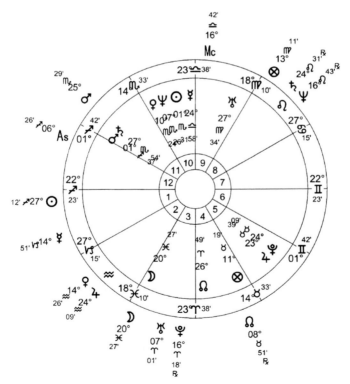

Figure 3: Gustave Natal (outer wheel) on Oct 24, 1632 Lunar Return

Having decided from the Solar Return that King Gustave was likely to die abroad during 1632, Morin further refined his timing by considering all the Lunar Returns that occurred during that Solar Return year. The Lunar Return preceding the king's death took place in Nurnberg, Germany on October 24, 1632 NS at 11:14:26 AM LMT, 49N27, 011E04. Except for the 12th and 6th houses, the same signs rule the cusps of the Lunar Return as in the natal chart. The most angular planet in the Lunar Return is Mercury, which rules the king's 7th house of wars and open enemies and his 9th house of foreign lands. Jupiter represents the king's body because it rules the Ascendant of both the natal chart and the Lunar Return. If we superimpose the natal and Lunar Return charts (Figure 3), we see a striking grand cross, involving Jupiter (the king), Saturn (death), and Mars (battles and also self-undoing since it rules the natal 12th).

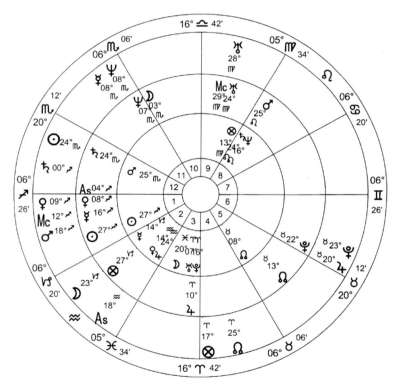

Figure 4: Gustave's Nativity with superimposed SR and Transits at Death

(Inner wheel= Natal. Middle wheel = SR. Outer wheel = Death)

In short, natal Jupiter in Aquarius squares Lunar Return Jupiter in Taurus and opposes Lunar Return Saturn in Scorpio in the 12th house. Natal Saturn, debilitated in Leo in the natal 8th house of death, squares the planets Jupiter, Pluto, and Saturn in the Lunar Return. The malefics Mars and Saturn conjoin in the Lunar Return on the cusp of its unfortunate 12th house. Clearly this is an ominous Lunar Return chart, which precedes and signifies the king's death in battle. On the day of Gustave's death, the transiting Sun in the 25th degree of Scorpio appeared to act as a trigger as it conjoined natal Mars and squared natal Saturn. At the same the transiting Sun conjoined annual Saturn in his Solar Return and opposed Jupiter in his Lunar Return (Figure 4).

Morin also comments that the king's primary directed Midheaven, which symbolizes the result of actions, pointed to a violent death. Using Solar Fire, I calculated the following directions involving the Midheaven to be in effect during 1632: primary directed Midheaven (at a rate of one year per degree) conjunct natal Neptune (fog) in the 8th; primary directed 12th ruler Mars (at a rate of one year per degree) square the natal Ascendant and conjunct the natal Midheaven; primary directed natal 8th ruler Sun (at the natal solar rate) conjunct natal 12th ruler Mars; solar arc directed Midheaven conjunct natal Mars in the natal 12th; Ascendant-arc directed Midheaven quincunx natal Pluto (co-ruler of the natal 12th); and Ascendant-arc directed Midheaven square natal Neptune (fog) in his natal 8th of death (this last direction became exact on November 10, 1632 just six days prior to his death).

Listed below are the major hard aspects of the directions by primary, solar arc, and Ascendant-arc calculated by the Solar Fire program for the months surrounding Gustave's final stand in the foggy battle of Lützen. Note the prominence of Mars, Saturn, Neptune, and Pluto during the year of his death in battle. The primary directions in this list are calculated at the rate of one year per degree of right ascension. If we use the Naibod rate of 59'08" per year (preferred by Morin), then the primary directed Midheaven exactly conjoins Neptune (fog) in the natal 8th house just weeks before his death on October 26, 1632 NS.

Pm = primary direction; Sa = solar arc direction; Na = natal; Sp = secondary progression

Conjunctions:

MC (8) Cnj Nep (8)	(X)	Pm-Na	Apr 9 1632 NS	12°Le32' D	16°Le43' R
Mer (2) Cnj Ven (2)	(X)	Aa-Na	Jun 24 1632 NS	14°Aq26' D	14°Aq26' D
Asc (2) Cnj Mer (2)	(X)	Sa-Na	Sep 4 1632 NS	14°Cp51' D	14°Cp51' D
Mar (9) Cnj MC (10)	(X)	Pm-Na	Oct 5 1632 NS	00°Cn00' D	16°Li42' D
MC (12) Cnj Mar (12)	(X)	Sa-Na	Jan 13 1633 NS	25°Sc29' D	25°Sc29' D

Oppositions:

MC (8) Opp Ven (2)	(X)	Pm-Na	Jan 12 1632 NS	12°Le16' D	14°Aq26' D	

Squares:

MC (12) Sqr Sat (8)	(X)	Sa-Na	Feb 2 1632 NS	24°Sc31' D	24°Le31' R
Plu (6) Sqr Jup (2)	(X)	Sa-Na	Feb 14 1632 NS	24°Ta09' D	24°Aq09' D
Sun (12) Sqr Mon (3)	(X)	Pm-Na	Jun 11 1632 NS	19°Ar51' D	20°Pi27' D
Plu (6) Sqr Sat (8)	(X)	Sa-Na	Jun 24 1632 NS	24°Ta31' D	24°Le31' R
Mar (9) Sqr Asc (1)	(X)	Pm-Na	Oct 5 1632 NS	00°Cn00' D	06°Sg26' D
MC (11) Sqr Nep (8)	(X)	Aa-Na	Nov 12 1632 NS	16°Sc43' D	16°Le43' R

As a modern astrologer, I also find it useful to consider the secondary progressions of the natal and annual charts during the Solar Return year. The secondary progressed natal Venus quincunx natal Neptune (fog) would have activated his natal Venus/Neptune opposition from the 2nd to 8th houses. The secondary progressed natal Ascendant semisquare natal Mars (wounds) would have activated his natal 12th house Mars square Saturn in the 8th. Natal Saturn in the 8th was activated by the secondary progressed natal Ascendant at the beginning of 1632. Below is a list of Gustave's secondaries (other than those formed by the secondary progressed Moon, which is useful for timing) for the year beginning December 19, 1631:

Asc (2) Sqq Sat (8)	(X)	Sp-Na	Jan 4 1632 NS	09°Cp31' D	24°Le31' R
Ven (3) Qnx Nep (8)	(X)	Sp-Sp	Apr 28 1632 NS	15°Pi52' D	15°Le52' R
Sun (2) SSq Mon (3)	(X)	Sp-Na	Jul 11 1632 NS	05°Aq27' D	20°Pi27' D
Asc (2) SSq Mar (12)	(X)	Sp-Na	Oct 25 1632 NS	10°Cp29' D	25°Sc29' D
Sun (1) Sqq Nod (5)	(X)	Sp-Sp	Dec 6 1632 NS	28°Sg11' D	13°Ta11' R

Firdaria and the Death of King Gustave

A common technique used by medieval astrologers, but discarded by Morin, is the method of Persian firdaria[19], which was first introduced into astrology by the renowned Muslim astrologer Abu Ma'shar (787-886). The 75-year lifespan of the individual is divided into nine unequal periods, each of which is ruled by one of the seven planets during the first 70 years of life. The remaining 5 years (ages 70–75) are ruled by the north and the south lunar nodes. Abu Ma'shar taught that the lunar nodes can rule only at the end of life because the seven planets, which rule the entire zodiac from Aries through Pisces, must first exercise their dominion over the life of the individual. In Abu Ma'shar's theory the pre-eminence of the planets over the lunar nodes is related to the fact that the world was created with the conjunction of the seven planets at the beginning of Aries and the world will end when the seven planets again conjoin at the end of Pisces.

In the system of firdaria, day births (Sun above the horizon) are ruled in Chaldean order by the Sun (10 years), Venus (8 years), Mercury (13 years), Moon (9 years), Saturn (11 years), Jupiter (12 years), Mars (7 years), North Node (3 years), and South Node (2 years), for a total of 75 years. Night births (Sun below the horizon) are ruled in Chaldean order by the Moon (9 years), Saturn (11 years), Jupiter (12 years), Mars (7 years), Sun (10 years), Venus (8 years), Mercury (13 years), North Node (3 years), and South Node (2 years). The sequence repeats after age 75. Each planetary period is subdivided equally among the seven visible planets (but not the lunar nodes because they do not have domiciles), beginning with the planet ruling that period.

For example, King Gustave died in 1632 at age 37, about a month before his 38th birthday. His is a night birth, so his firdaria follow the lunar sequence. At age 36 he is passing through his Mars firdar, which extends for 7 years from ages 32 to 39. A different planet rules each subdivision of his 7-year Mars firdar. Specifically, Mars rules ages 32-33; the Sun, ages 33-34; Venus, ages 34-35; Mercury, ages 35-36; the Moon, ages 36-37; Saturn, ages 37-38; and Jupiter, ages 38-39. Thus, at age 37 Gustave Adolphus was in the Saturn subperiod of his Mars firdar, and the influence of Mars and Saturn (as we have already seen in his solar and lunar returns and in the directions of his natal chart) was predominant when he died in battle.

Emerson's Point of Death

Finally, let us consider a more modern technique, namely, Emerson's Point of Death. There are two significant contacts made by the Death Point in the king's natal and annual charts. Using a one-degree orb, the natal Death Point, at 15° Cancer 44', opposes natal Mercury, ruler of the king's natal 7th of battle and 9th of foreign lands. The annual Death Point, at 28° Sagittarius 11', opposes Gustave's Sun, which occupies his annual 1st house of vitality and rules his natal 8th of death and 9th of faraway places. Had the king been born just 4 minutes earlier than the time used by Morin, these Death Point contacts would have been exact.

A Note on Primary Directions

In directing the natal chart, Morin relied principally on the Regiomontanus method of primary directions. In his discussion of Jerome Cardan's Solar Return, however, Morin may also have used Ascendant-arc and solar arc directions – or at the very least these latter two forms of directing produce results that are consistent with the primary directions (see the discussion of Cardan at the end of this chapter). Prior to Morin's time, astrologers utilized primary directions to identify periods when particular planets became prominent in the native's life.[20] According to astrologer Rob Hand:

> "primary directions were originally a period system, not a system for timing events with exact hits; this change occurred just before William Lilly."[21]

It seems that Morin de Villefranche and his immediate predecessors began to use primary directions not to identify time lords but rather to forecast specific dates when events might occur, much as modern astrologers use secondary progressions.

Because they require complex calculations and a sophisticated understanding of latitude, right ascension, oblique ascension, and the geometry of astrological house division, primary directions fell out of favor in modern astrology. In addition, primary directions are only valid for charts with precise birth times. If the birth time is off by even a few minutes, primary directions can be years off the mark. Another confounding factor is the various theoretical measures of the rate by which to primary direct the chart. Popular rates include equating one year of human life to:

1.   The time it takes one degree of right ascension to cross the Midheaven (proposed by Ptolemy).
2.   The average daily motion of the Sun measured in right ascension on the equator (the Naibod rate of 0°59'08").
3.   The actual daily motion of the Sun on the birthday, measured either in longitude on the ecliptic or in right ascension on the equator. Tycho Brahe preferred the latter of these two measures.[22]
4.   The sidereal actual daily motion of the Sun in right ascension.

These various rates are all close to one another; but as the native advances in age, the discrepancy in the dates when directed aspects will perfect at each particular rate can become substantial. I have experimented with these various rates in different case examples in this text and, in my limited experience, I have not found that one rate is more reliable than the others. Morin's experience, however, led him to prefer the Naibod equivalence of 59'08" of arc of right ascension to 1 year of life (or alternatively that one degree of right ascension is equivalent to one year, 5 days, and 8 hours).[23]

Perhaps the most commonly used primary directions are the Placidean or "primary mundane" directions derived from the daily rotation of the earth on its axis in which exactly one degree of the earth's rotation measured along the equator (in right ascension) is equated to one year of life. In other words, about four minutes of sidereal time, or one degree of right ascension over the Midheaven, symbolizes a year in the life of the native. Starting from its natal position, each planet or angle is directed along its own diurnal arc. Primary directed planets or angles form aspects with natal positions when the positions of the directed and natal points come into particular angular relationships in their diurnal arcs. Solar Fire describes this process as follows:

> Aspects are deemed to be formed between directed and natal planets when their relative positions in their diurnal arcs are in angular relationship. (Note that this is quite different from aspects of zodiacal longitude.) For example, if the Sun is natally situated in the 10th house at 90% along its arc from its rise to its culmination, then Saturn will be in natal mundane square to it when it is directed to a position in the 1st house which is at 90% along its arc from its nadir to its rise across the horizon. If this occurs after Saturn has been directed by 24.5 degrees along its diurnal arc, then it is deemed that directed Saturn makes a mundane square to the Sun when the individual is 24 and a half years old.[24]

Makransky has studied primary directions extensively and claims that most standard textbooks give misleading information. After carefully researching the topic, he concluded that primary directions produce accurate hits only about 67% to 75% of the time. To quote Makransky:

> The concept behind primary directions is that, in the hours after birth, the diurnal rotation of the celestial sphere brings the planets successively to the eastern horizon, upper meridian, western horizon and lower meridian. The space in time between the moment of birth and the moment of rising, culmination, setting, or lower culmination of a planetary body, converted to years of life at a rate of approximately 4 minutes of Sidereal Time to a year of life, yields a prediction which usually corresponds to a major life event consonant with the symbolism of the planet involved.... In an interplanetary primary direction, one planet (termed the promissor) is conceived as moving by the rotation of the celestial sphere along its diurnal circle until it reaches the position originally occupied by another planet (termed the significator) in the birth horoscope.[25]

In summary, we can say the following about the technique of primary directions:

• They are a method to forecast how the birth chart will unfold based on the movement of natal planets and cusps as they are carried forward in the heavens by the daily rotation of the earth on its axis. Originally primary

directions were a method to identify periods during which certain planets were especially active as "time lords" during one's life.
•   According to Makransky's research, primary directions produce meaningful hits about 70% of the time.
•   The time it takes about one degree of right ascension (depending on the measure chosen) to pass over the meridian is equated to one year of life; that is, approximately every four minutes after birth equals one year of life. An entire human lifetime corresponds to the earth's movement during the first six hours after birth.
•   The planets retain their original natal positions and are merely directed or carried forward by the rotation of the earth. Significant times occur when the directed planets or directed cusps form "mundane" aspects with natal planets or cusp positions.

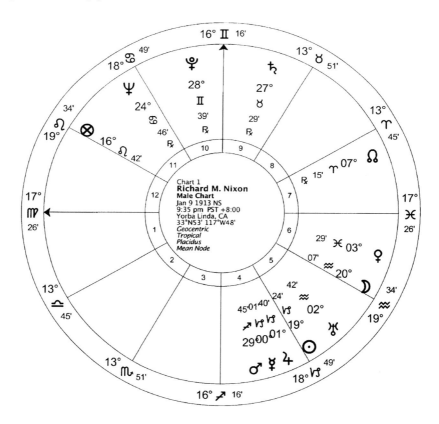

Figure 5: Richard Nixon Natal Chart

•   The calculations of primary directions are complex and vary depending on the house system being utilized. The modern favorite is Placidus as calculated by the Solar Fire program. Morin preferred the system of Regiomontanus, which produces a different timing than Placidus of the primary directed aspects.[26]

Malefics, Unfortunate Houses, and Richard Nixon's Resignation

Because of the Watergate scandal and the threat of impeachment, Richard Nixon announced in a nationally televised speech at 9 PM EDT on August 8, 1974, that he would resign the presidency at noon the following day. According to AstroDataBank, President Nixon was born on January 9, 1913 at 9:35 PM PST in Yorba Linda, California (Figure 5). As far as I can tell from newspaper accounts, President Nixon probably spent his 1974 Solar Return at the White House in Washington, DC.

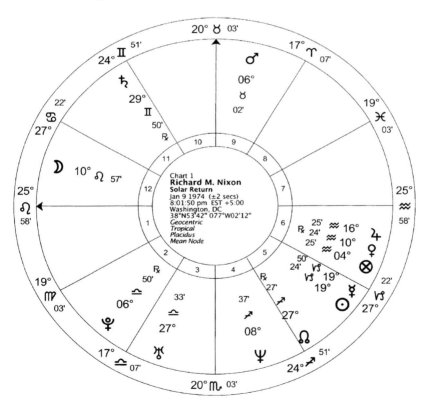

Figure 6: Richard Nixon 1974 Solar Return

Nixon's ambition, secrecy, and desire for power are shown by his natal Pluto in the 10th of career. His natal Mercury, which rules his 10th house, opposes Pluto in the 10th and conjoins Mars and Jupiter in the 4th house. Herein lies the natal promise of difficulties with his public standing (Mercury ruling the 10th house) and drive for power (Pluto in the 10th) due to rash action (Mars) and arrogance (Jupiter). Natal Saturn retrograde in the 9th house of the law shows the potential for legal difficulties at some time in his life.

Nixon began 1974 with his secondary progressed Sun semi-square his secondary progressed Uranus – an aspect that perfected on January 10, 1974, within 24 hours of his Solar Return. Progressed aspects that become exact so close to the Sun's return to its natal position are highly significant. This secondary progressed Sun/Uranus semi-square marks 1974 as a stressful year

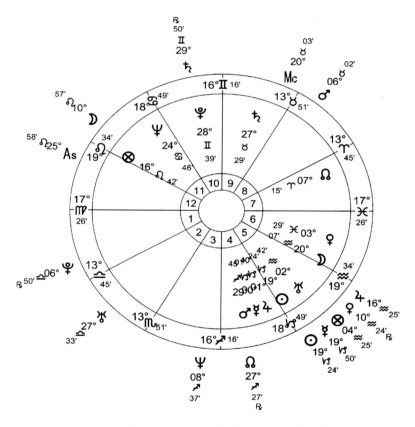

Figure 7: Nixon 1974 Solar Return on Natal Chart

of surprises and disruption (Uranus) with regard to his reputation and honor (Sun). It is also noteworthy that the Sun rules his natal 12th house of resignation and undoing.

On August 11, 1974, just two days after Nixon's resignation his secondary progressed natal Moon perfected a sesqui-square to natal Mercury, ruler of this 10th of public reputation. Nixon's primary directed Uranus (at the natal solar rate) semi-squared his natal Sun on May 30, 1974, repeating the signification of his secondary progressed Sun semi-square progressed Uranus. Although I don't usually consider Chiron in Solar Returns, on July 28, 1974, eleven days before his resignation, Nixon's primary directed Chiron (at the natal solar rate) semi-squared his natal Moon, which Solar Fire delineates as:

> "an emotionally frustrating time during which you are being forced
> to slow down and reconsider your actions in the light of past events.
> Your usual sources of comfort seem to have dried up…"

Nixon's other primary directions (calculated at a rate of one year per degree) are also telling. On May 19, 1974 primary directed Neptune (at one year per degree) conjoined natal Saturn, signifying the dissolution of long-established structures in his life. On September 5, 1974 his primary directed Ascendant (at one year per degree) opposed his natal Sun (honor, dignity), the ruler of his natal Leo 12th house of self-undoing.

Nixon's 1974 Solar Return (Figure 6) has Leo rising in Washington, DC. The sign Leo, ruled by the Sun, is the sign on the cusp of his natal 12th house of sorrow and self-undoing. Thus, the Sun carries a 12th house significance throughout Nixon's life. During a Solar Return year with Leo rising, Nixon's 12th house issues become major factors that are likely to manifest in his life. A striking feature of the 1974 Solar Return is that Mercury, ruler of his natal 10th of career and public image, conjoins the Sun within 25 minutes of arc. In traditional astrology, Mercury so close to the Sun is considered combust (burned by the Sun) and thereby seriously debilitated. He is likely to "get burned" and to experience significant sorrow (Sun ruling the natal 12th) in career matters (Mercury ruling the natal 10th).

If we superimpose Nixon's natal and 1974 Solar Return charts (Figure 7), we see that the annual Ascendant in Leo (ruling his 12th of undoing) squares natal Saturn in the 9th house of legal affairs, highlighting Nixon's problems with the law in 1974. Those who use Abu Ma'shar's system of firdaria will note that Nixon was passing through the Saturn subperiod (Sep 1973 – Aug 1975) of his Mercury firdar (Mercury rules his natal 10th of career) at the time of his resignation. Saturn is particularly important in Nixon's natal chart because it rules his Sun-sign Capricorn. Morin tells us that the Sun "acts according to the nature of the sign that it occupies, and the nature and state of its ruler.[27] "

The fact that the Solar Return Leo Ascendant squares natal Saturn with Saturn disposing the Sun, ruler of the annual Leo Ascendant, makes Saturn highly prominent in Nixon's life during 1974. In addition, his natal

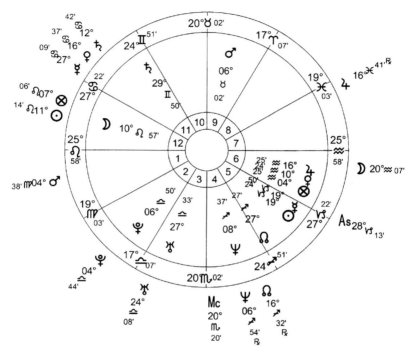

Figure 8: Nixon Lunar Return on 1974 Solar Return

Saturn is almost exactly quincunx the annual lunar north node; and his annual Saturn is debilitated by being retrograde, which renders its malefic action even more unfortunate. Finally, the first solar eclipse of 1974 took place on June 20, 1974 with the Sun at 28° Gemini 30' tightly conjunct Nixon's natal 10th house Pluto and his Solar Return Saturn – in a sense supercharging this annual Saturn/natal Pluto conjunction in the natal 10th of career during the summer of 1974. As mentioned previously, the first solar eclipse of the Solar Return year typically highlights major issues in the year ahead.

Thus, the Solar Return Ascendant and other significant chart factors tell us to pay special attention to Saturn this Solar Return year. Annual Saturn, supercharged by the June 1974 solar eclipse, sits right on top of natal Pluto in the natal 10th of career, exactly opposite natal Mars in the natal 4th house of endings. Annual Saturn in retrograde motion perfects the conjunction with natal Pluto on January 27, 1974. Also striking is that annual Saturn will exactly oppose natal Mars within 24 hours of the Solar Return, making this opposition of the traditional malefics an earmark of 1974. Before the year is over, Nixon will feel the full force of this opposition between annual Saturn and natal Mars, which happens to rule his natal 3rd house of news reports – the basis of the Watergate investigation into his illegal activities. Annual Saturn also opposes natal Mercury and conjoins the contrascion[28] of natal Mercury, ruler of his natal 10th of career and of the natal Ascendant. No doubt the Watergate investigation took a heavy toll on him personally.

Superimposing Nixon's Lunar Return, which occurred 5 days before his resignation, onto his 1974 Solar Return is also revealing (Figure 8). The lunar return Sun (ruler of the annual Ascendant and the natal 12th house) conjoins his annual Moon (ruler of the Solar Return 12th) in the annual 12th house of undoing. The Midheaven of the lunar return lies on the annual IC (endings) and almost exactly opposes the annual Midheaven (career). The lunar return Mercury (which rules the natal 10th of career) almost exactly conjoins the annual 12th cusp of exile. The lunar return Ascendant closely opposes the annual 12th cusp. Finally, the lunar return Moon (which by definition has the same position as the natal Moon) almost exactly squares both the annual and lunar return Midheavens, suggesting a crisis in career and public standing.

Antiscia and Contra-antiscia

For those unfamiliar with traditional astrology, the antiscion (or solstice point) of a planet refers to its reflection, due east or due west, across the 0° Cancer - 0° Capricorn cardinal axis of the natural zodiac. Thus, the midpoint of a planet and its antiscion is always a solstice point (0° Cancer or 0° Capricorn). Similarly, the contrascion (or contra-antiscion) of a point or planet refers to its reflection, due north or due south, across the 0° Aries-0° Libra cardinal axis of the natural zodiac. The midpoint of a planet and its contra-antiscion is always an equinoctial point (0° Aries or 0° Libra). It is considered a harmonious relationship when one planet aligns with the antiscion or another, and stressful or inharmonious when one planet aligns with the contra-antiscion of anther.

Imagine the natural zodiac, with Aries occupying the 1st house, as a mirrored wheel. Look at the accompanying diagram and picture a beam of light emanating from 20° Aries and traveling horizontally across the wheel, parallel to the horizon in an east-west direction. That light will hit the point at 10° Virgo. It will then reflect vertically, in a north-south direction, so that it hits 20° Libra. From there it will reflect horizontally across the wheel until

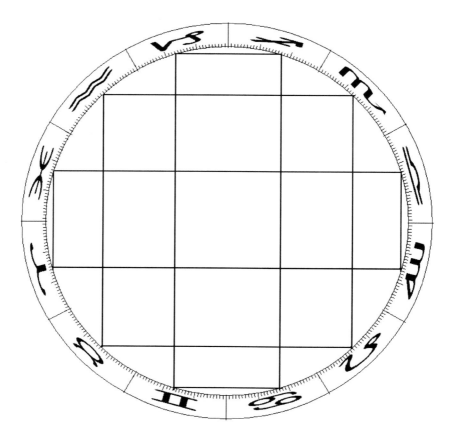

Antiscions (horizontal lines) & Contrascions (vertical lines) in the Natural
Zodiac

it hits 10° Pisces, and from there it will again reflect on a vertical north-south line to return to 20° Aries, its starting point. Essentially, antiscia and contra-antiscia are mirror images across the cardinal axes of the natural zodiac, and the rectangles embedded in the diagram of the natural zodiac make contact with the four points that reflect each other's light in the natural zodiac. Whenever a transiting, directed or progressed planet touches one of these points, it illuminates all four corners of the rectangle (the antiscions and contrascions) through the reflection of its light across the solstice and equinoctial axes.

Nixon's natal Mercury at 0° Capricorn 01' has its reflection (antiscion) at 29° Sagittarius 59'. The point opposite the antiscion is the contra-antiscion or contrascion, which for Nixon's Mercury is at 29° Gemini 59'. Solar Return Saturn contacting the contrascion of natal Mercury has the force of an

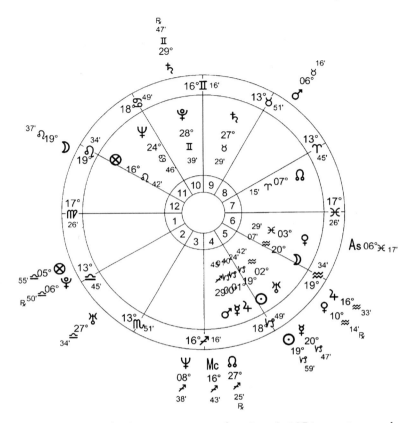

Figure 9: Nixon Solar Return progressed to Aug 8, 1974 superimposed on his Natal Chart

opposition aspect. Thus, in the 1974 Solar Return Saturn makes two important contacts with natal Mercury, ruler of the 10th of career: return Saturn opposes natal Mercury and at the same time conjoins the contrascion of natal Mercury. This double assault of Solar Return Saturn on 10th house-ruler Mercury spells trouble for Nixon's career in 1974.

Nixon's sudden fall from power is also reflected in an almost exact quincunx between natal Saturn (ruling legal difficulties in the birth chart) in the Solar Return 10th house of career and Solar Return Uranus, which is about to turn retrograde in the return 3rd house of news events. Transiting Uranus perfects the quincunx to natal Saturn on February 26, 1974. These significations are reinforced by Solar Return Moon, which rules and occupies the annual 12th of self-undoing, very closely opposing Solar Return Venus, ruler of the annual 10th house of career and public standing.

This Solar Return demonstrates the value of Morin's dictum that the

Solar Return must always be interpreted in the context of the natal chart. As a stand-alone chart, Nixon's 1974 Solar Return looks troublesome but not particularly ominous. None of the malefic planets conjoin the angles. The 1st and 10th houses are unoccupied. There are two troublesome career-related aspects: the opposition of the annual Moon, ruling the 12th of sorrow, to annual Venus, ruling the 10th of reputation, showing trouble with his public image; and Solar Return Mars, ruling and occupying the annual 9th of legal affairs, mutually applying to a square of a debilitated retrograde 6th house Venus, ruling the Solar Return 10th of career, showing legal problems related to his career. The quincunx of annual Mars in the 9th to annual Pluto in the 2nd also suggests costly legal complications, perhaps leading to a significant ending since both Mars and Pluto rule the annual 4th house of the end of things. Only when we compare the Solar Return to the natal chart, however, do we see the major role played by Saturn, which is symbolically more indicative of his fall from power in 1974.

The Timing of Nixon's Resignation

If we progress Nixon's 1974 Solar Return to the day of his resignation speech, using the conversion table in the Appendix, we find that 211 days have elapsed between his Solar Return of January 9, 1974 and the resignation speech of August 8, 1974, corresponding to 13 hours 49 minutes 37 seconds on the day of his Solar Return. Adding this time interval to the "birth time" of the original Solar Return chart (9:01:50 PM EDT) we find that the progressed Solar Return chart should be calculated for January 10, 1974 at 10:51:27 AM EDT. If we then superimpose the progressed Solar Return chart onto the natal chart (Figure 9), we see some striking hits.

On August 8, 1974, the progressed Solar Return Moon, which acts as a timing device, exactly conjoins the natal 12th cusp of exile, resignation, and self-undoing. The progressed Solar Return Moon, which rules the annual 12th house of exile and resignation, closely opposes the natal Moon at the cusp of the natal 6th house. At the same time the progressed Solar Return Moon is exactly quincunx the midpoint of the natal Sun/annual Mercury conjunction, with Mercury ruling the natal 10th house of public reputation. The progressed Solar Return Midheaven (career, public standing) almost exactly conjoins the natal IC (final endings). The progressed Solar Return Ascendant in the natal 6th house forms part of a yod (finger of fate) configuration with Solar Return Mars in the natal 8th house, both forming a quincunx with Solar Return Pluto in the natal 1st house of personal initiatives. At the same time annual Saturn sits prominently on top of natal Pluto in the public 10th house, indicating that the time has come for him to pay the piper.

Jerome Cardan's Solar Revolution of 1534

Jerome Cardan (1501-76) was a mathematician, physician, and astrologer. Born in Pavia, Italy, Cardan became a professor of mathematics at Padua and a professor of medicine at Pavia and Bologna. A prolific writer, Cardan penned more than a hundred works on such topics as astrology, astronomy, natural history, physics, mathematics, rhetoric, ethics, dialectics, history, medicine, and music. He is one of the forefathers of the modern algebra. Cardan used his knowledge of mathematical probability to win at gambling, to which he eventually became addicted (5th ruler Sun in the 6th square Neptune, Jupiter ruling the 12th conjunct the natal Ascendant). In 1570 he ran afoul of church law and was imprisoned for heresy because he cast the chart of Jesus Christ, a no-no during the Roman Catholic Inquisition which went on to persecute Galileo early in the next century.

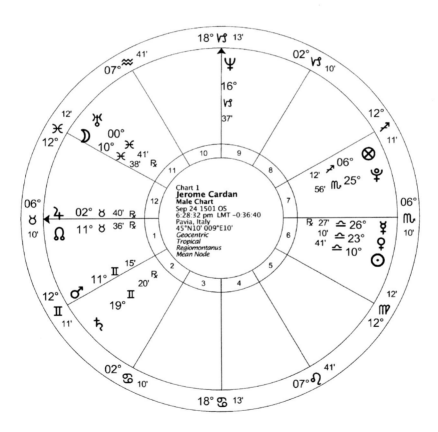

Figure 10: Cardan Natal Chart (Regiomontanus Houses)

Like Morin, Cardan published a book on solar revolutions in which he espoused the dictum that the Solar Return chart must be always judged with reference to the nativity. In his own book Morin cites Cardan's example that if a marriage is not promised in the birth chart, then no revolution can possibly bring it about. Nonetheless, in Cardan's book on solar revolutions he delineated two of his own Solar Returns without reference to his nativity, as if the returns were new natal charts. Morin takes Cardan to task for ignoring his natal chart, pointing out that:

> "it is rash and erroneous to judge the figure of a revolution with-out any consideration of the natal figure, since the revolution is subordinated to it in its force, significations, and effects, and since it depends upon it."[29]

Morin tells us that if the annual chart appears to promise marriage but the natal chart indicates celibacy, then there may be activity related to marriage during that year but a wedding will not take place.

As mentioned, Morin held that nothing will come to pass, regardless of what is happening in a Solar Return, unless it is first promised in the nativity. Factors that are active in an annual revolution can only trigger events in conformity with the promise of the natal chart. If the annual chart contradicts the birth chart, the nativity takes precedence. Robert Corre, a contemporary teacher of Morin's methods, expresses this idea by making a distinction between prediction and forecasting. Prediction is based on the potentials of the natal chart whereas forecasting refers to any method that indicates when those potentials are likely to manifest. The Solar Return is a method of forecasting but not of prediction, because prediction is only possible from the birth chart.

It is illustrative of Morin's approach to consider his delineation of Jerome Cardan's 1534 Solar Return. The following data is based on close approximations to the charts used by Morin in his book on solar returns. Cardan was born on September 24, 1501 OS, at 6:28:32 PM LMT in Pavia, Italy (Figure 10). His solar revolution occurred on September 24, 1534 OS at 6:25:31 PM LMT in Milan, Italy (Figure 11). The bullet points below refer to Cardan's account of what happened. The accompanying explanations summarize Morin's delineations of Cardan's annual chart with reference to his nativity. Morin used Regiomontanus houses, and the modern calculations give results that are slightly different from those of Morin.

Morin's Delineation of Cardan's Solar Return:[30]

•   Cardan reports that during the year spanned by his 1534 solar revolution he was perfectly healthy; nonetheless, he suffered anxiety about his health.

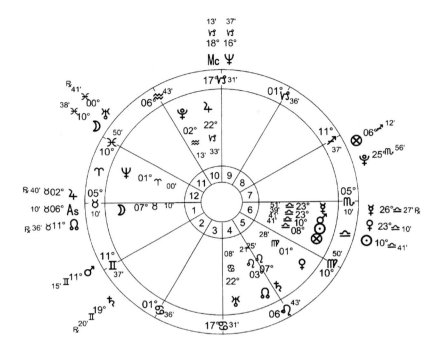

Figure 11: Cardan's Natal Chart on his 1534 Solar Return

Morin notes that natal Jupiter (good fortune) conjoins the Taurus Ascendant (the physical body and life force) of both the natal and annual charts. Any planet in the 1st house has reference to the native's health and life. Benefic natal Jupiter also conjoins the annual Moon in Taurus in the 1st house. The annual Moon trines annual Venus, which rules Taurus and thus disposes the Moon. Hence the dispositor of the annual Moon is benefic Venus, which forms a favorable aspect with the annual Moon. No malefics conjoin the annual Moon. All these factors promise good health. (When we discuss James Eshelman's work, we will revisit the importance of the Moon as a general significator of the native's health in the Solar Return chart.)

•   Regarding Cardan's anxieties about his health, Morin notes that the natal Moon, which is disposed by Jupiter, occupies the radical 12th house (fears, anxieties, illness) – in Morin's calculations the annual Moon lies at 11° Pisces 53'. In the Solar Return chart the annual Moon has moved to conjoin natal Jupiter on the Ascendant and at the same time trines annual Venus. These favorable aspects of the annual Moon/Ascendant conjunction with the greater and lesser benefics protects the native from the signification of the natal ruler of the 12th conjoining the Ascendant of the annual and return charts. Cardan's anxiety stems comes from the annual Moon and annual Ascendant receiving a square from annual Saturn, the greater malefic. Again natal Jupiter conjunct the annual Ascendant and annual Venus trine the annual Ascendant protect against the malefic effects of the annual Saturn square.

•   Morin also refers to a direction of the natal Ascendant to natal Saturn as accounting for Cardan's anxiety about his health that year. Solar Fire, which uses the method of Placidus, calculates the primary directed Saturn as conjoining the Ascendant in August of 1637. Initially I was puzzled that this primary direction did not take place until 1637. Then, I calculated Cardan's primary directions by hand in the Regiomontanus system and found the arc between natal Saturn and the Ascendant to be 31.88 degrees. This arc equates, at the Naibod rate, to about 32 years and 4 months. In other words, the primary directed Saturn/Ascendant conjunction occurred in early February of 1534, about 8 months prior to Cardan's 1534 Solar Return.

•   There is also an Ascendant-arc direction[31] on March 3, 1534 (seven months before Cardan's 1534 Solar Return) in which the Ascendant-arc directed natal Ascendant conjoined natal Saturn at 19° Gemini 19'. This made me wonder whether Morin had also used the Ascendant-arc technique.

Because Morin's calculations placed Cardan's natal Saturn a degree later than computer-generated position, that is, at 20° Gemini 20', he would have timed this Ascendant-arc direction as occurring about a year later or in March of 1535 in the midst of the Solar Return year that he was studying. Since natal Saturn rules Cardan's natal 10th house of career and dignities and also occupies his natal 2nd house of income, one would expect an Ascendant/Saturn direction to highlight these areas of his life at this time.

•   Cardan says that he dissipated his assets (2nd house) in pursuit of a dignity (10th house), but he also gained substantially from his practice of medicine and astrology. Morin notes that natally Cardan has Jupiter conjunct the Ascendant with impulsive Mars on the cusp of his 2nd house, so he is naturally inclined to dissipate his wealth. In the Solar Return, Mercury rules the 2nd house of income, and annual Mercury in the annual 6th house squares annual Jupiter, in its fall in Capricorn in the annual 10th house of dignities. Stressful aspects involving Jupiter often signify wastefulness. In addition, annual Mars squares annual Jupiter and conjoins annual Mercury, activating his natal tendency to dissipate assets. Jupiter has moved from its natal position on the Ascendant (personal striving) to the annual 10th house (dignities), suggesting that he will be ambitious for dignities this year. Morin attributes Cardan's successes to the fact that Mars rules Capricorn by exaltation and thus rules both annual Jupiter and the annual Midheaven. The annual Mercury/

Mars conjunction brings the ruler of his natal 2nd house of income, Mercury, into contact with Mars, the ruler by exaltation of benefic Jupiter. Morin neglects to mention that the annual Mercury/Mars conjunction also conjoins natal Venus, the lesser benefic, in her home sign of Libra – a fortunate influence on his career and income.

•   A blood relative (3rd house) intervened on Cardan's behalf in his pursuit of a dignity (10th house). According to Morin, the Moon is the ruler of the Cancer 3rd house of blood relations in both the natal and annual charts. As mentioned in the discussion of Cardan's health, the annual Moon is favorably disposed by its conjunction with natal Jupiter and trine with annual Venus. In addition, Jupiter rules both the annual and natal 3rd houses (kin) by exaltation and occupies the 10th house (dignities) of the Solar Return, suggesting that the efforts of his blood relations will be directed toward his achieving some dignities.

•   Cardan says that he kept his immovable goods (4th house) with difficulty, and there were not enough of these goods to be sold. Morin attributes this difficulty to the fact that the annual Moon, ruler of the 4th house (landed property, the parents), receives a square from annual Saturn (deprivation) in detriment in Leo. Morin also attributes the fact that Cardan's mother (Moon, 4th house) was not harmed by the square between annual Saturn and the Moon to the annual Moon being exalted in Taurus and receiving a protective trine from annual Venus.

•   Cardan's wife (7th house) conceived a daughter (5th house), who suffered an intrauterine illness (Cardan's 4th, which is his daughter's derived 12th of bodily affliction). Morin notes that Venus rules the Solar Return Ascendant (Cardan's life force) and also disposes the annual Moon in the annual 1st house. It is good that the annual Moon does not conjoin any malefics. Annual Venus occupies the annual 5th house of children and trines both the annual Moon and the Solar Return Ascendant, thus promising offspring this year. Mercury disposes annual Venus in Virgo in the 5th of children, and annual Mercury occupies the 6th house conjunct annual Mars, the lesser malefic and ruler of the unfortunate 12th house – suggesting an infirmity of his child. Morin neglects to mention that annual Saturn, the greater malefic in detriment in Leo, conjoins both the annual and natal 5th house cusps of children. Annual Saturn also squares the annual Moon, which rules Cardan's annual and natal 4th house – the derived 12th of sickness of his natal 5th house children.

•   Cardan's servants and animals (6th house) were a source of trouble (12th house) and underwent many changes. Morin attributes these effects to annual Mercury, which rules the 2nd and 6th houses of both the annual and natal charts, conjunct annual 12th ruler Mars in the 6th house in the cardinal (changeable) sign of Libra. Cardinal signs were thought to be active, energetic, initiatory, and changeable – his servants and animals started feeling their oats this year.

•   Some harm came to Cardan's wife. Mars and Jupiter rule the wife because Mars rules the 7th house cusp (marriage partner) of both the natal and annual charts, and Jupiter rules Sagittarius, part of which occupies the 7th house of marriage in both charts. The annual Moon also has reference to the wife because it occupies the annual 1st house opposite the 7th house cusp (the principle of ricochet). Annual Mars (the wife) lies in its detriment in Libra in the unfortunate annual 6th house. Annual Jupiter (the wife) lies in its fall in Capricorn and forms a square to annual Mars (the wife) in the unfortunate Solar Return 6th House. The annual Moon (the wife) is afflicted by a square from annual Saturn (hardship) in its detriment in Leo. Morin adds that "open enemies are suppressed by fear of the prince and hindered by just men so that they cannot do harm."[32] His explanation is that annual Mars, ruler of the 7th of open enemies, is in detriment in Libra in the debilitating 6th and closely squares Jupiter in its fall in Capricorn in the 10th of dignified princes and magistracy.

•   Cardan says that he achieved several dignities (10th house) in that year (October, 1534 – October, 1535), but they were impeded by open and secret enemies (7th and 12th houses). According to Morin, Cardan received dignities because the natal Midheaven was by direction in right trine to the Midheaven-ruler Saturn.[33] By primary direction, the natal Midheaven actually opposed natal Saturn (at the Naibod rate) around January of 1533, indicating impediments to career matters. There did, however, occur a trine by solar arc direction, which became exact in November of 1532. Recall that Morin had calculated Saturn to be a degree later than in the modern computer chart, so that in Morin's calculations the solar arc directed Midheaven/Saturn trine would have occurred at the very end of 1533, and would still have been within orb at the time of Cardan's 1534 Solar Return. This example made me wonder whether Morin consulted solar arc directions in his work.

•   Continuing to examine Cardan's dignities this year, we see that Jupiter had moved from its position on the natal Ascendant to the annual Capricorn 10th house of honors where it aspects (by square) the Sun, Mars and Mercury in Libra. Furthermore, the benefic annual Ascendant-ruler Venus disposes this conjunction of annual Sun, Mars, and Mercury, and also disposes the annual Moon. Venus is doubly benefic because of its favorable placement oriental of the Sun (rising before the Sun), which is a traditional dignity. Cardan's enemies caused problems because annual 12th ruler Jupiter lies in its fall in the 10th and squares annual Mars, which rules the 7th of open enemies and also rules the 12th of secret enemies by ricochet.

•   As an interesting aside, let us consider the technique of firdaria (not used by Morin). We find that Cardan entered the Sun subperiod of his Mars firdar on September 24, 1534 NS. Thus, issues signified by Mars and the Sun come into prominence during this Solar Return year. The planet Mars rules his natal 12th (fears, illness) and 7th (his wife), lies on the cusp of his natal 2nd (wealth), and is exalted in his natal 10th (dignities). The Sun, a natural signifier of honors, rules his natal 5th (pregnancy, children), is exalted in his natal 12th house, and occupies his natal 6th (animals, servants, health concerns). In the system of derived houses, Cardan's 6th and 12th houses also refer to the health of his 7th house wife.

NOTES

1.   Morin, Book 23 of *Astrologia Gallica: Revolutions*, 2nd Edition, translated by James Holden, AFA, 2003, p. 129.

2.   For a excellent discussion of Morin's influence read Tom Callanan's essay on Morin at http://www.skyscript.co.uk/morin.html.

3.   Morin, Book 23 of *Astrologia Gallica: Revolutions*, 2nd Edition, translated by James H. Holden, AFA, 2003, p. 6.

4.   See *Late Classical Astrology: Paulus Alexandrinus and Olypiadorus*, translated by Dorian Greenbaum, ARHAT, 2001. In his introduction to this book Rob Hand writes:

> "We see in the combination of Paulus & Olympiodorus that late Greek Astrology was in fact much closer to early Arabic than has generally been recognized. While the Arabic tradition clearly picked up much from the Persian that was not to be found in the Greek tradition, some of the methods that achieved such prominence in the Arabic tradition are already found in the Paulus-Olympiodorus tradition. The two outstanding instances of this are the use of large numbers of Lots and at least the beginnings of the elaborate Persian-Arabic doctrine of Solar Revolutions. The Paulus-Olympiodorus material shows us much of the Greek tradition just before the Arabic invasions of the Byzantine empire carried Greek Astrology into the Middle Eastern world where it combined with Persian & Indian traditions, giving rise to the Arabic & later Latin medieval traditions of Astrology from which much of Western Astrology is descended."

5.   Morin, *Book 23*, translated by Holden, ibid, p. 6.

6.   Morin, *Book 23*, ibid, p. 8.

7.   Robert Corre at http://www.forumonastrology.com/ascendant.html
8.   Morin, *Book 23*, ibid, p. 23.
9.   Morin, *Book 23*, ibid, p. 22.
10. Morin, *Book 21*, translated by Richard S. Baldwin, AFA, 1974, p. 23.
11. Morin, *Book 21*, p. 44.
12. Morin, *Book 21*, ibid, p. 47.
13. Morin, *Book 22*, op. cit., p.19.
14. The source of Gustave's "toward 1 PM" time of death is http://en.wikipedia.org/wiki/Battle_of_L%C3%BCtzen_%281632%29.
15. The Battle of Lützen at http://www.fortunecity.com/victorian/riley/787/30/war/lutzen.html .
16. Morin, *Book 21*, ibid, p. 46.
17. Morin, *Book 23*, ibid, p. 28.
18. Vivian E. Robson, *TheFixed Stars and Constellations in Astrology*, 1923, pp. 181-184.
19. Steven Birchfield presents a scholarly discussion of firdaria at http://www.astrologiamedieval.com/firdaria.htm.
20. Medieval astrologers used numerous techniques to identify periods when particular planets were active during an individual's life. Such techniques included Ptolemy's seven ages of man, the Persian firdaria, and the directing of the natal Ascendant through the Egyptian terms to identify time lords. Morin dismissed such techniques as superstitions.
21. Rob Hand speaking on the "Classical Method of Solar Revolutions" at the ISAR Astrology Conference, Illinois. August 2005.
22. Morin in *Book 22*, op. cit., p.78, writes:
     "Tycho Brahe meant the diurnal motion of the right ascension of the Sun and not the diurnal motion of its longitude. And I, who am unable to assign fictitious causes to real times of effects, had long since conceived the same thing ..."
23. Morin, *Astrologia Gallica* Book 22, translated by James Holden, AFA, 1994, pp. 81-83.
24. Solar Fire Dexlue v. 6.0.25, Help File on Primary Directions. Esoteric Technologies, 2005.
25. Makransky, 'Primary Directions – An Overview', *NCGR Journal* Winter 1988-89, pp. 131-135.
26. James Holden gives instructions for calculating Regiomontanus primaries in his translation of *Book 22* of *Astrologia Gallica*, AFA, 1994, pp. 203-206. I have not found a computer program that calculates Regiomontanus primaries.
27. Morin, *Book 23*, ibid, p. 128.
29. Morin, *Book 23*, ibid, p. 24.
30. For a detailed account of Morin's delineation the reader is referred to James Holden's translation in Morin, *Book 23*, pp. 24-26.

31. In Ascendant-arc directions, the longitudinal distance moved by the secondary progressed ascendant is added to all points in the original chart. Thus, on March 3, 1534, Cardan's secondary progressed Ascendant had moved to conjoin his natal Saturn.

32. Morin, *Book 23*, ibid, p. 26.

33. Rather than using a solar arc direction, Morin may have been directing the trine of natal Saturn to the natal Midheaven. Saturn at 19° Gemini 20' has a trine at 19° Aquarius 20'. The right ascension of the trine point is 321°46' and the right ascension of the Midheaven is 289°44', so the difference in arc between them is 32°02'. Hence the trine of Saturn would be carried to the natal Midheaven by primary direction in the year 1533. A helpful table for calculation oblique and right ascension can be found at http://www.worldastrology.net/table.php

9

The Death of Jean-Baptiste Morin

As mentioned previously, Jean-Baptiste Morin is said to have predicted his own death. Astrologer Thomas Callanan gives the following account of Morin's demise:

> In the middle of October 1656, Morin was told by a chiromancer that the following month would be fatal to him. He was in altogether good health, but smiled. He'd seen it in his chart. A little more than a week later he was taken with fever, and urged his doctors not to trouble themselves too much. His end was inevitable. At 2:00 AM on November 6, in Paris, Jean-Baptiste Morin passed away leaving many to wonder what might have been had he been born at a time when his greatest gifts would have received greater appreciation.[1]

In this chapter we will reconstruct what Morin might have seen in his natal chart that fateful month and further elaborate his system of interpreting Solar Returns.[2] Let's begin by considering the birth chart Morin used for himself (Figure 1), which I cast with a computer using the following data: 23 February 1583 NS, 8:47:33 AM LMT, Villefranche, France, 45N25, 004E43. Modern computer calculations differ very slightly from Morin's own published chart.

We begin by asking whether the potential for death by febrile illness is shown in the natal chart. The planet Mars rules his natal Aries Ascendant and thus governs Morin's body, life, and state of health. Taurus is intercepted in the 1st house, making Venus a co-ruler of Morin's corporal well being. Venus on the cusp of the 12th house shows a tendency to illness. Because the Sun is exalted in Aries, it rules the Ascendant (his body) through exaltation. Like Venus, the hot Sun also conjoins the 12th cusp of bodily ailments, suggesting a proneness to febrile illness.

Jupiter rules Morin's natal 8th house of death and occupies the natal 12th house, suggesting death due to illness or in confinement. Jupiter, ruler of the 8th (his death) and Venus ruler of the 1st (his body), are each combust the Sun, raising the possibility of a febrile illness (combustion). In addition, Mars (fevers) conjoins the 4th house cusp (final endings) and occupies the

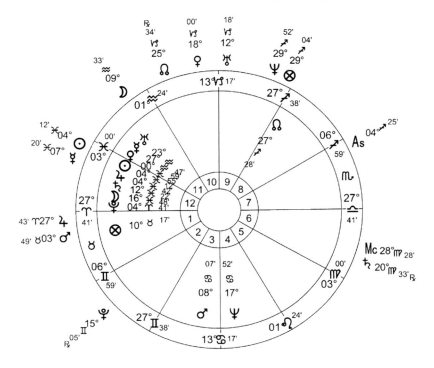

Figure 1: Jean-Baptiste Morin Solar Return on Natal Chart

whole sign 4th house (end of life). Mars is debilitated in Cancer, which is opposite Capricorn, its sign of exaltation. The natal trine from Mars (fevers) to the stellium of Venus, Sun, Jupiter, Saturn and the Moon in the 12th house, though a beneficial aspect, carries the malefic sting of a debilitated Mars. Though Morin was unaware of it, his natal Mars also squares Pluto in Aries in the natal 12th house. The potential for a febrile death due to illness is thus presaged in the natal chart.

Let us now turn our attention to the Solar Return set for Paris in 1656, the year of his death (Figure 2). Sagittarius rises in the Solar Return, making Jupiter the annual Ascendant-ruler by domicile. In Morin's natal chart Jupiter rules the natal 8th house of death. Annual Jupiter at 27° Aries 43' (the natal lord of death) has moved to the exact position of the birth Ascendant (his body and life). In addition, the Solar Return Ascendant (the life of the native) almost exactly squares his natal Sun (at the natal 12th cusp) and also conjoins the natal 8th house cusp of death.[3] By secondary progression of the annual chart, the progressed Sun squares the annual Ascendant in May of 1656 and squares the secondary progressed annual Ascendant in November of 1656,

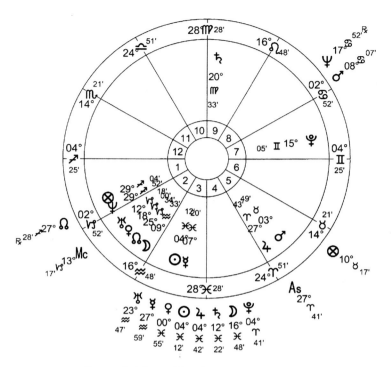

Figure 2: Morin Natal on 1656 Solar Return

the month of his death. The emphasis on the 8th and 12th houses in the 1656 solar revolution must have alarmed Morin. Could the stars have been any clearer in their warnings about death?

Morin emphasized that the Ascendant-ruler acts through the sign that it occupies. The annual Ascendant-ruler Jupiter in Aries thus acts through the nature and state of Mars. Recall that natal Mars is debilitated in Cancer, the sign of its fall, which enhances its malefic nature. Annual Mars is also debilitated in Taurus (the sign of its detriment opposite its home sign Scorpio). In addition, this debilitated annual Mars rules the Solar Return 12th house of illness and occupies the natal 1st house (his body), suggesting that he might suffer a febrile illness or a piercing wound during the year. The signification of a life-threatening fever is reinforced by the Solar Return Moon ruling the annual 8th house of death and squaring annual Mars.

This signification is further repeated in the sesqui-quadrate between Solar Return Mars (ruling the return 12th) and Solar Return Saturn (which occupies the natal 12th). The two malefics, each associated with the 12th house and forming a hard aspect, suggest an illness or injury during the year. Finally his natal debilitated Mars (fever) occupies the annual 8th house (death), raising the possibility of death through Mars-related causes. The Solar Return Mars occupying Taurus in the annual 5th house together with annual Ascendant-ruler Jupiter at the cusp of the 5th makes one wonder whether Morin had contracted a venereal disease that led to the fatal fever. We may never know. Nonetheless, we can see why Morin thought that he might die of a fever or a piercing injury in 1656.

How did Morin forecast November 6th as the likely date of death? Let's recap his technique to put things in perspective. First, Morin studied the birth chart to determine the natal potentials that would be in effect for the entire life of the individual. Nothing significant occurs in one's life unless it is presaged in the birth chart. Our entire life history is reflected in the unfolding of the birth chart. All subsequent progressions, directions, returns, and transits merely act through the principle of similarity to manifest the promise of the birth chart.

After studying the birth chart, Morin next looked at the directions of the natal chart for the year. As we saw in our discussion of Cardan's Solar Return, Morin certainly used primary directions, and may also have considered Ascendant-arc and solar arc directions. He did not, however, use secondary progressions, which were popularized by his younger contemporary, the Italian Benedictine monk Placido de Titus (1603-1668).

By way of review, the system of primary directions (one degree of the earth's rotation on its axis equals a year of life) was initially used to determine time lords, that is, planets that govern specific periods of one's life – the so-called planetary periods. Only much later in Western astrology, and not long before the time of Morin, did primary directions come to be used for timing events. After Placido de Titus popularized secondary progressions (a day equals a year of life), which are much easier to compute, the method of primary directions fell into relative disuse.

Despite the difficulty with their calculation, the idea behind primary directions is quite simple. The birth chart represents the native's potential. The primary directions are one method to forecast when and how that potential will unfold. After birth, the earth continues to turn on its axis and the heavens appear to rotate around the birthplace. Primary directions are based upon this apparent motion of the sky around the place of birth during the several hours after the nativity. As the earth's rotation carries the planets, angles, and house cusp positions of the natal chart around the wheel, they will eventually contact (or be directed to) the positions of the planets and points of the natal chart.

Morin would have calculated his primary directions for 1656-1657 and would have noted any significant directions perfecting during the course of his 1656 Solar Return year. It is difficult to reconstruct Morin's primary directions because of variations in calculations between modern computers and those done manually with the use of tables in Morin's time. In addition, each house system has its own particular method for dividing three-dimensional space. Thus each house system gives rise to a specific and distinct definition of what it means for planets to be "conjunct" in three-dimensional space, that is, to be brought into alignment on the celestial sphere by the rotation of the earth. As a result, each house system has "its own unique method of computing primary directions.[4]"

Using *Solar Fire*, I generated the following list of the primary directions (at the natal solar rate) that were active during Morin's last year of life. This list of prismaries most likely differs from that used by Morin, who preferred Regiomontanus houses and the Naibod rate in right ascension. *Solar Fire* uses the Placidean method to calculate primary directions and not the method of Regiomontanus. Hence the following list is for illustrative purposes only.

DYNAMIC REPORT
Jean Baptiste Morin - Male Chart
Feb 23 1583 NS, 8:47:33 am, LMT -0:18:52
Villefranche France, 45°N59', 004°E43'
Geocentric Tropical Zodiac
Regiomontanus Houses, Mean Node

Primary Directions (at natal solar rate)

Mon (9)Opp Mar (3)	(X)	Pm-Na Aug 6 1656 NS	098°13'	08°Cn07'
Mer (9) Sqr Mon (12)	(X)	Pm-Na Sep 21 1656 NS	118°02'	06°Pi48'
Ven (9)Cnj Nod (8)	(X)	Pm-Na Nov 9 1656 NS	114°28'	27°Sg28'

Using the Placidean method of calculation, we see that the primary directed Moon (at the natal solar rate) opposes natal Mars on August 6, 1656; primary directed Mercury squares the natal Moon on September 21, 1656; and primary directed Venus opposes the natal South Lunar Node on November 9, 1656. Such aspects would have troubled Morin because the Moon signifies his natal 4th house of final endings and occupies his natal 12th of illness. The Moon also rules the 8th house of death in his annual chart. The planet Mars, debilitated in Cancer – the sign of the Moon – rules his natal Ascendant and is a natural signifier of fevers. Venus – a co-ruler of his natal 1st house – conjoins his natal 12th house cusp and, through its position in the annual 2nd house, has an 8th house significance through ricochet. The Moon's North Node is debilitated by its fall in Sagittarius in the natal 8th house and is conjoined by primary directed Venus, which co-rules his body and life-force in the natal chart.

Not having a computer program to do the math, I used James Holden's instructions[5] to calculate Morin's primary directions by hand, following the method of Regiomontanus. If my calculations are correct, the primary directed natal Moon came to the opposition of natal Mars in the late summer of 1656 (at the Naibod rate), a few months before Morin's demise. Morin would have been aware of this primary direction. The planet Mars, ruler of Morin's natal Ascendant and of his natal 6th house (Scorpio intercepted), falls in the 1656 annual 8th house of the solar revolution. The Moon (a co-ruler by exaltation of his natal 1st house with Taurus intercepted therein) rules Morin's natal 4th of final endings as well as his annual 8th of death in the 1656 Solar Return.

After studying the natal chart and its primary directions, and next the Solar Return and its directions, Morin would look for any concordant Lunar Returns, and finally he would consider the transits to pinpoint the time an event was likely to occur. The Lunar Return set for Paris prior to his death

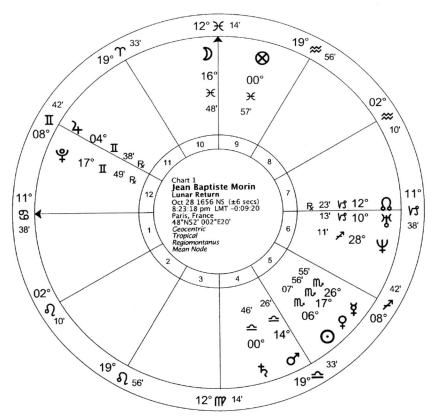

Figure 3: Morin Lunar Return for Oct 28, 1656

occurred on October 28, 1656 (Figure 3). Morin's natal IC (cusp of the natal 4th house of the grave) conjoins the Lunar Return Ascendant (his body and life); thus the symbol of his life force in the Lunar Return conjoins the symbol of final endings in the natal chart.

His natal Mars (fevers) also conjoins the Lunar Return Ascendant, and his Lunar Return Mars squares the Lunar Return Ascendant and the natal IC of endings (see Figure 4). His natal Saturn almost exactly conjoins the Lunar Return Midheaven in the unfortunate natal 12th house. The two traditional malefics of his natal chart are highly angular in the Lunar Return, and Saturn rules the 8th house of death of the Lunar Return chart. In addition, Lunar Return Jupiter, which rules his natal 8th of death, is almost exactly square his natal Jupiter/Sun conjunction in the natal 12th house. Lunar Return Jupiter also opposes the natal 8th cusp of death. The South Lunar Node in the

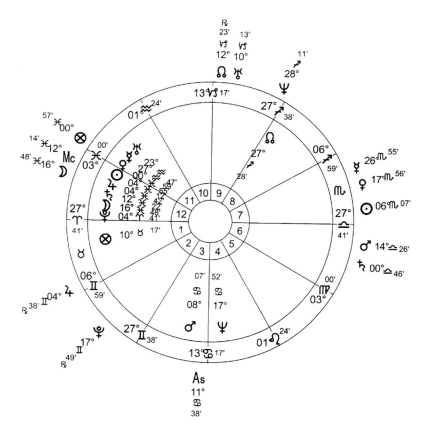

Figure 4: Morin Oct 1656 Lunar Return on his Natal Chart

Lunar Return, which occupies the Solar Return 8th house of death, conjoins the natal 4th house cusp of the grave. Seeing this Lunar Return, Morin would have expected death to occur during this lunar revolution.

The Solar Eclipses and Morin's Death

Morin most likely was aware of the impending partial solar eclipse of December 15, 1656, which took place in late Sagittarius in his natal 8th house of death. The planet Jupiter, his natal 8th house ruler, ruled that eclipse and fell in late Taurus in his natal 1st house. The eclipse itself squared annual Saturn as well as the meridian axis of his Solar Return chart.

More significant was the total solar eclipse of July 21, 1656 – the first solar eclipse of his Solar Return year, which is usually quite informative when superimposed on the annual chart. The total solar eclipse fell in the 8th house of the annual chart (see Figure 5). This eclipse squares annual Jupiter, ruler of the natal house of death and of the return Ascendant. The eclipse also squares

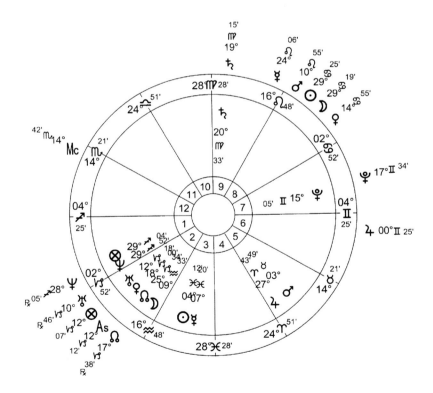

Figure 5: July 21 1656 Total Solar Eclipse on Solar Return

the natal Ascendant. Venus and Mars of the eclipse chart, which rule his natal 1ˢᵗ house, occupy the return 8ᵗʰ house of death. The Midheaven of the eclipse chart for Paris conjoins the unfortunate 12ᵗʰ cusp of the annual chart, suggesting illness and confinement. When Morin died at 2 AM on November 6, 1656, the transiting Sun at 14° Scorpio 23' almost exactly conjoined the annual 12ᵗʰ cusp and the eclipse Midheaven. At the same time the transiting Moon, ruler of the annual 8ᵗʰ house, at 0° Cancer 43'closely conjoined the annual 8ᵗʰ cusp of death.

Transits at the Time of Death
In studying the transits for the time of his death, I am not sure what Morin might have regarded as an indicator of his demise. On November 6, 1656, transiting Mercury (ruler of his 2ⁿᵈ and accidental ruler of the 8ᵗʰ) was on the 8ᵗʰ house cusp. This does not seem a significant enough transit to represent a death. Transiting Jupiter (natal ruler of the 8ᵗʰ of death) had squared his natal Sun in the 12ᵗʰ house on November 1ˢᵗ, suggesting the possibility of death around the beginning of November. During the evening of November 5ᵗʰ transiting Mars sesqui-squared natal Sun and then continued on to semi-square natal Jupiter in the natal 12ᵗʰ house. Morin died about five hours after this last aspect reached perfection. Interestingly, at 1:52 AM (8 minutes before the reported time of death) the transiting Ascendant in Paris conjoined the natal Emerson's Point of Death at 17° Virgo 32'.

Directing the Lunar Return
The following discussion of Lunar Returns is presented for the obsessive among us. Most astrologers are quite busy and rarely have the time to erect a series of Lunar Returns for the entire year, let alone to progress each of them. The reader can safely skip this section on progressing Lunar Returns without fear of missing an essential technique. It is offered mainly to stimulate curiosity among those who might wish to further investigate an interesting idea.

According to Morin, "the directions of the revolutions may indicate the day of an effect by of the proportion of the daily motion of the Sun or the Moon to the whole circle for a year or a month..."[6] Morin felt that it was important in directing a revolution to make an equivalence between two distinct but related complete cycles. For Solar Returns, Morin used a method similar to primary directions and considered the ratio of one daily cycle of the Sun to one yearly revolution of the Sun.

Morin used a similar method to direct Lunar Returns by mapping a sidereal lunar month (lunar revolution) onto the time it takes the Moon to make a complete 360-degree circuit of the chart. The Moon's orbital period (the sidereal month) has a length of about 27.3 days (27 days, 7 hours, 43 minutes, 11.6 seconds). Interestingly, the human gestation cycle of 273 days is exactly ten sidereal months in length. For those of us who are technically challenged, Morin's instructions for directing a return chart can be intimidating. I will enumerate Morin's four steps below but will not further elaborate his technique for directing Lunar Returns:

1.   Count the number of days from the beginning of the Lunar Return up to the day that an event occurs.
2.   Calculate (or look up in Morin's tables) the number of degrees corresponding to the number of days in step #1.
3.   Add the number of degrees from step #2 to the right ascension or oblique ascension of the significator being directed.
4.   Then, to find the ecliptic longitude of the directed significator, look in a table of right or oblique ascensions for the altitude of the pole above the circle of position of the significator.

Daily Progressed Lunar Returns (Lunar Mansions)
Instead of directing the Lunar Return by the Morin's method, I find it easier to do some type of progression. Recall that in directing a chart we add the same number of degrees of arc to every point in a chart to obtain to the new directed positions. In directions the entire chart is shifted backward or forward by a predetermined fixed arc. As we saw with primary directions, calculating the new directed positions and accounting for latitude can be mathematically challenging.

Progressions, on the other hand, simply recalculate the chart and all its points for a new time that is proportional, by some theoretical measure, to the original time for which the chart is cast. In secondary progressions, for example, the chart is recalculated at a rate of one day after birth equals one year of life. It would be reasonable then to progress a Lunar Return in daily increments so that, at the end of a complete lunar cycle, the Moon has returned to its original zodiacal position. After experimenting with various ways to progress the Lunar Return, I came up with the following useful method, which is essentially a system of lunar mansions based on the sidereal lunar cycle.

The Moon repeats its location in the zodiac roughly every 27 calendar days. For example, whatever zodiac longitude the Moon occupies at 0 hours on the 1st of any month, it will again occupy on morning of the 28th day of the month. From a sidereal perspective the Moon completes one full cycle as measured against the backdrop of the fixed stars in a *sidereal month*, which has a duration of 27.321661 days (27 days, 7 hours, 43 minutes, 11.5 seconds). At the end of the sidereal month the Moon returns to its original position among the fixed stars (in Latin *sidus* means star).

If we divide the sidereal month into 27 equal segments, one segment for each of the 27 solar calendar days, we can determine a reasonable progression rate for the Lunar Return. In other words, the Lunar Return can be progressed at a rate of 27.321661 divided by 27, which equals 1.01191337 "lunar days" of the sidereal month per solar calendar day. This amounts to advancing the Lunar Return chart daily by 24 hours 17 minutes 9 seconds.[9] At this rate the Lunar Return Midheaven progresses at approximately 5½ degrees per day.

Such a daily progressed chart gives the current transits for each day but has the advantage of producing meaningful progressed daily angles and house cusps, which correspond to the start of a new "lunar day". To repeat, we are dividing the sidereal month into 27 equal "lunar days" and erecting a progressed lunar return chart for the start of each new lunar day (sidereal lunar mansion). Each progressed daily lunar chart remains in effect for 24 hours, 17 minutes, and 9 seconds, at which time the next progressed daily lunar chart becomes active.

In Hindu astrology the cusps of the lunar mansions are considered critical degrees. Events during the sidereal month associated with the current Lunar Return can be located to one of these 27 lunar mansions, and the progressed daily lunar return chart for that "lunar day" or mansion will have meaningful angles and house cusps related to that event.

Table for Daily Progressed Lunar Returns

"Lunar Day" or Mansion of the Lunar Return	Days	Hours	Mins	Secs
1st "Lunar Day" begins at	0	0	0	0
2nd "Lunar Day" begins at	1	0	17	9
3rd "Lunar Day" begins at	2	0	34	18
4th "Lunar Day" begins at	3	0	51	27
5th "Lunar Day" begins at	4	1	8	37
6th "Lunar Day" begins at	5	1	25	46
7th "Lunar Day" begins at	6	1	42	55
8th "Lunar Day" begins at	7	2	0	5
9th "Lunar Day" begins at	8	2	17	14
10th "Lunar Day" begins at	9	2	34	23
11th "Lunar Day" begins at	10	2	51	33
12th "Lunar Day" begins at	11	3	8	42

13th "Lunar Day" begins at	12	3	25	51
14th "Lunar Day" begins at	13	3	43	1
15th "Lunar Day" begins at	14	4	0	10
16th "Lunar Day" begins at	15	4	17	19
17th "Lunar Day" begins at	16	4	34	29
18th "Lunar Day" begins at	17	4	51	38
19th "Lunar Day" begins at	18	5	8	47
20th "Lunar Day" begins at	19	5	25	56
21st "Lunar Day" begins at	20	5	43	6
22nd "Lunar Day" begins at	21	6	0	15
23rd "Lunar Day" begins at	22	6	17	24
24th "Lunar Day" begins at	23	6	34	34
25th "Lunar Day" begins at	24	6	51	43
26th "Lunar Day" begins at	25	7	8	52
27th "Lunar Day" begins at	26	7	26	2
End of sidereal month	27	7	43	11

To illustrate the technique, let's apply the Table for Daily Progressed Lunar Returns to the lunar revolution in effect at the time of Morin's death on November 6th around 2 AM. The Lunar Return just prior to his death occurred on October 28th at 8:23:18 PM. Doing the arithmetic, we see that 8 days 5 hours and 37 minutes have elapsed from the exact time of the Lunar Return to the time of his demise. Looking at the Table, we can see that Morin died during the 9th "lunar day," of his Lunar Return chart.

To find the daily progressed Lunar Return Ascendant for the 9th "lunar day," we check the Table and find that we must add 8 days 2 hours 17 minutes 14 seconds to the time that we cast the original lunar revolution to get to the start of the 9th lunar day. In other words, we calculate a "daily progressed" lunar chart for November 5, 1656 (8 days later) at the original time of 8:23:18 PM of the Lunar Return *plus* 2 hours 17 minutes 14 seconds, which takes us to 10:40:32 PM on November 5th (see Figure 6). This new chart is the daily progressed lunar chart that was in effect on the day of Morin's death. This new chart, which went into effect at 10:40:32 PM on November 5, 1656, gives a progressed Ascendant of 13° Leo 37'.

For additional practice, let's calculate the progressed chart for the next day of the Lunar Return. A similar calculation for November 6 (the original 8:23:18 PM plus 9 days 2 hours 34 minutes 23 seconds = 10:57:41 PM) gives a progressed daily Ascendant of 17° Leo 26' for the 10th "lunar day." Between November 5th and November 6th, the progressed daily Ascendant advanced from 13° Leo 37' to 17° Leo 26', or approximately 4 degrees, and the progressed daily Midheaven moved from 27° Aries 54' to 3° Taurus 26', or about 5½ degrees. The November 6th daily progressed angles and house cusps remain in effect until the next progressed lunar chart, which goes into effect a day later on November 7th at 8:23:18 PM plus 2 hours 51 minutes 33 seconds, and so on.

Superimposing Morin's natal chart onto the progressed daily Lunar Return at the time of his death (Figure 6), we see that his natal stellium of 12th house planets has migrated to the progressed lunar 8th house of death. The Sun, which rules the progressed Lunar Return Ascendant by domicile and also rules his natal Ascendant by exaltation, exactly conjoins the progressed lunar 8th house cusp. The natal Ascendant (his body) closely opposes the progressed Lunar Return 4th house cusp of the grave. At the same time the progressed daily Lunar Return Ascendant squares the progressed lunar Sun in the progressed lunar 4th house of the final endings. Although Morin was unaware of it, the modern planet Neptune, which rules the progressed lunar Pisces 8th cusp of death and the natal Pisces 12th cusp of illness, closely conjoins the progressed lunar 12th house cusp.

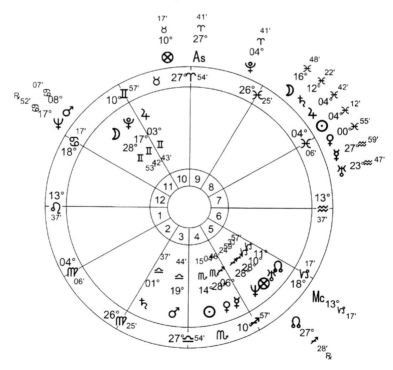

Figure 6: Morin Natal Chart on Progressed Lunar Return for Nov 5, 1656

Morin's Twelve Steps for Judging a Revolution

This chapter concludes with a synopsis of Morin's recommendations for judging a return chart, which he outlines in Chapters 19 and 20 of his *Book 23* on revolutions. In reviewing Morin's twelve principles, the reader will appreciate the origins of many modern techniques for interpreting returns.

1st: In judging Solar or Lunar Returns, note whether the heavens are disposed in the return chart as they are in the birth chart. Natal potentials are triggered into action by a similarity between the return chart and the nativity. Also note whether the zodiacal signs ascending in the return and the nativity form an opposition, square, or trine (see Morin's aphorism #6 in the next chapter). Consider the houses of the return to which the signs governing the houses of the birth chart relocate. Morin's final point is the origin of Volguine's method of superimposing the natal and return charts.

2nd: The cusps of the astrological houses are powerful points within the chart. Note whether the house cusps of the return chart conjoin or form an aspect with the natal planets. Consider the nature, determinations, and the state of those planets. Also consider the nature, state, and determinations of the planets ruling the houses. This rule of Morin became a cornerstone of Volguine's method of studying conjunctions and aspects involving house cusps in the natal and return charts.

3rd: Note which natal house(s) each planet occupies or rules, and determine what can be forecast on the basis of these natal positions and the celestial state of each of the planets in the birth chart. (Celestial state refers to whether a planet is fortified or debilitated according to its zodiacal location on the ecliptic.)

4th: Note whether any of the planets in the return chart conjoin or aspect their own natal positions or the positions of any other birth planet. How are these planets related to each another or determined in each chart?

5th: Note the house position of each planet in the birth chart and to which house the natal planet relocates in the return chart. Also note which house(s) each planet rules in the natal and return charts. Consider to which house of the return chart the planet's natal house relocates and study how it is disposed in the return chart.

6th: Consider the dispositor of each planet (the planet ruling the sign occupied by the planet) and how each planet relates to its dispositor in both the natal and the return charts. Ray Merriman makes extensive use of this rule as part of his system for interpreting Solar Returns.

7th: Note whether the celestial state of each planet in the natal and return charts are similar or contrary in nature, and to what extent. Similarity tends to manifest natal potentials. Contrariety causes hindrance, stress, and friction.

8th: Note whether a planet has the same or a similar determination in the Solar Return as in the birth chart. A similarity of determinations is especially important for any planet involved in natal directions that will perfect in the coming year.

9th: Note whether the same house in each chart presages the same or related matters or whether they have contrary indications. This is similar to the 7th step above.

10th: Note whether the current directions favor or contradict what is signified by the Solar Return. Morin taught that "directions alone do nothing without the agreement of annual revolutions, or at least monthly revolutions with transits in agreement...."[10] Modern astrologers can apply this same principle to secondary progressions.

11th: Note what each planet signifies in the birth chart according to its celestial state and determinations in the nativity. In a similar way, study the return chart and note whether the natal and return significations of each planet agree or disagree among themselves and how these significations relate to any directions involving the planet that will perfect in the coming year. Judge the effects of each planet in the return chart by synthesizing all of these factors.

12th: Note any directions of the birth chart that will perfect in the coming year and compare them with any directions of the return chart that will also perfect during that year. [Morin directed the Solar Return at a rate of the mean daily motion of the Sun, and the Lunar Return at a rate of the mean daily motion of the Moon.] Check whether any direction in the return chart is concordant with a natal direction. Then check whether the Lunar Return that is in effect when the annual direction perfects has a similar signification. If so, the matter will come to pass during that Lunar Return and on a day when a Lunar Return direction is in agreement, especially if a concordant transit occurs at the same time. This same rule can be applied to other types of directions and to secondary progressions.

To be thorough the astrologer can erect all the Lunar Returns for a given Solar Return year and select the one that is most concordant with a natal direction. Before considering any Lunar Returns for the year, however, it is important first to judge the Solar Return. The only significant Lunar Returns will be those that accord with the annual chart as well as with the natal significations and directions. If there is no conformity between the Solar Return and the birth chart and its directions, then the Lunar Returns generally will be ineffectual, unless the matter is strongly signified both by the natal chart and its directions and also by the Lunar Return.

In Chapter 20 of *Book 23* Morin offers additional considerations regarding the judgment of revolutions. He notes that if one calculates all the directions of the Solar and Lunar Return charts for a one-year cycle, the number of perfected aspects will be enormous. He advises focusing only on the most salient factors to avoid getting caught up in trivia. Morin notes that because clients consult astrologers "only for accidents of major importance … relating to life, dignities, marriage, journeys, etc., the astrologer should therefore see in a particular year which effects are signified by the radical directions in that year that are more significant in type or in kind, and whether the solar revolution confirms that signification."[11]

After Morin has identified a natal potential that is likely to manifest in a given year because of a currently active direction, he looks to the Solar Return for a concordant signification. If a concordant direction of the annual chart exists, Morin then looks to the Lunar Return for a similar signification to decide in which month the matter is likely to occur. He then considers the directions of the Lunar Return to pinpoint the day of manifestation and confirms his forecast with a concordant transit. When studying an event that has already occurred, Morin reverses this process to deduce its astrological antecedents. He locates the event to one of the twelve houses and then looks to the directions of the Lunar and Solar Returns that are active on the day of the event to determine its astrological correlations.

By way of illustration, Morin offers the following advice for specifically forecasting matters of health and life on a particular day:

• Consider the directions of the natal Ascendant (the body, life force) and the Ascendant-ruler on that day.

• Consider the directions of the annual Ascendant and Ascendant-ruler on the same day.

• Consider the directions of the current Lunar Return Ascendant and its ruler on that day.

• Consider the houses in which these various directions fall in the return charts and especially in the birth chart.

• Consider how the current transits affect each return chart and especially the natal chart.

• In matters of health and life, pay special attention to planets occupying the 1st (the life of the native), 8th (death, or danger to the life of the native) and 12th (illness of the native) houses. Study the directions of those planets.

- Also study the rulers of the 1st, 8th, and 12th houses and their directions.
- Finally, synthesize all of the above information in making any forecast on the basis of the radical chart, its Solar and Lunar Returns, and the current transits.

In addition to the above twelve principles, Morin left us thirty-one aphorisms for judging revolutions. These are summarized in the next chapter. Though it can be slow going, it is worth the effort to study Morin's method in detail. The authoritative source for Morin's ideas about revolutions is James Holden's translation of *Book 23* of *Astrologia Gallica*.

NOTES

1. Thomas Callanan, "The Astrology of Jean Baptise Morin" at http://www.skyscript.co.uk/morin.html.
2. For an excellent summary of Morin's approach to judging Solar and Lunar Returns, see James Holden's translation Chapter 18 of *Book 23* at http://www.forumonastrology.com/book23resume.html.
3. Morin used a rule derived from Ptolemy that any planet or point within 5 degrees of a house cusp is strongly conjunct that cusp and acts as if it belongs in that house, even if technically it resides in the preceding house.
4. Makransky, 'Primary Directions', *NCGR Journal*, Winter 1988-89, p. 132.
5. Morin, *Book 22*, Holden translation, AFA, 1994, pp. 203-206.
6. Morin, *Book 23*, Holden translation, AFA, 2003, p.112.
7. Morin, *Book 22*, Holden translation, AFA, 1994, p.164.
8. Morin, *Book 23*, ibid, p.139.
9. Instead of dividing the *sidereal* month into 27 equal segments (mansions), it is also possible to measure the exact span of time elapsed from a Lunar Return to the next in the tropical zodiac and divide that time period into 27 equal segments. The results will produce progressed lunar return angles that are slightly different from the method described in this chapter.
10. Morin, *Book 22*, Holden translation, AFA, 1994, p.164.
11. Morin, *Book 23*, ibid, p.139.
12. Robert Corre's website is www.forumonastrology.com.

10

Morin's Thirty-One Aphorisms for Judging Revolutions

In Morin's view predictions are always rooted in the birth chart. The return chart is merely a key that unlocks the natal potentials through its similarity to the birth chart. To forecast when a particular birth potential will manifest, Morin advised astrologers first to consider the directions of the natal chart, then its solar and lunar revolutions and their directions, and finally the current transits. He also looked at the effect of eclipses and the contacts between return charts and important fixed stars.

Morin identified several universal laws that apply to the judgment of nativities and revolutions. His thirty-one aphorisms for judging returns are reviewed below so that the reader can glimpse into the mind of this astrological genius. Having tried to read Morin in the original Latin as well as in Spanish and English translation and having translated Morin's *Book 18* of *Astrologia Gallica* into English, I can attest to the density and pithiness of his writing. For that reason I have summarized Morin's aphorisms in modern English, and I must take responsibility should there be any misunderstanding in my rendering of Morin's ideas. James Holden's authoritative English translation of Morin's writings offers a detailed and literal account of these principles.[1]

The Author's 2005 Solar Return

The reader may find it helpful to check Morin's guidelines against a case example. I have provided my own Solar Return for 2005 (Figure 1), which covers the period when much of the first draft of this book was being researched and written. The writing began under the influence of my 2004 Solar Return (not shown) whose Ascendant in the first degree of Capricorn fell in my natal 3rd house of communications in trine to both natal and annual Mercury, the ruler of my natal 9th of publishing. At the same time my natal Ascendant occupied the 2004 annual 9th house of publishing with annual Jupiter conjunct the annual 9th cusp.

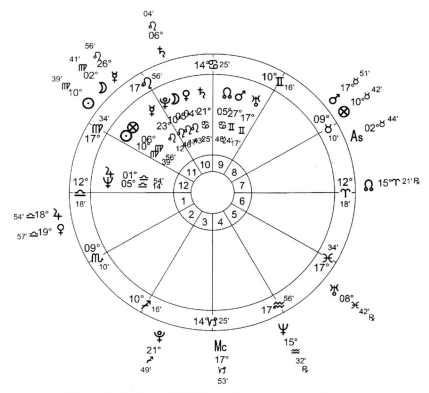

Figure 1: Author's 2005 Solar Return on Natal Chart

The bulk of the work on the initial draft of this book was done from early 2005 through the end of 2006. The primary directions active during that period are telling. The planet Jupiter – a general signifcator of publishing – rules my natal 3rd house of writing. By primary direction (Placidus system, one year per degree) Jupiter perfected a sextile to its natal position in October of 2005. Pluto, a general signifier of in-depth research, perfected a sextile by primary direction to natal Mercury (ruler of my 9th of publishing) in April of 2006. Finally, Saturn (ruler of my 10th house of professional undertakings) perfected a primary directed trine to my natal 3rd house ruler Jupiter in September of 2006. Here is the list of primary directions generated by *Solar Fire*:

DYNAMIC REPORT

Anthony Louis - Natal Chart
Sep 3 1945, 9:05:36 am, EWT +4:00
Waterbury CT, 41°N33'35", 073°W03'35"
Geocentric Tropical Zodiac
Placidus Houses, Mean Node

Primary Directions (rate of one year per degree of RA on MC) for 2005-2006:

Mon (8)Tri Asc (12)	(X)	Pm-Na	Jan 5 2005	120°00'	12°Li18'
Ura (7)Tri PF (11)	(X)	Pm-Na	Feb 27 2005	161°31'	06°Vi56'
Ura (7)Sqr Mon (10)	(X)	Pm-Na	Mar 3 2005	161°32'	05°Le17'
Nep (10)Sxt Nep (12)	(X)	Pm-Na	Mar 17 2005	069°40'	05°Li14'
Jup (10)Sxt Jup (12)	(X)	Pm-Na	Oct 30 2005	073°39'	01°Li54'
Ura (7)Sqr Ven (10)	(X)	Pm-Na	Dec 8 2005	162°09'	04°Le43'
Plu (9)Sxt Mer (11)	(X)	Pm-Na	Apr 6 2006	115°00'	23°Le12'
Sat (8)Tri Jup (12)	(X)	Pm-Na	Sep 6 2006	133°39'	01°Li54'

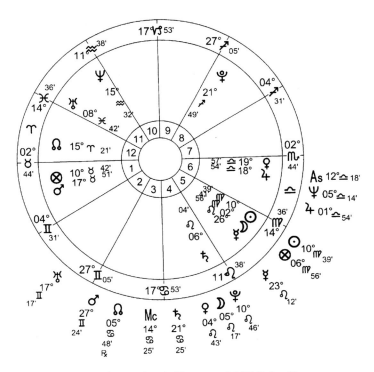

Figure 2: Author's Natal Chart on 2005 Solar Return

The 2004 Solar Return and the primary directions of 2005-2006 had set the stage for writing. Would the 2005 Solar Return also support such an undertaking? The annual 2005 Ascendant falls in Taurus (see Figure 2). The annual Ascendant-ruler Venus conjoins annual Jupiter, and this conjunction lies in the natal 1ˢᵗ house, suggesting personal initiative directed into writing. Mars moves from the 9ᵗʰ house of publishing of the birth chart to the 1ˢᵗ house of the Solar Return, again suggesting much energy expended on writing and publishing matters. Natal Mars almost exactly conjoins the 3ʳᵈ house cusp of the 2005 return chart. Annual Mars occupies the natal 8ᵗʰ house of death, suggesting research into matters of death and dying. The Sun occupies the 2005 annual 5ᵗʰ house of creative endeavors and is about to be conjoined by the annual Moon, symbolizing a New Moon or new beginning in 5ᵗʰ house matters. With this example in mind the reader can now review Morin's advice on how to delineate a Solar Return chart.

Morin's Thirty-One Aphorisms for Judging Revolutions

1.   Nothing should be predicted on the basis of a revolution unless it is originally promised in the nativity or in the directions of the birth chart. Always consider how the planets of the revolution relate to the natal chart and how the houses of each chart determine the significations of the planets. According to Morin, the planets are determined by the houses in four ways – by their actual locations in houses, and by their dignities (domicile, exaltation, or triplicity), aspects, or antiscion in the houses. In judging revolutions, Morin especially notes the determinations of the planets by the houses they occupy or rule. These determinations allow the astrologer to identify what the planets signify in both the natal and return charts. Morin next considers whether the significations of the planets are similar, dissimilar, or contrary to one another between the two charts – the lock and key metaphor. Similarity of planetary significations activates the natal potentials related to those planets, whereas dissimilarity hinders manifestation. Contrariety of significations between the nativity and the revolution brings stress and difficulty. If the key fits the lock, you can open the door. If the key and the lock have nothing in common, you can't get in. If the key fits, but the shape of the key runs contrary to the tumblers of the lock, then turning the key causes stress and friction.

2.   Similarities between what is signified in the birth chart and in the revolution indicate which natal promises will manifest in a given year. Dissimilarities of significations between the revolution and the nativity reveal those factors in the natal chart that will remain dormant or will manifest only partially or inadequately. Lack of similarity between the revolution and the

birth chart means that the natally pre-signified matters that find no similar signification in the revolution will not happen in that year. To gain a fuller perspective it is useful to study the solar revolutions that immediately precede and follow the one under consideration.

3. The more closely the return chart resembles the natal chart with regard to the positions of the signs and planets, the more likely the natal potentials will manifest – for good or for evil – especially if a direction of the natal chart also signifies the same natal potentials during that year. Planets in the revolution act according to their natal determinations. Hence, planets that are badly disposed at birth will act badly in the revolution, and planets fortified at birth will act favorably in the revolution. Especially powerful are revolutions that have the same degree on the Ascendant as the birth chart. An individual can choose which natal potentials will manifest by traveling to a location where the revolution more or less resembles the natal chart. This aphorism appears to be the origin of the modern idea of celebrating one's astrological birthday in a more favorable location to modify the influence of the Solar Return on the year ahead.

4. If a matter is strongly signified by the birth chart or its directions, even a weak Solar Return with the same significations will bring it to pass; but a weak analogous Lunar Return will not perfect the matter. On the other hand, something only weakly signified by the birth chart or its directions can be brought to fruition by a strong solar revolution of the same signification but probably cannot be made manifest even by a strong analogous lunar revolution. If a matter is weakly signified in the birth chart and also weakly signified in the solar revolution, it is unlikely to come about. In making predictions one must combine an understanding of the celestial influences with an awareness of the individual's typical interests, dispositions, and activities. This last point is well taken because astrological symbols are multi-determined and the astrologer must come to understand how they play out specifically in an individual's chart.

5. It is stressful and possibly harmful for the native when opposite zodiacal signs rise in the natal and return charts (solar or lunar), especially when the degrees of the Ascendants are in opposition. Natal potentials, for good or evil, can only manifest when there is a similarity between the natal and return charts. Inhibition of natal potentials results from dissimilarity between the birth chart and the revolution. When the natal and return Ascendants are 180 degrees apart, all the signs in the revolution are positioned contrarily around the wheel in opposite relationship to those of the birth chart. In such a case, the signs in the revolution carry significations exactly contrary to what

they mean in the nativity – a stressful configuration. Such marked contrariety is analogous to the ill effects one sees when icy Saturn, the ruler of Aquarius, transits the opposite sign Leo, ruled by the hot Sun. It is generally unfortunate when the planets and signs of the revolution carry significations exactly opposite to those of the natal chart. If, however, a benefic – Jupiter or Venus – occupies the 1st house of the revolution and does not govern the unfortunate 8th or 12th houses (making it an accidental malefic) of either the revolution or the nativity, then the stress caused by opposing Ascendants is mitigated and some benefits can accrue regarding 7th house matters (partnerships, lawsuits, contracts). Recall that each house accidentally signifies the one opposite. When there are opposing Ascendants, the natal 7th house (marriage, open enemies) becomes the revolution's 1st house (body, life, health), and any negative potentials of the birth chart or its directions with regard to health, lawsuits, rivals and so on, are likely to manifest – especially if ill-disposed planets occupy the 1st house of the revolution. This principle of the stressful nature of signs opposing one another in the natal and return charts also applies to the meridian axis and to all the intermediate house cusps.

6.   It is generally fortunate for 1st house matters if the natal and return Ascendants are in a trine relationship, and it is generally stressful if the respective Ascendants are in square. This rule should not be applied in isolation but must always be interpreted in the context of the entire chart, which will modify the influence of the aspect between the two Ascendants.

7.   A natal planet occupying the ascending sign of the return chart, especially if that natal planet conjoins the Ascendant of the revolution, has a marked impact on 1st house matters (life, health) according to its nature, state, and determinations in both the natal and return charts. This principle also applies to the Midheaven and to the intermediate house cusps. For example, if a person has a malefic – Mars or Saturn – in the natal 8th house and if that malefic, or the ruler of the natal 8th house, occupies the ascending sign in the solar revolution, then the native will be at risk of dying during the Solar Return year, especially during a month when the Lunar Return also has the same ascending sign as the Solar Return.

8.   For a given individual each zodiacal sign carries with it the significations determined by the houses it spans in the birth chart. These natal significations must be combined with the meanings of the houses that the sign occupies in the revolution, especially if the directions of the birth chart are in agreement. Volguine make extensive use of this principle of Morin in his writing on Solar Returns. Thus, for example:

- If the natal Ascendant sign falls on the 8th or 12th houses of the return, there is risk of illness, death, imprisonment, danger to life, trouble from enemies, etc.; if on the 11th house of the return, dealings with friends; if on the 10th house of the return, undertakings, actions, dignities, and so on.

- If the natal 2nd house falls on the 7th house of the return, one can expect income or expenses deriving from contracts, lawsuits, or marriage – depending on the state of the 7th house and its ruler in both the natal and return charts.

9.   In both solar and lunar revolutions, the planets act primarily according to the nature of the house that they occupy in the revolution; but the planets can also act according to the nature of the houses that they occupy in the nativity and these meanings must be combined. A planet is more strongly determined by its presence in a house than by its rulership of a house. Morin gives the following examples:

- If Mars (action) moves from the 2nd house of the birth chart to the 5th house of the revolution, then one can expect spending (2nd house) on pleasurable activities or children (5th house).

- If Jupiter (expansion) moves from the natal 5th house to the return 2nd house, one can expect increased wealth or income deriving from children, lovers, games, or pleasurable activities.

- If the planet ruling the natal 2nd house lies in the natal 5th house but occupies the return 12th house, there is a risk of illness or imprisonment due to pleasures or to money spent on 5th house matters (pleasures, speculative risks).

10.   When judging a planet in the revolution, look first to its house position in the birth chart and then to its house position in the revolution. The return chart must always be judged against the significations of the nativity. For example, if Saturn is the killing planet in the birth chart and in the revolution Saturn falls on the natal Ascendant, there is a danger to life, regardless of which house of the revolution contains the natal Ascendant. On the other hand, the house containing the natal Ascendant can describe the type of danger. For example, if the natal Ascendant lies in the 5th house of the revolution, the danger may come from pleasures. If the natal Ascendant and Saturn occupy the 8th house of the return, there is a potential for a sudden or violent death, or a danger to life, because Saturn doubly signifies death due to its roles in both the natal and the return charts. Morin recommends reviewing

the following seven considerations regarding each planet in the Solar Return:

- The nature of the planet.

- The celestial or zodiacal state of the planet in the nativity.

- The natal determinations of the planet according to the birth house that it occupies or rules.

- The house of the natal chart that the return planet occupies (superimposing the Solar Return on the birth chart).

- The annual determinations of the planet according to the return house that it occupies and the return house that it rules.

- How the natal and return determinations of the planets can be combined, taking into account their similarities, dissimilarities, and contrarieties.

11.   In any given year a planet fulfills it natal significations in accord with the house that it occupies in the solar revolution. The effects of a planet must be judged from the celestial and terrestrial state of that planet in both the natal and return charts. The celestial state refers to a planet's position in the zodiac; the terrestrial state refers to the planet's relationship to the horizon and meridian axes and to the houses. The astrologer needs to study what changes in sign, house, rulership, and configuration the planet undergoes in moving from the natal to the return chart. For example, if a planet that occupies or rules the natal 1st house relocates to the 5th house of the revolution – especially Venus – then native will pursue pleasures; or if a planet that occupies or rules the 1st house of the nativity relocates to the return 10th house – especially Jupiter – the native will be ambitious for honors; and so on.

12.   The significations of a planet in the revolution depend on its house position in the birth chart as well as on the significations of the house it occupies in the return chart. The astrologer must also account for the significations of derived houses when considering whether the planet refers to the native per se or to some other person. According to Morin, some astrologers have incorrectly claimed that a planet moving from the natal 11th house to the annual 8th house signifies the death of a friend. This notion, says Morin, is mistaken because the 8th house refers specifically to the death of the native and not to the death of others. Hence, a natal 11th house planet occupying the annual 8th house does not signify a friend's death but rather a danger to the life of the native on account of a friend. The death of a friend can be determined from the derived 8th of the natal 11th house of friends, which is the natal 6th house. Thus when the annual chart is superimposed on

the natal chart, if an ill-disposed planet occupies the natal 11th house of friends and in the revolution falls in the natal 6th house of the death of friends, then the death of a friend may be signified.

In addition, a distinction must be made between the relocation of a planet from the natal 11th house of friends to the annual 8th house of death versus that planet migrating from the natal 8th house of death to the annual 11th house of friends. In the former case, especially if the planet signifying the friend is malefic, the natal 11th house friend goes to act in the return 8th house of the death, and the native's life is intentionally put in danger through the agency of a friend. In the latter case, the natal house of death happens to visit the return house of friends, and a friend unintentionally gets involved, for good or ill, in matters related to the native's death or danger to the native's life.

Similarly, a natal 11th house planet or ruler occupying the annual 7th house may have several significations, including:

- that a friend has intentionally become an open enemy,

- that a friend will intentionally bring or settle a lawsuit against the native,

- that a friend may marry the native, or friends may find a spouse for the native.

On the contrary, a natal 7th house planet or ruler occupying the annual 11th house may signify that a rival may become a friend, or that a friend may help settle a lawsuit, and so on. In making a judgment the astrologer must take into account the nature of the planet, and in the above examples, how that planet relates to the Ascendant of the annual and especially the natal chart.

13.   Consider whether in a revolution a planet returns to the zodiacal sign or house it occupies in the birth chart. If the planet returns only to its natal sign but not to its natal house, then its current effects will depend on its natal significations combined with those of its house position in the revolution. If a planet returns only to a similar house in the revolution but not to its natal sign, then its current effects will depend on its natal significations combined with those of the house and house-ruler in the revolution and also the house that the planet's return sign governs in the nativity. If a planet happens to return to both the same sign and the same house it occupies in the natal chart, its current influence will be quite strong, often producing effects from unexpected sources. If a planet returns neither to its natal sign nor to its natal house, one must check whether it returns to the sign or house opposite its

natal position, since opposition is very stressful, especially if the planet returns to the sign opposite its natal sign. Similarly, it is fortunate if a planet returns to trine its natal position but stressful if it returns to square its natal position. Ray Merriman offers detailed delineations of such configurations in his book on Solar Returns. If a planet returns without any aspect to its natal position, it is generally weak and less effective during the period covered by the revolution.

14.   When a planet in the revolution shares the same location as a planet in the nativity, one must combine the natal significations of the two planets with the signification of the annual house that the planet occupies. The astrologer should note which planet is stronger in that location, whether the two planets are friends or enemies either by nature or by natal determination, that is, whether the two planets are determined in similar or contrary ways in the birth chart. When a planet in the revolution forms an aspect with a planet in the natal chart, the influence of the return planet is affected by that aspect according to the type of aspect and the nature and natal determinations of the natal planet being aspected. For example, if the Ascendant-ruler of the birth chart relocates to the 12th house of the revolution and forms a square to natal Saturn, which happens to rule the natal 8th house of death, then a life-threatening illness can be expected. Similarly, if Venus moves from the natal 7th house (spouses) to the annual 5th house (children) and trines natal Jupiter, which happens to be the natal Ascendant-ruler, then in that year the native's wife may bear a child.

15.   If in the revolution a planet forms a stressful aspect (e.g., square, opposition) with a planet that it also stressfully aspected in the nativity and there is no reception between the two planets by domicile or exaltation, then bad things will happen. Reception, however, can mitigate the harm of such an aspect. If two planets form a stressful aspect in the natal chart but form a favorable aspect (e.g., sextile, trine) in the revolution, little benefit will accrue or, if there is reception, there will be only a small benefit that cannot be counted on. If two planets favorably aspect each other in the natal chart but stressfully aspect each other in the revolution but are in mutual reception, there will be benefit through contrary means; without reception, however, bad things will happen.

16.   If two natal planets are conjoined in the birth chart and again conjoin in the revolution, or are otherwise similarly configured in the two charts, their natal potentials will manifest for good or evil, as signified by their natal configurations and in accordance with the meaning of the house of the revolution that they occupy. If the two planets are configured dissimilarly in

the two charts (e.g., square in the nativity but trine in the revolution) and there is no reception by domicile or exaltation, then their favorable aspect in the revolution will not benefit the native and their stressful aspect in the revolution will cause problems. Should there be reception, however, especially mutual reception, their favorable aspect in the revolution will produce positive results and their unfavorable aspect in the revolution will produce little harm. This principle is similar to Guido Bonatti's aphorism that reception abates all malice.

17.   If a planet has the same celestial state in the revolution as it does in the birth chart, its natal potentials and significations are highly likely to manifest during the current Solar Return year. The astrologer can judge the celestial state of a planet to be fortunate according to the following considerations:

- whether the planet occupies its own domicile or exaltation,

- whether the planet forms favorable aspects with other planets, and

- whether the planet is direct, swift in motion, oriental of the Sun, occidental of the Moon, not under the sunbeams, diurnal by day above the earth, and so on.

If a planet changes from a favorable celestial state in the birth chart to an unfortunate state in the revolution, the effects of that planet will do harm. If a planet's celestial state changes only partially from the birth chart to the revolution, a judgment must be made according to whether the resulting state is predominantly fortunate or harmful.

18.   If a planet has the same significations in the nativity and the revolution and if a natal direction, or some other concordance between the charts, agrees with these significations, then the matters so signified will manifest in that Solar Return year. Without a concordant direction, however, little or nothing is likely to happen.

19.   If two planets have similar significations in the birth chart, and if in the annual chart they are conjunct or concordant in aspect or location, then the matters that they signify will come to pass during that Solar Return year.

20.   One must consider the ruler (dispositor) of any given planet in both the natal and return charts. It is more difficult to forecast accurately the annual influence of a planet that has different rulers (dispositors) in the natal and return charts because the astrologer must take into account whether the two

dispositors are harmonious or contrary with regard to their natures, aspectual connections, and determinations in the two charts.

21.   The Sun is the most important "planet" in a Solar Return and always acts according to what it signifies in the birth chart, regardless of whether there is a currently active direction of the Sun. In Morin's nativity the Sun occupies the natal 12th house, together with Jupiter, the Moon, and Saturn. As a result, Morin notes that every year, in everything he does, his actions are limited or opposed by people in power (Sun in the 12th). In a similar way the Moon is the most important "planet" in a Lunar Return. Morin notes that it is bad for the native when Saturn in a Lunar Return occupies the same or opposite sign as the Moon, especially if Saturn forms a partile (in the same zodiacal degree) conjunction or opposition with the Moon. In cases where Saturn signifies death and the Moon signifies life or illness in the lunar revolution, the native may die during such a month, especially if there is a confirmatory current natal direction. As a rule, in solar and lunar revolutions, the directions of the Sun and the Moon of the nativity are especially important and efficacious.

22.   A person who has many planets in a single house of the birth chart will experience many things related to that house throughout life. Annually that cluster of natal planets in a single house acts according to their determination in the birth chart and causes matters of the natal house to manifest. Morin notes that in his own nativity he has five planets – Venus, Sun, Jupiter, Saturn, and the Moon – clustered in the natal 12th house, and so each year he must endure and overcome matters related to the unfortunate 12th house. A corollary to this aphorism is that each year the cluster of natal planets may also highlight a particular house of the annual chart. We will see an example of this principle when we consider the solar revolution of my friend Don for the year he was battling colon cancer.

23.   This aphorism deals with the directions that are in force during a given year. Morin's language is difficult to follow but he appears to be saying that the astrologer should note which directions of the natal chart are currently active and then check how those same planets in the return chart relate to the directed natal planets, either by conjunction or aspect.

24.   Consider the ruler of the revolution, that is, the planet that is most powerful in the annual chart because of its celestial and terrestrial state. If the ruler of the year is benefic and strong in both the natal and annual charts, good fortune will manifest in matters signified by the revolution and any directions involving the ruler of the year. If the ruler of the year is malefic and

strong, bad things signified by the annual chart will come to pass. In a similar way, one can judge the ruler of the month, which is the ruler of the Lunar Return.

25.   If the ruler of the solar or lunar revolution is combust the Sun, it is unfortunate for matters that the planet signifies in either chart, and also for hidden things; the native may suffer because of people in positions of power (the Sun). According to William Lilly in *Christian Astrology*, "a Planet is said to be Combust of the Sun, when in the same Sign where the Sun is in, he is not distant from the Sun eight degrees and thirty minutes, either before or after the Sun." In horary astrology when the planet ruling the querent is combust the Sun, Lilly says that it "shows him or her in great fear, and overpowered by some great person."

26.   If the planet ruling the natal chart also rules the solar or lunar revolution, it will be very powerful – for good or evil. A similar principle applies when the ruler of the Lunar Return also rules the Solar Return.

27.   If the planet ruling the revolution conjoins or forms an aspect with a natal planet, it should be judged according to principle #14 above, but in this case the influence of the annual chart ruler will be more effective.

28.   In every revolution, pay special attention to the Ascendant-ruler, the Midheaven-ruler, and also to the Sun and the Moon. Note the nature and determinations of the planets ruling the return Ascendant and Midheaven, to which places these planets return in the natal chart, also the state of these planets in the revolution and to which planets they apply and how they are determined in the return chart.

29.   If any house is well disposed in both the natal and return charts and that house is not affected by planets with a contrary signification in the nativity, then there will be good fortune in the matters related to that house; but if the natally well disposed house is badly disposed in the revolution, especially by malefic planets that are natally determined to a contrary signification, then one can expect misfortune in the matters related to that house. If a natal house signifies misfortune and is badly disposed in the revolution, then the bad fortune will surely manifest; but if the unfortunate natal house is well disposed in the revolution, the misfortune either will not occur or else it will be diminished.

30.   Also study the solar revolutions that immediately precede and follow the current revolution. If the same matter is signified in two succeeding returns, especially if the primary directions are in agreement, then that matter is likely

to manifest. It may begin during one year and conclude in the next. Consider the example of the writing of this book, which was presented at the beginning of this chapter.

31.   Judge a solar revolution only after studying the natal chart and its directions for the year. Pay careful attention to what the Solar Return chiefly and most powerfully signifies, for those are the matters that are most likely to manifest. To this last aphorism of Morin I would add, on the basis of my own experiences, to always consider the first solar eclipse of the return year and how it relates to the annual chart.

NOTES

1.   Holden's translation of Morin's 31aphorisms and other material about Solar Returns can be found online at http://www.forumonastrology.com/book23resume.html

11

Tales of Two Musicians

Musicians John Lennon and Bob Dylan each suffered tragic events in the course of their lives. Despite the morbid nature of such happenings, they are worthy of study because they are well documented and show up prominently in the horoscopes of the individuals. In this chapter we will consider the Solar Returns for three such events: Bob Dylan's broken neck in 1966, John Lennon's mother's fatal accident in 1958, and Lennon's own tragic demise in 1980. In analyzing these charts we will make use of paran aspects, and these will be further elaborated in the next chapter.

Bob Dylan's Motorcycle Accident and Period of Seclusion

Early on the morning of July 29, 1966 Bob Dylan had a motorcycle accident near his home in Woodstock, New York. Apparently he was blinded by the sun and, unable to see where he was going, he panicked. As Dylan tells it, he then "stomped down on the brake and the rear wheel locked up on me and I went flyin'."[1] Dylan was thrown to the ground, injuring the vertebrae in his neck and suffering a concussion. Reflecting on the accident in 1984 in *Rolling Stone*, Dylan said that when he woke up he came to his senses: "I realized that I was workin' for all these leeches. And I didn't wanna do that."[2] The accident marked a turning point in his career. Dylan became quite reclusive and entered into twenty months of seclusion after the accident. He eventually re-emerged into public view with a transformed vision of his role as a performer.

Features of Dylan's natal chart (Figure 1) that show the potential for a motor vehicle accident include:

- The natal Sun at the cusp of the 6th house square natal Mars in the Whole Sign 3rd house.
- A prominent angular natal Mercury (transport) in Gemini square natal Neptune (carelessness, not seeing clearly) in the 9th, with Neptune ruling the Pisces 3rd cusp.
- A stellium of natal Saturn, the Moon, Uranus, and Jupiter – all in Taurus (the neck) – quincunx the natal Ascendant (the body). Uranus figures prominently in accidents.

•   The natal Uranus/Jupiter conjunction joined to the cusp of the 6th house, with Jupiter ruling the natal Ascendant, the 3rd house of local travel, and the unfortunate 12th house.

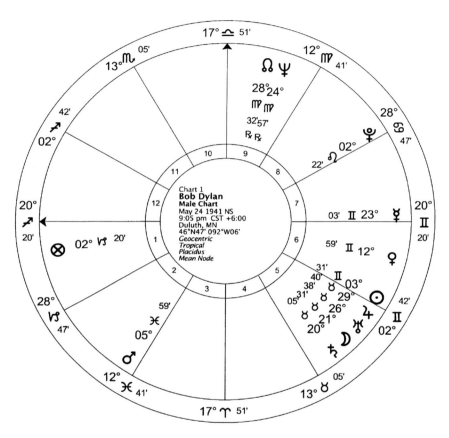

Figure 1: Bob Dylan Natal Chart

Sometimes it is difficult to determine where a celebrity spends his or her Solar Return, and by default the astrologer must use the birthplace as the location for the annual chart. Fortunately we know from press releases that Bob Dylan spent his 1966 Solar Return in France where he gave a concert at the Olympia in Paris. According to news accounts, a recording of Dylan's 25th birthday show at the Olympia was to be broadcast on French radio on May 29th but Dylan vetoed it at the last minute.[3] We will therefore cast his 1996 Solar Return for Paris, France.

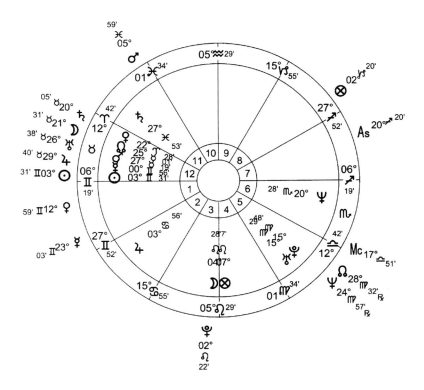

Figure 2: Dylan Natal Chart Superimposed on 1966 Solar Return

Superimposing Dylan's birth positions onto his 1966 Solar Return (Figure 2), we see a striking stellium of planets in the 12th house of bodily affliction and hospitalization. Even a novice astrologer would notice this emphasis on the 12th house, suggesting seclusion and poor health in the year ahead. Further highlighting Dylan's 12th house is the solar eclipse of May 20, 1966, just five days prior to his Solar Return and well within orb of conjoining his Solar Return Sun.[4]

The May 20th solar eclipse (at 28° Taurus 55') conjoined not only the annual Sun but also the annual Mars and Mercury in the Solar Return 12th house. In the eclipse chart Neptune almost exactly opposes Mercury, the annual Ascendant-ruler. The eclipse Neptune/Mercury opposition (not seeing clearly during travel) fell across the unfortunate 6th and 12th houses of the annual chart. In addition, the May 20th solar eclipse conjoined the natal 6th cusp and fell upon his natal Uranus/Jupiter conjunction at the end of Taurus, with Jupiter ruling his natal 1ˢᵗ (his body), 3ʳᵈ (local travel), and 12ᵗʰ (hospitalization) and with Uranus ruling his natal Placidean 2ⁿᵈ and Whole Sign 3ʳᵈ houses. Finally, this eclipse activated the conjunction of his natal Jupiter with Alcyone of the Pleiades (Weeping Sisters), a fixed star associated with accidents and sorrowful circumstances.[5]

The annual Gemini Ascendant occupies the natal 6ᵗʰ house of health concerns and closely squares natal Mars. The potential for a motor vehicle accident is shown by annual Mars (raw energy, motor vehicles) conjoining natal 5ᵗʰ house Uranus (accidents) in Taurus (the neck) in the Solar Return 12ᵗʰ house. The natal 5ᵗʰ house of pleasures (riding his motorcycle for fun) is entirely encompassed within the unfortunate Solar Return 12ᵗʰ.

The Solar Return Sun in the annual 12ᵗʰ house of confinement conjoins the annual Ascendant. An angular Sun always signifies a significant year. In Dylan's case the Sun rules his natal 8ᵗʰ house (Leo intercepted) of intensive medical therapy as well as his Solar Return 4ᵗʰ house of home and endings. Dylan's natal Sun also rules health problems and hospitalization by virtue of its conjunction with his natal 6ᵗʰ house cusp, opposite the natal 12ᵗʰ house cusp.

The Solar Return Moon, which always relates to one's health, is prominent as it conjoins natal Pluto at the annual 4ᵗʰ house cusp. The annual Moon, ruler of the annual 3ʳᵈ of local travel, and natal Pluto are both in paran-square to the Sun in the Solar Return. Paran connections between the Moon and Pluto commonly appear in Solar Returns for years when the individual requires intensive medical or surgical treatment. In general I would advise Dylan against celebrating his Solar Return in Paris because that location creates several potential paran-squares between his natal Pluto and other natal planets, including Saturn, Uranus, the Moon, Jupiter, and the Sun – and these were all activated by his 1966 Paris Solar Return. The Moon rules Dylan's natal 8ᵗʰ house of death and, with its angular emphasis in the return chart, warns of a potential near-death experience, especially with the Solar Return Moon conjunct natal Pluto, which occupies the 8ᵗʰ house in the natal chart. Natal Midheaven lies in the annual 6ᵗʰ house (health concerns), suggesting that his health may come to public attention (the Midheaven) in the year ahead.

As for timing, the accident occurred on July 29, 1966 – 65 days after the Solar Return in Paris on May 25ᵗʰ. Using the conversion table in the Appendix, we need to advance the Solar Return chart by 4 hours 35 minutes 45 seconds to get the progressed Solar Return corresponding to July 29ᵗʰ. Since the 1966 Solar Return took place at 5:12:48 AM in Paris, France, the progressed Solar Return chart should be cast for 4 hours 15 minutes 35 seconds later than 5:12:48 AM, that is, for 9:28:23 AM in Paris. The progressed Solar Return chart for July 29th (not displayed) has a Midheaven of 12° Aries 57', virtually in exact conjunction with the annual 12th house cusp, on the day of his hospitalization for a serious injury and his entry into a period of professional seclusion. In addition, Dylan's Lunar Return on July 13, 1966, in Woodstock, New York, has an Ascendant of 14° Virgo 09', closely conjunct the Uranus/Pluto conjunction of the Solar Return and opposite the natal 3rd cusp.

An alarming feature of the Solar Return chart is Emerson's Point of Death at 6° Sagittarius 02' closely opposing the Ascendant at 6° Gemini 18'. Not uncommonly such an angular Point of Death occurs in the Solar Return of the year of one's demise. Fortunately, the progressed Solar Return Moon lies at 6° Leo 59', where it conjoins the Solar Return Part of Fortune and sextiles the Solar Return Ascendant. The Moon rules local travel in the Solar Return chart and rules death in Dylan's natal chart. These fortunate lunar aspects probably had a protective influence, preventing what might have resulted in their absence.

The Fatal Accident of John's Mother, Julia Lennon

John Lennon's mother, Julia, was fatally struck by a car at 9:40 PM on July 15, 1958, when John was only 17 years old. The accident occurred near the home where John grew up with his aunt and uncle, Mimi and George Smith, at 251 Menlove Avenue in the Liverpool suburb of Woolton. Although this was an emotionally depressing time for John, the loss of his mother served to further cement Lennon's friendship with Paul McCartney, whose own mother had died of breast cancer in 1956.

There is some disagreement in the literature about Lennon's exact time of birth. Based on various reports, many astrologers use 6:30 PM BST in Liverpool. Author Ray Coleman, however, in his book *Lennon*,[6] quotes Aunt Mimi as saying, "At 6:30 [PM] on 9 October I phoned and they said Mrs. Lennon had just had a boy." Aunt Mimi's firsthand account that the baby was already born when she telephoned places Lennon's birth a few minutes before 6:30 PM – the time of the call – and accordingly I cast a chart for 6:24 PM, a few seconds before sunset, as a reasonable approximation.

The resulting 6:24 PM chart describes the native (see Figure 3). With Aries rising, he is feisty, independent, and somewhat rebellious. The stellium of planets in Taurus in the 1st house suggest vocal talent and, with Uranus among them, a bit of personal eccentricity. Saturn retrograde and rising in the 1st house lends a depressive cast to the personality. The angular Sun in Libra prominent on the Western horizon conveys showmanship and artistic sensibilities. Venus and Mercury favorably aspecting the Midheaven imply

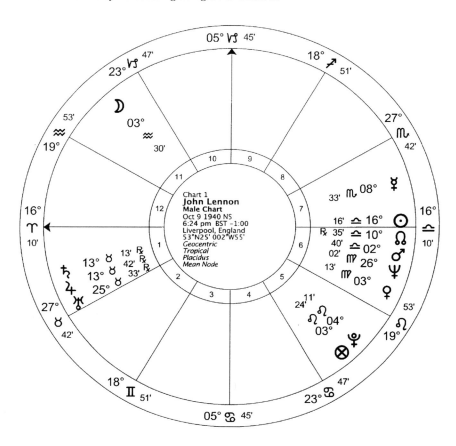

Figure 3: John Lennon Natal Chart (estimated 6:24 PM birth time)

musical and literary talent and give potential for a career in the performing arts.

If we apply the technique of secondary progressions to this 6:24 PM natal chart, we find that the secondary progressed angles (progressing the longitude of the Midheaven by the same longitude arc as the Sun) for July 15, 1958 (the date of his mother's fatal accident) are: Ascendant at 25° Taurus 26' and Midheaven at 23° Capricorn 23'. Strikingly the secondary progressed Ascendant conjoins his natal Uranus (sudden separations) and his secondary progressed Midheaven conjoins this natal 11th cusp (the formation of important professional friendships). In addition, the secondary progressed natal

Ascendant at 25° Taurus 26' conjoins the malefic fixed star Caput Algol (associated with violent death) at 25° Taurus 20'. This secondary progressed Ascendant/Algol conjunction would be exact with a birth time of 6:23:45 PM, which one could use as a possible rectified birth time. According to Robson, Caput Algol "causes misfortune, violence, decapitation, hanging, electrocution and mob violence, and gives a dogged and violent nature that causes death to the native or others."[7] The symbolism of the secondary progressions fits quite well with the loss of his mother in a fatal car accident and also the bond with Paul McCartney at this time.

Since we are looking at the topic of death in these charts, we would do well to calculate Emerson's Point of Death, which happens to fall at 16° Leo 18' in the 6:24 PM birth chart.

Let's consider Lennon's Solar Return prior to his mother's accident (see Figure 4). At first glance the Solar Return chart is not particularly striking. The annual Moon (a general signifier of mothers) in the 11th house stands out as a singleton planet in the southeastern segment of the annual chart. Morin would note that the natal 11th house of friends is the derived 8th of death of the 4th house parent. Both the natal and the annual charts have an 11th house Moon, which in the birth chart actually rules the 4th house parent. There are several potential paran configurations between the annual Moon and the other annual planets. At moonrise, a few hours before the exact time of the Solar Return, the annual Moon was in paran-opposition to annual Mars, Mercury, the Sun, Jupiter, Pluto, and Neptune across the horizon. A few hours after the time of the Solar Return, the Moon occupied the Midheaven in paran-square to annual Uranus and Pluto, which were rising, and in paran-opposition to annual Neptune at the IC. These potential parans placed Lennon's annual Moon (ruling his natal 4th house parent) under tremendous astrological pressure during his 1957-1958 Solar Return year.

Solar Return Neptune (ruler of Pisces, which is intercepted in his natal 12th house) closely conjoins the Solar Return 6th house cusp, so we might expect health problems or a period of grief since Neptune rules the natal 12th house and opposes the annual 12th cusp of sorrow. When we compare the 1957 Solar Return with the natal chart, we find that Emerson's natal Death Point at 16° Leo 18' conjoins the annual 4th house cusp, symbolizing the mother. Furthermore, Emerson's 1957 Solar Return Death Point at 16° Aries 04' closely conjoins the natal Ascendant and opposes the natal Sun. The prominence of the annual and natal Death Points in the superimposed charts indicate that 1957-1958 is a Solar Return year when an important death might affect the native.

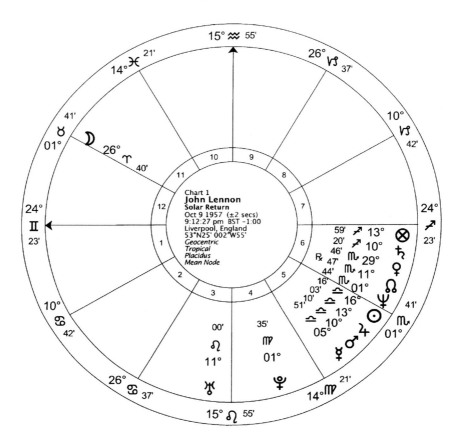

Figure 4: John Lennon 1957 Solar Return for Mother's Death

John Lennon's Death

On December 8, 1980 at 10:50 PM, Mark David Chapman shot John Lennon outside the Dakota apartment complex in Manhattan. Lennon died a short time later at about 11:30 PM. The superimposition of the 1980 Solar Return (for Manhattan) onto his natal chart gives many hints of danger (see Figure 5). Perhaps most prominent is the Solar Return conjunction of annual Mars with Uranus (sudden violence) straddling the natal 8th house cusp, with annual Mars (the ruler of his birth Ascendant) in almost exact conjunction with the natal 8th cusp (the death of the native).

The 1980 Solar Return Midheaven closely conjoins the natal IC suggesting that his public image will be linked with significant endings. The

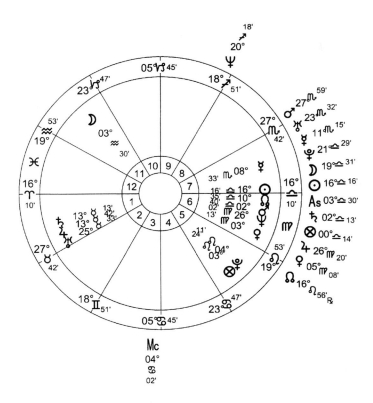

Figure 5: John Lennon 1980 Solar Return on Natal Chart

Solar Return Midheaven on the natal 4th house cusp of final endings also squares natal Mars, the natal ruler of the 8th house of death. Recall that both Volguine and Morin observed that an activated IC was common in the year of the native's passing. Furthermore, annual Saturn (ruler of the natal 12th) conjoins the Solar Return Ascendant, and both conjoin natal Mars (ruler of the natal Ascendant and the natal 8th) in the unfortunate 6th house. On the day of the shooting (December 8, 1980) the secondary progressed Moon of the Solar Return exactly conjoined annual Pluto, modern ruler of Lennon's natal 8th house. The Moon rules Lennon's natal 4th house of endings.

The daily progressed Lunar Return also points to 8th house issues (see Figure 6). John Lennon's Lunar Return prior to the assault occurred on November 13, 1980, at 10:38:10 PM EST in Manhattan. The shooting occurred at 10:50 PM EST on December 8, 1980 – 25 days and 20 minutes after the

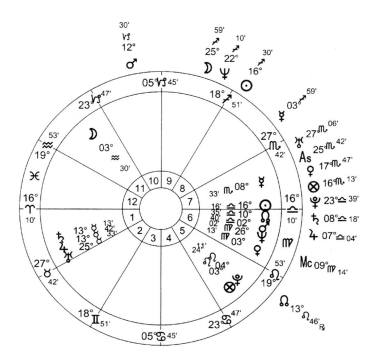

Figure 6: John Lennon Daily Progressed Lunar Return on Natal Chart

Lunar Return, that is, during the 25th "lunar day" (mansion) of his sidereal month. From the table in Chapter 9, we see that to progress the Lunar Return we must add 24 days, 6 hours, 51 minutes, 43 seconds to its "birthtime" (November 13, 10:38:10 PM EST) of the Lunar Return, which means we must cast the progressed daily Lunar Return for December 8, 1980 at 5:29:53 AM EST in New York City.

The Ascendant of the daily progressed Lunar Return for the day of the murder lies at 25° Scorpio 42' almost exactly opposite natal Uranus at 25° Taurus 33', and it traverses about 4 degrees over the next 24 hours. During the day of December 8th the Ascendant progresses to conjoin transiting Uranus at 27° Scorpio 06', the natal 8th house cusp at 27° Scorpio 42', and annual Mars at 27° Scorpio 59'. Thus, an unexpected event (Uranus) involving Mars and the 8th house is about to unfold. As the Ascendant progresses during the day, it triggers into action whatever it encounters on its 4-degree path. The next day – December 9, 1980 – the daily progressed lunar return Ascendant advances to 29° Scorpio 53' to start the 26th "lunar day" or mansion of Lennon's sidereal month.

NOTES

1. Bob Dylan gives details of the accident in an interview quoted at http://doctormooney.blogspot.com/2007/09/bob-dylan-crackers-complete-basement.html

2. Dylan is quoted at http://www.punkhart.com/dylan/reviews/self_portrait.html

3. See http://bobdylan.com/etc/wilentz.html and http://www.bjorner.com/1966%20Skeleteon%20Keys.PDF

4. Although my usual practice is to consider the first solar eclipse to occur *after* the Solar Return, this eclipse is just a few days before the Solar Return and conjoins the annual Sun, so its effects will certainly be felt by the native during this Solar Return year.

5. At http://www.moonvalleyastrologer.com/special_points.htm, Celeste Teal notes that Alcyone is associated with accidents to the face and with "tragedies ranging from blindness to disgrace and ruin or even violent death". She also discusses the astrological significance of the fixed stars in ther book *Predicting Events with Astrology*, Llewellyn, 1999.

6. Ray Coleman, *Lennon*, McGraw-Hill, 1985.

7. See Vivian E. Robson, *The Fixed Stars and Constellations in Astrology*, 1923, pp. 181-184.

12

Some Influential Modern Writers

Two of the most influential books about *tropical* Solar Returns in English during the latter part of the 20th century were *Planets in Solar Returns* by Mary Shea and *The New Solar Return Book of Predictions* by Raymond A. Merriman. In addition, the 1979 book *Interpreting Solar Returns* by James A. Eshelman has become a classic text about Solar Returns in the *sidereal* zodiac. This chapter will review key contributions of these modern authors, and the reader would do well to study each of these approaches in depth. Also worthy of note are Marc Penfield's *Solar Returns in Your Face,* which we discussed in an earlier chapter, and Celeste Teal's *Predicting Events with Astrology*[1] in which she discusses the revolutions not only of the Sun and the Moon but also of each of the planets.

Mary Fortier Shea

Mary Shea delineates return charts primarily from the point of view of a counseling astrologer. She believes that the Solar Return chart is "more closely related to psychological influences and patterns of growth than it is to the events which allow these influences to manifest themselves."[2] Unlike Volguine and Morin, Shea believes that the Solar Return chart can be read by itself without reference to the birth chart, especially as regards its psychological implications for the year ahead. Like Merriman, she considers the influence of the Solar Return to begin three months before the actual date of the return and in some cases to continue its influence for three months beyond the next return. Also like Merriman, she uses the tropical zodiac and does not adjust for precession. When superimposing the natal and annual charts, Shea puts the natal placements around the outside of the Solar Return chart. As for where to cast the annual chart, Shea offers three options:

- The birth location
- The current residence
- The current location if you are away from home

She points out that using the natal location is essentially a type of progression, using the formula that one day after birth equals one day of life. Such progressed charts for the birth location are always meaningful and can be read in addition to reading the Solar Returns cast for the residence or the actual location at the time of the return. According to Shea, the annual chart for your current residence reflects the internal shifts you have made as your life has progressed. Shea also believes that casting the Solar Return for your actual location at the time of the Sun's return is "the most accurate because it most closely reflects your present state of mind and any free-willed choices you have made."[3]

Like Morin who propounded the idea, and like Merriman who popularized it, Shea believes that you can travel to a new location on the day of your Solar Return to choose the annual angles and houses that will be in effect for the year ahead. In this way you can maximize favorable aspects between planets and shift difficult configurations to less problematic houses. According to Shea, you begin to feel the effect of the relocated Solar Return as soon as you begin to make travel plans for the new Solar Return location.

An important contribution of Shea is her observation of patterns that recur among subsequent Solar Returns. To quote Shea directly (with her kind permission):

"The house placement of a solar return planet is more important than the sign it is in. ... The Sun is always in the same sign and degree; that is the nature of the solar return chart. Because of the eclipse cycle, the Moon is limited to nineteen placements in the solar return chart. After nineteen years, the Moon begins to repeat itself; therefore, the lunar placements are limited and repetitive. Mercury can only be at most one sign away from the Sun, and consequently, the placement of Mercury is limited. Venus has only eight placements in the solar return. If you do eight solar returns in a row, you will have all eight of your solar return Venus placements for your lifetime. On the ninth year, the Venus placement will begin to repeat itself, usually within a degree. In fact, if you look at these placements and how they aspect your natal planets, you will discover a lot of information about your love life and why your relationships feel more comfortable some years than others.

Saturn, Uranus, Neptune, and Pluto are slow moving planets, and are usually in the same sign in everyone's solar return chart during any given year. That leaves Jupiter and Mars. Jupiter spends approximately one year in a sign and chances are you will experience a new sign every year. Reason tells us that Jupiter's sign cannot possibly be important when everybody else has it; however, experience has shown that Jupiter's sign can be important when Jupiter is in aspect to the Sun, Moon or in a major configuration such as a T-square, Grand Cross or Grand Trine. In these situations, it is worth noting Jupiter's sign. Mars, and possibly the Moon, are the only other planets that can have significance by sign.

As a general rule, concentrate your interpretation on the house placement of the planet rather than the sign."[4]

Mary Shea also points out that if you stay at the same location, the Sun follows a particular pattern of "clockwise rotation and counterclockwise slippage" from year to year in the Solar Return charts. This pattern occurs because the difference in sidereal time between consecutive tropical Solar Returns is 5 hours 48 minutes 46 seconds. Hence, the Sun appears to move three houses clockwise in each subsequent Solar Return, as does the Midheaven by about three signs less a few degrees each year corresponding to the 5 hours 48 minute 46 second increment. After spending ten years in any given mode (angular, succedent, cadent), the Sun appears to slip into the next mode. In other words, the Sun appears to move clockwise through the angular houses (1, 4, 7, 10) for ten years, then clockwise through the succedent houses (2, 6, 8, 11) for ten years, and then clockwise through the cadent houses (3, 6, 9, 12) for ten years.

Shea offers a psychological interpretation for the retrograde status of the faster moving planets. When Mercury is retrograde in a Solar Return, it is important to review and consolidate one's thinking. When annual Venus is retrograde, again the focus is inward on Venus-related qualities rather than outward on money, adornments, fashion, and other Venus-ruler matters. When annual Mars is retrograde, Shea advises learning to handle one's anger and aggression constructively in the year ahead.

As regards the timing of events from the Solar Return, she notes that such timing must be coordinated with information from other predictive techniques such as transits, progressions, and directions. Like Volguine and Merriman, Shea uses the secondary progressed (day for a year) annual Moon as a timing device by progressing the Moon at the speed it is traveling on the day of the Solar Return. She also times events by noting the passage of the transiting outer planets over the angles and house cusps of the Solar Return chart.

James A. Eshelman

Unlike Shea, Eshelman prefers the sidereal zodiac because it is does not require any adjustment for precession.[5] Eshelman also uses the Campanus house system because he believes that Campanus houses are the most appropriate for determining angularity.[6] In the tradition of Morin and Volguine, Eshelman casts the Solar Return for the exact longitude and latitude where the person is located when the Sun returns to its birth position in the sidereal zodiac.

Following the lead of Cyril Fagan,[7] Eshelman divides the sidereal chart into twelve segments labeled *foreground, middleground* and *background.*[8] Foreground planets (centered around the angular cusps) are most prominent and likely to manifest whereas background planets (centered around the cadent Campanus cusps) are the least emphasized and represent qualities that are held in abeyance. Middleground planets (centered around the succedent Campanus cusps) occupy an intermediate position in terms of their emphasis and power to manifest in the year ahead.

An important difference between the approaches of Eshelman and Volguine is the importance of cadent house cusps. Eshelman believes that in the sidereal zodiac the cadent cusps are extremely weak and that planets conjoining these "background" cadent cusps are the least likely to manifest. Volguine and Morin, on the other hand, believe that in the tropical zodiac all the house cusps are powerful points and that a planet conjunct the cusp of any house will be extremely important in the year ahead. My own experience agrees with the findings of Morin and Volguine, at least in the tropical zodiac. I do not use the sidereal zodiac; and it may be that different rules apply depending on one's choice of a zodiac.

Eshelman's stress on the importance of the angles of the Solar Return chart is common to all systems of interpretation. He recommends that astrologers pay attention to the auxiliary angles of the chart, including the East Point, West Point, Vertex, and Antivertex.[9] Planets that are conjunct or square to any of these angles in the Solar Return chart are strongly accented.

Eshelman reads the Solar Return twice, first as a stand-alone chart and then with reference to the birth chart. When he considers the Solar Return alone, he regards it as an alternate birth chart for the year and uses the same techniques one would use to analyze a natal chart. When he compares the annual chart to the natal chart, he reads the Solar Return planets as transits to the natal chart and considers primarily the hard aspects (conjunction, opposition, square, semi-square, and sesqui-square) to compare the two charts.

In addition, Eshelman pays particular attention to *parans* (short for the Greek *paranatellonata*), which occur when pairs of planets simultaneously occupy any of the angles (horizon or meridian axes) of the chart. Planets are in paran relationship when they conjoin each other on any given angle (a paran-conjunction), when they oppose each other (a paran-oposition) across the meridian or horizon axes, or when they occupy adjacent angles (a paran-square) of the chart. Paran relationships also exist when two planets have the *potential* to simultaneously conjoin the angles of a chart at the geographic latitude for which the chart is cast, that is, when at some point during the day the two planets will simultaneously conjoin the horizon and/or meridian axes. Potential paran-squares are often revealed, for example, when we superimpose the natal and return charts, or the lunar and solar return charts.

Parans are measured along the great circle known as the Prime Vertical, which is specific to the individual's geographical location on the globe. The Prime Vertical rises due east of the person's location, passes directly overhead, and sets due west of the individual's spot on earth. When measured along the prime vertical, the meridian and horizon axes form an exact 90° angle. By way of review, the Midheaven is the intersection of the Ecliptic with the upper meridian, the IC is the intersection of the Ecliptic with the lower meridian, the Ascendant is the intersection of the Ecliptic with the horizon in the east (except at extreme arctic latitudes), and the Descendant is the intersection of the Ecliptic with the horizon in the west (again with the exception of polar latitudes).

An example from Eshelman's own life illustrates some of these points. *AstroDataBank* gives his birth data as 4:10 AM CST, October 10, 1954, Rochester, Indiana, and reports that he started a computer business in 1983. In his book Eshelman tells us that 1983-1984 was an arduous period in his life. For example, when he moved from San Diego to Los Angeles to start the business, he learned that the office he had rented would not be vacated for at least another month.

If we lay his October 1982 tropical Solar Return for San Diego over his tropical natal chart (Figure 1), we see a close conjunction of his annual Ascendant with his natal Midheaven, symbolizing a new 10th house professional endeavor. Annual Neptune conjoins the natal 4th cusp, indicating confusing circumstances surrounding his base of operations. The tropical Solar Return Ascendant and annual Neptune also form a paran-opposition across the meridian axis of the natal chart. An annual Saturn/Pluto conjunction in the natal 2nd house conjoins natal Neptune and squares his natal Jupiter/Uranus conjunction in the natal 10th of carrer, suggesting financial difficulties at the start of this new venture. Annual Jupiter (ruler of his annual 10th cusp) conjoins the natal 10th ruler Mercury (which rules the annual Ascendant), indicating the opportunity to expand professionally. The annual Part of Fortune conjunct the natal Ascendant most likely exerted a protective influence over the enterprise.

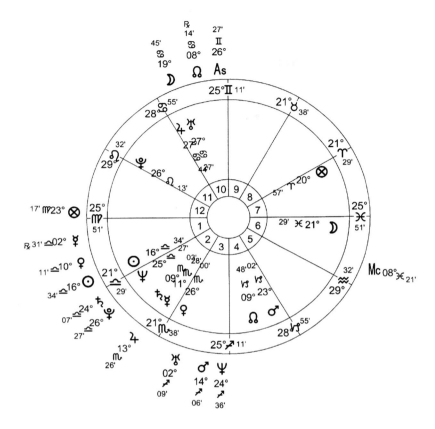

Figure 1: Eshelman 1982 Solar Return on Natal Chart

The importance of the paran-square can be seen in the Solar Return of illusionist Roy Horn, who was bitten in the neck by one of his tigers while performing on stage in Las Vegas around 8:15 PM on Friday October 3, 2003, a few hours before he celebrated his 59th Solar Return. News reports stated that emergency crews were dispatched to the Mirage Hotel and Casino at 8:21 PM and that paramedics arrived at the scene of the attack by 8:25 PM. According to *AstroDataBank*, Roy Horn was born October 3, 1944 in Nordenham, Germany, at 11:57 PM (see Figure 2). At the time of the tiger attack his 2002 Solar Return was still in effect but barely. He actually celebrated his 2003 Solar Return at 10:44:30 PM PDT on the operating table in Las Vegas. Doctors said it was a miracle that he survived.

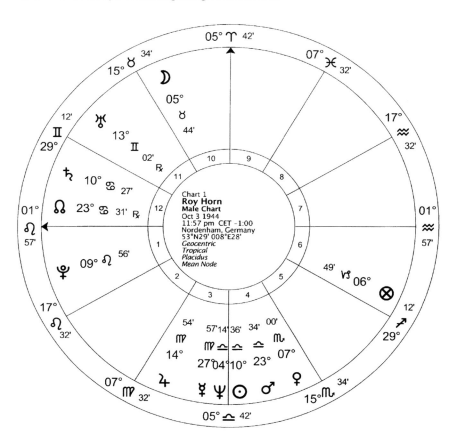

Figure 2: Roy Horn Natal Chart

Horn's 2002 Solar Return (Figure 3) has an angular Pluto conjunct the annual Midheaven and an angular Moon conjunct the annual Descendant. As measured along the Prime Vertical[10], annual Uranus conjoins the return Ascendant within 7 degrees. Thus the annual Moon forms a paran-square with annual Pluto in the 9th and a paran-opposition with annual Uranus in the 12th – a compelling paran-T-square configuration involving the annual Moon, Pluto, and Uranus falling on the horizon and meridian axes of the chart. According to Eshelman, the Solar Return Moon has potent medical implications, and the placement and aspects of the annual Moon typically manifest in terms of personal health. Eshelman was "extremely impressed by how often years of important illnesses showed afflictions to the solar Moon"[11]

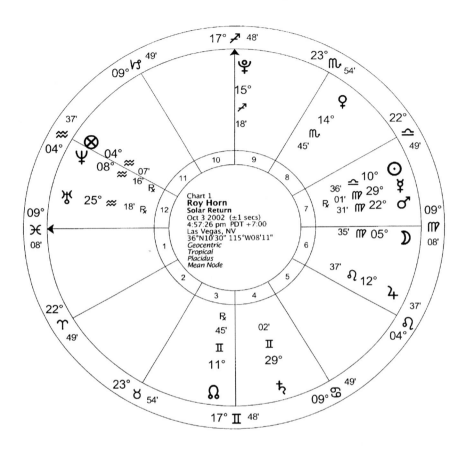

Figure 3: Roy Horn 2002 Solar Return

whereas a strong foreground Sun in the sidereal return implies a year of physical well being.

In Horn's tropical Solar Return (Figure 3) the Moon is foreground and is afflicted by an angular Pluto. Interestingly, Horn was born with natal Moon in Taurus (the neck) in the 10th square natal Pluto in Leo (the lion) in the 1st house of the physical body. The Moon rules Cancer, which is intercepted in Horn's natal 12th house of large animals and hospitalization. The paran-square of the annual Moon with annual Pluto appears to have activated the promise of the natal Moon square Pluto in his birth chart. Also noteworthy is Horn's annual Saturn, which rules the annual 11th and 12th houses, falling exactly on Horn's natal 12th house cusp. Finally, annual Jupiter and annual Neptune, the rulers of his 2002 Solar Return Pisces Ascendant, oppose each other across the unfortunate 6th and 12th houses of the annual chart, suggesting health problems in the year ahead.

While on the subject of the annual Moon, I should mention that astrologer Lynn Bell[12] has observed that the astrological sign, house, and aspects of the annual Moon in the Solar Return chart reflect the types of people who will play an important role in your life during the coming year. Ray Merriman made a similar point when he said that the annual Moon signifies "areas of life in which one may form significant relationships (intimate ones) for the year."[13] Horn's annual Moon in Virgo in the annual 6th house suggests contacts with doctors or healers. Morin regarded one's servants and "cattle" (livestock of any kind) as belonging to the 6th house and one's secret enemies and bodily afflictions as 12th house matters. With Leo (the lion) ruling Horn's annual 6th cusp, perhaps his annual Moon in the 6th, with its paran-square to annual Pluto and its quincunx to the annual 12th cusp, signifies hidden danger from his felines. The paran-square between the annual Moon and annual Pluto also suggests an intense relationship with a Pluto-ruled person such as a healer, surgeon, or someone connected with life and death issues.

Eshelman on Timing

Eshelman believes that the annual chart is operative only for 365¼ days, and whatever it promises will occur at some time during that Solar Return year.[14] Using the sidereal zodiac, he recommends four techniques to time events from the Solar Return chart:

1.   Quarterly charts cast for when the transiting Sun exactly squares or opposes the natal Sun. He finds the opposition chart to be the most significant.

2.   Lunar Return charts of the Solar Return Moon: every 27.3 days the transiting Moon returns to its position in the sidereal Solar Return. In the tradition of Morin, Eshelman compares these Lunar Returns of the annual Moon to the Solar Return chart.

3.   Eshelman finds, like most authors, that the aspects of transiting planets (representing outside influences on the individual) to Solar Return planets or angles correspond to events during the year.

4.   Progressions of the Solar Return chart.

•   Solar Quotidian Secondary Progressions: This is essentially the same as the method detailed in the Appendix to this book.
•   Progressed Sidereal Solar Return (PSSR). Cyril Fagan pioneered this method in 1956 using the sidereal zodiac.[15] Fagan noted that the earth actually rotates 366¼ days from one Solar Return to the next. Distributing this annual

difference of 30 hours 9 minutes 12.8 seconds over the year, Fagan progresses the Midheaven of the Solar Return chart by approximately 1¼ degrees per calendar day and progresses the Moon at a rate of about 1° 23' per month. Eshelman finds Fagan's method very reliable with sidereal Solar Returns.

Raymond A. Merriman

Merriman's text *The New Solar Return Book of Prediction* (1998) first appeared in print in 1977, a year after the death of Volguine in France. Merriman's interest in Solar Returns began years earlier when he was searching for astrological correlates of the time when he first met his future wife. Apparently unaware of the work of Morin and Volguine on timing events with Solar Returns, Merriman experimented with applying the formula for secondary progressions (a day equals a year of life) to his Solar Return and found that the progressed Solar Return accurately pinpointed his first encounter with his wife-to-be.

Merriman appears to have independently re-discovered and verified Volguine's system, which was not available in English when Merriman was first studying Solar Returns. In fact, in Chapter One of his book Merriman tells us that, at least in English, "very little literature is available on the subject." It speaks to the validity of Volguine's method that two astrologers, working independently fifty years apart on opposite sides of the Atlantic, and in different languages, developed almost identical systems for interpreting Solar Returns based on their empirical work with numerous charts.

Merriman starts with the premise that "in the 24-hour period following the return of the Sun to its natal placement – for any given year – lies an astrological outline of what the next year portends – just like the method used in secondary progressions."[16] Thus, the transits for the 24 hours following the Sun's return to its natal position can be projected onto the year ahead. Merriman divides the daily motion of the planets and the angles of the Solar Return by the 365 days of a year to determine the rate at which to progress them. He also uses the simplified technique of "one degree per day" to progress the Midheaven (which would move the Midheaven a total of 365 degrees rather than 360 degrees in a year) and finds that this rate of progression of the Midheaven provides hits that are accurate within three days. Like Volguine and Morin, he uses the actual location of the person at the time of the Solar Return to cast the chart. Merriman adds, "one's Solar Return is the most personally sacred of all days of the year."[17]

According to Merriman, the interpretation of any horoscope is an art, and he offers not absolute rules but rather guidelines for delineation. The astrologer must rely on her or his skill and experience to synthesize the chart into a meaningful whole. Merriman begins his interpretation of a Solar Return by noting which types of houses are emphasized according to the number of planets that they host. Like Volguine, Merriman uses Placidus Houses.

In Merriman's view a majority of planets in the initiatory angular houses (1, 4, 7, 10) suggests an important or eventful year with much activity, excitement, adventure, accomplishment, self-assertion, personal attention, and new beginnings. Many planets in the conservative succedent houses (2, 5, 8, 11) puts the focus on building, follow-through, development, responsibility, consolidation, stabilization, making permanent, the completion of projects, dealing with conditions that are hard to change, and frustration or resistance to change. The succedent houses are also closely tied to the realm of emotions since they have to do with money, love, sex, death, and friendship. Finally, when the diffusive cadent houses (3, 6, 9, 12) are highlighted, it will be a year of transition, change, fluctuation, flux, communication, new ideas, learning, adaptation, mental activity, travel, taking care of health, and preparation for something new.

Following is an outline of Merriman's guidelines for interpreting a Solar Return chart. His book, which I highly recommend, contains detailed and well researched delineations for all of the combinations mentioned.

• Judge the *overall tone of the year* by noting which types of annual houses (angular, succedent, cadent) contain the largest number of planets. Merriman superimposes the birth chart on top of the Solar Return and includes both natal and annual planets in his count. The maximum count is 20 since he includes the Sun, the Moon and the eight planets from Mercury out to Pluto. Like the other planets, the Sun is counted twice since it has both a natal and an annual position.

• Consider the *annual house position of the Sun*. Because we are dealing with a *Solar Return*, the house placement of the Sun is extremely important and identifies which area of life will "light up" in the year ahead.

• Consider all *conjunctions of annual house cusps with natal or Solar Return planets or angles*. Merriman uses an orb of 3° 45' either side of the Placidus house cusp. His delineations combine the general nature of the planet or angle with the meaning of the annual house cusp. For example, natal or Solar Return Uranus (disruption) conjunct the annual IC (home, family) could mean an unexpected separation from a family member. Unlike Morin and Volguine, Merriman does not appear to use the significations the planets deriving from their position or rulership in the birth chart.

• Also consider the *placement of natal or annual planets or angles in the Solar Return houses*. Merriman uses the same delineations as for the conjunctions with house cusps but emphasizes that the conjunctions carry more weight in interpretation than simple placement within a house.

• Consider close *aspects between natal or annual planets and the Solar Return horizon* (ASC/DSC axis), using an orb of up to 7 degrees. The horizon has to do with how we initiate activity, perceive the world, project our personalities outward, and how we cooperate or do battle with others. For example, in a year when annual Mars trines the Ascendant, you may feel highly motivated to start a new project and work hard as part of a team.

• Consider close *aspects between natal or annual planets and the Solar Return meridian* (MC/IC axis), using an orb of up to 7 degrees for major aspects (conjunction, opposition, trine, sextile, square) and 3 degrees for minor aspects (semi-square, sesqui-square, quincunx). The meridian has to do with family, home, parents, authority, career, public reputation, sense of purpose, and accomplishment. For example, in a year when the annual Sun forms a 45° semi-square with the Midheaven, your authority at work may be challenged.

• Consider the *gender of the signs containing the same natal and annual planet.* The Fire (Aries, Leo, Sagittarius) and Air (Gemini, Libra, Aquarius) signs are considered "masculine" or yang in gender. The Earth (Taurus, Virgo, Capricorn) and Water (Cancer, Scorpio, Pisces) signs are considered "feminine" or yin in gender. Merriman has found that when the same planet occupies signs of the same gender in both the natal and annual charts, "there is a sense of being compatible and in synch with the planetary principle."[18] When the same planet occupies signs of opposite gender in the natal and Solar Return charts, especially if those planets form a 45° or 90° angle, the person will feel out of synch with that planetary energy. For example, when natal and annual Mercury fall in signs of opposite gender, one may feel restless, distracted, and mentally unfocused during the year.

• Consider the aspects *between the same natal and Solar Return planet.* When the positions of the same planet in the natal and annual charts form a harmonious aspect (sextile, trine, most conjunctions), one feels in synch with that planetary energy. When the aspect is inharmonious, a sense of feeling out of synch applies. Merriman uses an orb of 9° for conjunctions, square, oppositions, and trines; 6° for the sextile, and 3° for the minor aspects.

• Consider the *aspects between the annual and natal planets contained in a Solar Return house and the planet ruling the sign on the cusp of that house.* Morin also used this technique of noting aspects between house-rulers and planets occupying their houses. Harmonious aspects between house rulers and planets in the house imply that matters related to the house will go well, whereas inharmonious aspects suggest that the affairs of that house will be associated with stress or difficulty.

•   Using the above principles, Merriman (like Morin and Shea) believes that you can travel to a new location to *choose your Solar Return*, thereby maximize its positive features, minimize the negatives, and highlight particular issues in the year ahead. For example, it may be possible to travel to a location where you alter the house emphasis (angular, succedent, cadent), where the majority of planets form harmonious aspects to the Solar Return angles, and where the annual house rulers favorably aspect the planets occupying their houses. Specifically, Merriman suggests traveling to a location where beneficial planets (Sun, Venus, Jupiter) make exact favorable aspects with the Solar Return angles and where potentially malefic planets (Mars, Saturn, Uranus, Neptune, Pluto) avoid making close hard aspects to the Solar Return horizon or meridian. Unlike Eshelman, Merriman does not consider potential paran configuration in selecting a location for the Solar Return. Identifying a favorable location may require the skills of a professional astrologer.

Regarding forecasting via the Solar Return, Merriman uses the following techniques:

•   The *progressed Solar Return Moon*. As mentioned previously, Merriman progressed the annual Moon via the method of secondary progression in which one day, or one rotation of the earth on its axis, is equivalent to one year of life. At this rate the annual Moon will progress somewhere between 12° and 15° per year, or roughly one degree per month. Merriman considers all the exact aspects that the progressed annual Moon makes with both natal and Solar Return planets and their solstice points (antiscia). Recall Morin's comment that the planets are determined by the houses in four ways – by actual location in the houses, or by dignities, aspect, or antiscion in them. Like Morin, Merriman finds antiscia (solstice points) very revealing. He allows an orb of up to six weeks before and after a progressed lunar aspect becomes exact. Merriman also feels that the Solar Return is in effect for three months before the date of the Sun's return and for three months after the next return, and he calculates his aspects accordingly.

•   Ongoing *transits of the Sun* during the year. Merriman follows the transiting Sun as it moves though the annual chart, highlighting those houses of the Solar Return chart during the year. He finds that for three days before and after the transiting Sun conjoins a Placidus house cusp of the annual chart, the matters related to that house become especially prominent. I have found that whenever the Sun or any planet, by transit or progression, enters a new zodiacal sign, the matters of the house(s) with that sign on the cusp become a focus of attention.

•   *Progress the Midheaven by about 1° per day* through the Solar Return chart. Merriman progresses the Midheaven at the same rate as the transiting

Sun, which is approximately one degree per day. He then calculates the corresponding Ascendant. Using an orb of three days before and after the exact conjunction, he finds that when the meridian or horizon axis conjoins a planet, significant events unfold that are symbolically related to the nature of the planet, the house it occupies, and the nature of the angle making the conjunction. For example, when the progressed annual Descendant conjoins natal or annual Neptune, one may be prone to deception in a relationship.

•   *Keep a diary of the day of your Solar Return.* As mentioned, Merriman considers the day of the Solar Return – one's annual astrological birthday – to be sacred. Since the theoretical basis of the method is that the astrological events of the day of the Sun's return will be projected onto the year ahead, a diary of the day should also reflect the year's feeling tone and happenings. Merriman begins his diary 6 hours before the Sun's actual return and continues for 30 hours after.

Timing with the Progressed Annual Meridian
A college student consulted me around the time of his 2005 Solar Return. According to his birth certificate he was born on October 16, 1984, at 5:44 PM EDT in Bridgeport, Connecticut. He spent his 2005 Solar Return (Figure 4) in New York City, where he had recently transferred to a new university.

Because his Solar Return has Mars, Saturn and Neptune in angular houses, we talked about how this could be a stressful year. The annual Saturn/Neptune opposition falling across the 10th and 4th houses particularly stood out. Saturn opposing Neptune can indicate a crisis of confidence, as it tends to undermine important structures that one takes for granted. The 4th and 10th houses have to do with home, family, parents, career, and public standing. We discussed the importance of good study habits so that he could succeed at his new university.

Because annual Saturn was occupying his Solar Return 4th house, we reviewed how things were going in his family. His mother had died in 2002, his father was elderly, and the student was having difficulty with one of his brothers. Noting that the meridian axis (progressing at Merriman's suggested rate of 1° per day) would cross over Saturn in 7 days and over Neptune in 11 days, I told him that family issues might come to a head seven days hence, that is, between October 23 and October 27, 2005.

On October 24, 2005, the student called to say that his father had been struck by a car around 7 or 8 AM that morning and was now being treated in the hospital. The accident occurred 7½ days after his Solar Return.

Using the Conversion Table in the Appendix, we see that we must add 29 minutes and 28 seconds to the "birth time" of the Solar Return to progress

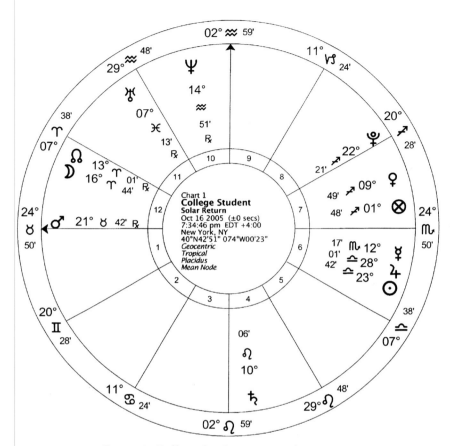

Figure 4: College Student 2005 Solar Return

it to the morning of October 24th.[19] Alternatively, we could do a secondary progressed chart at the mean quotidian rate for October 24th at 7 or 8 AM. The progressed chart (Figure 5) shows Saturn almost exactly on the IC at the time of his father's accident (it was exact at 4:30 AM). Mars in the Solar Return 12th near the annual Ascendant often signifies sorrow related to violence or excessive force. Annual Mars is quincunx the Sun, which rules the annual 4th cusp, signifying his father. Fortunately, the student's father recovered after several days in the hospital. The student called me again toward the end of the academic year and said that he indeed had had difficulty with his studies and was put on academic probation during the year (annual Neptune in the 10th opposing Saturn).

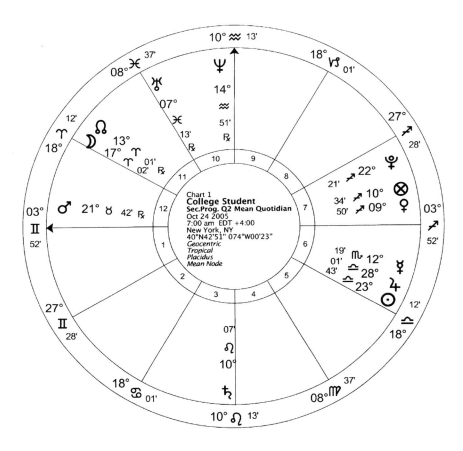

Figure 5: College Student 2005 SR progressed to the morning of
Oct 24, 2005

Weird Hector Comes to America

The following case illustrates many of the principles espoused by Merriman.
Hector, a young man from Mexico, and I became pen pals through a cultural
exchange site on the Internet. He was trying to improve his English and I
wanted to practice my Spanish. One of the first things Hector told me was
that his friends had nicknamed him "Weirdo" because of his penchant for
unpredictability, risk-taking, fast driving, sexual adventures, and pursuit of
adrenaline rushes. Explaining that I was an astrologer, I ventured a guess that
Uranus, the planet of weirdness, must be prominent in his chart.

Hector provided me with the data from his birth certificate and kindly gave permission to use it in this book. He was born on July 11, 1980 at 2:05 PM in Mexico City where he had lived all his life and was working as a taxi driver (see Figure 6). Sure enough Hector has quirky Uranus rising in Scorpio in the 1st house – a mark of independence, originality and unconventional behavior. Uranus is even more prominent because of its trine to the 9th house stellium including the Moon, Mercury, and the Sun, all in Cancer. Uranus is also square to the Lunar Nodes and sextile to Saturn.

Noticing the 9th house stellium, I asked Hector if he was fond of travel. He responded that he loved to travel and he frequently took trips within Mexico. His dream, however, was to travel to the United States and live there for an extended period so that he could perfect his English and help his family

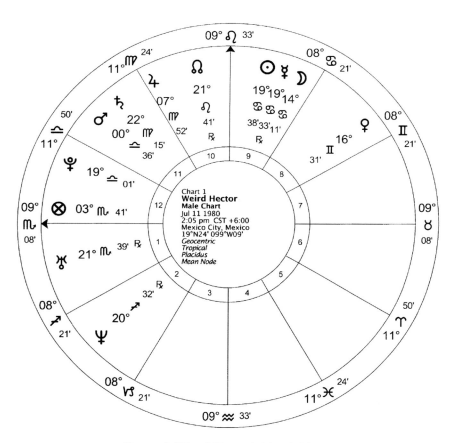

Figure 6: Weird Hector's Natal Chart

economically back home. With the Sun in family-oriented Cancer in the 9th house of long-distance travel, his dream was consistent with his natal chart. Mercury, the ruler of his 11th house of hopes and wishes, tightly conjoins his natal Cancer Sun in the 9th.

During the course of our Internet chats Hector experienced a Solar Return. In the context of our conversations, a couple of things immediately stood out in his 2005 Solar Return (Figure 7). First, the annual Ascendant lies directly on top of his natal Uranus, making 2005 the year when the natal promise of his Uranus is likely to manifest. Second, the Solar Return Sun closely conjoins the Solar Return 9th cusp of long-distance travel. Hence, 2005 would be a year characterized by unexpected events (Uranus) that foster personal independence (1st house), possibly through long-distance travel (9th house).

Around the time of his 2005 Solar Return, Hector received a call from his uncle who had moved to the United States years earlier and who now

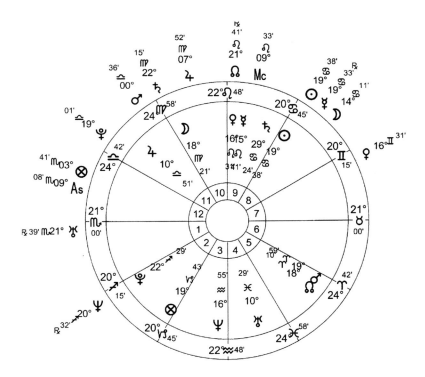

Figure 7: Hector's Natal Chart on his 2005 Solar Return

owned a successful Mexican restaurant in Texas. The uncle was inviting Hector to work in his restaurant and was offering to help him enter the United States.

Hector's dream was manifesting in true Uranian fashion. Note that natal Uranus is not only highly activated by the conjunction of the Solar Return Ascendant but also that annual Uranus occupies the 4th house (sudden changes in the home environment) of the Solar Return chart.

Mars rules the annual and natal Ascendant and 6th house of both charts. The 6th house is the derived 3rd (siblings) of the natal 4th (parents) and signifies the uncle. Annual Mars makes a trine to annual Pluto, the co-ruler of the Solar Return and natal Ascendants. Annual Mars also trines the Solar Return Midheaven (career) and receives trines from annual Mercury and annual Venus, both in the Solar Return 9th house (travel abroad), completing a grand trine in adventurous Fire signs. Annual Pluto conjoins the Solar Return 2nd house cusp, suggesting dramatic changes in how he earns his income in 2005.

Timing Hector's Arrival with the Progressed Solar Return Moon

Hector arrived in Texas on August 17, 2005 just as the progressed Solar Return Moon was perfecting a sextile to the Sun and a trine to the annual Part of Fortune. The Solar Return Moon progresses at a rate of approximately one degree per month, which equates to about one day for each 2 minutes of arc. The Moon rules both the annual and natal 9th houses and occupies the Solar Return 10th house of career. These favorable progressed lunar aspects perfected within days of Hector arriving in the USA to work at his uncle's restaurant in Texas.

In addition, two transiting non-lunar aspects perfect during the day of his Solar Return. On July 11, 2005, transiting Venus opposes his Solar Return Neptune at 10:55 PM CST, and the transiting Sun squares his annual Mars at 11:36 PM CST. Since the Solar Return occurred at 2:58 PM CST, the transiting Venus to annual Neptune opposition takes place 7 hours 57 minutes later and the transiting Sun to annual Mars square occurs 8 hours 39 minutes after the return.

Recall that Merriman equates the 24 hours following the Solar Return with the 12 months of the coming year. Approximately every 2 hours following the Solar Return corresponds to a month, every hour to about 2 weeks, and every half-hour period to about a week. Thus, 8 hours is equivalent to roughly 4 months. We can thereby estimate that the Solar Return Venus/Neptune opposition will manifest about 4 months (the equivalent of 8 hours) after the July 11th Solar Return, that is, around the second week of November of 2005. The progressed Sun to annual Mars square will manifest about 10 days later.

We should warn Hector that the period of a few weeks around mid-November of 2005 is likely to be a stressful time of this Solar Return year.

A quick and more precise method to find the above dates for when the progressed Solar Return aspects become exact is to use computer to do the secondary progressions of the Solar Return chart for the coming year. For example, in *Solar Fire* one would run a dynamic report for progressed to radix aspects of the secondary progressions to the Solar Return chart for a year beginning on the date of the Solar Return. In Hector's case that report looks like this:

DYNAMIC REPORT (Secondary Progressed to Radix):

Mon (10)	Sxt Sun(8)	(X) Sp-Re	Aug 19 2005	19°Vi38'D	9°Cn38'D
Mon (10)	Tri PF (2)	(X) Sp-Re	Aug 22 2005	19°Vi43'D	19°Cp43'D
Mon (10)	Qnx Mar (5)	(X) Sp-Re	Aug 30 2005	19°Vi58'D	19°Ar58'D
Mon (10)	Sxt Asc (1)	(X) Sp-Re	Sep 30 2005	21°Vi00'D	21°Sc00'D
Ven (9)	Opp Nep (3)	(X) Sp-Re	Nov 9 2005	16°Le55'D	16°Aq55'R
Mon (10)	Sqr Plu (2)	(X) Sp-Re	Nov 14 2005	22°Vi28'D	22°Sg28'R
Sun (8)	Sqr Mar (5)	(X) Sp-Re	Nov 20 2005	19°Cn58'D	19°Ar58'D
Mon (11)	Sxt Sat (9)	(X) Sp-Re	Jun 11 2006	29°Vi24'D	29°Cn24'D

A quick glance at the Dynamic Report shows two periods of intense activity indicated by the secondary progression of the Solar Return for the coming year. We already know that in mid-August, 2005, Hector left Mexico and traveled to Houston to work with his uncle. The span of time from November 9th to November 20th still lay in the future at the time of this writing. Unfortunately, I lost touch with Hector until June 11, 2006, when I again encountered him on the Internet. He could not recall the specifics of what happened in November of 2005, except to say that he greatly disliked the weather in Texas and left for California to find work and a better climate around that time. On June 11, 2006, Hector was again in Mexico City where he had returned to take part in his sister's wedding. The final aspect of the progressed Moon (in the annual 11th) sextile annual Saturn (in the return 9th) perfected on June 11, 2006, just one day after his sister's wedding and the very same day that he and I reconnected on the Internet. Perhaps I represent a Saturnian figure in his life.

Marie Curie and the 1911 Nobel Prize for Chemistry

Marie Curie was the first person and only woman to win two Nobel Prizes. In 1903 she and her husband Pierre Curie, together with Antoine Henri Becquerel, shared the Nobel Prize for physics for the discovery of radioactivity in 1896. While working at the Sorbonne University in Paris, Marie Curie was again awarded a Nobel Prize in 1911, this time in chemistry, for her discovery of the elements radium and polonium and her study of the nature of radium. She delivered her acceptance speech on December 11, 1911. In January 1912, just a month after accepting the Nobel Prize, she was hospitalized with depression and kidney disease. These events should be apparent in her 1911 Solar Return.

According to her birth certificate, Marie Curie was born Maria Sklodowska on November 7, 1867, at 10:36 AM GMT in Warsaw, Poland (see Figure 8). She has a stellium of planets – Sun, Saturn, Venus, Mars – in Scorpio (investigation, research) clustered near the Midheaven (career). The Sun (prominence, honors) in the 9th house (universities) conjoins the natal Midheaven. Also angular are Uranus (modern science) exactly on the horizon and Pluto (atomic power) closely conjunct the Taurus IC as well as conjunct

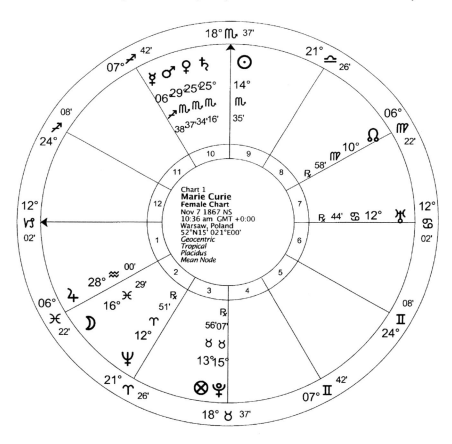

Figure 8: Marie Curie Natal Chart

the Part of Fortune. In addition, Uranus is trine her Sun/MC conjunction and Pluto lies opposite this same conjunction, indicating that these modern planets and what they signify will play a major role in her career. This is truly a remarkable chart.

Marie Curie's 1911 Solar Return (Figure 9) is equally remarkable. Annual Pluto (atomic energy, radical transformation) almost exactly conjoins the Solar Return Midheaven (public recognition). Pluto on an angle often marks a year that you will never forget, one that divides your life into before and after. The annual Moon conjunct a retrograde annual Mars puts a strain on her health and her emotional life. Annual Saturn in the Solar Return 8th house opposes her Sun, suggesting the potential for both illness and depression.

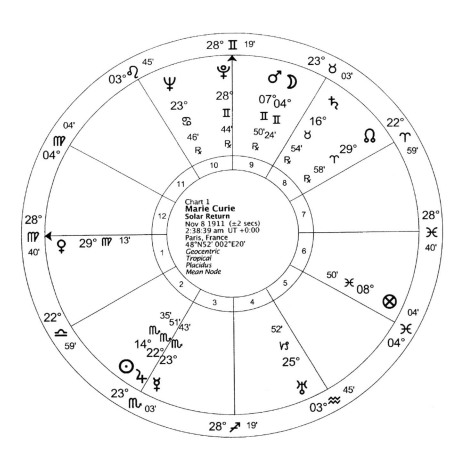

Figure 9: Marie Curie 1911 Solar Return

Annual Venus (the lesser benefic) almost exactly conjoins the Solar Return Ascendant and zodiacally squares the annual Pluto/MC conjunction. Annual Venus and annual Pluto also form an almost exact paran-square. The annual Venus/Ascendant conjunction also trines annual Uranus, so that these two outer planets – Uranus and Pluto – that were angular in her natal chart are again prominent during this Solar Return year. As the ruler of Libra, the sign associated with the kidneys, Venus on the annual Ascendant (the body, one's health) stressfully aspecting Pluto (healing) probably signifies the kidney ailment she would suffer this year.

Annual Jupiter (the greater benefic) conjoins the natal Midheaven (honors) and conjoins the natal Saturn/Venus/Mars conjunction in the 10th house (career). In addition, annual Jupiter conjoins annual Mercury (ruler of the Solar Return 10th house of honors), sextiles annual Uranus in the 4th house, and trines annual Neptune in the Solar Return 10th house. Annual Jupiter almost exactly conjunct the Solar Return 3rd cusp (communication, travel) together with annual Mercury (ruler of the Midheaven) suggests good news and favorable travel related to career.

As for timing, if we calculate the secondary progressions of this 1911 Solar Return for the year ahead, we obtain the following list in *Solar Fire*:

Marie Curie Secondary Progressions:

Mer (3)	Tri Nep (10)	(X)	Sp-Re	Nov 19 1911	23°Sc45'D	23°Cn45'R
Asc (1)	Sqr Plu (10)	(X)	Sp-Re	Dec 12 1911	28°Vi44'D	28°Ge44'R
Mon (9)	Cnj Mar (9)	(X)	Sp-Re	Jan 31 1912	07°Ge49'D	07°Ge49'R
Mon (9)	SSq Nep (10)	(X)	Sp-Re	Feb 23 1912	08°Ge45'D	23°Cn45'R
MC (10)	Sqr Asc (12)	(X)	Sp-Re	Mar 13 1912	28°Ge39'D	28°Vi39'D
MC (10)	Cnj Plu (10)	(X)	Sp-Re	Apr 9 1912	28°Ge44'D	8°Ge44'R
Ven (1)	SSq Sun (2)	(X)	Sp-Re	Apr 10 1912	29°Vi34'D	14°Sc34'D
Mon (9)	Sqq Ura (4)	(X)	Sp-Re	Apr 15 1912	10°Ge51'D	25°Cp51'D
Mon (9)	Qnx Sun (2)	(X)	Sp-Re	Jul 16 1912	14°Ge34'D	14°Sc34'D
Asc (1)	Cnj Ven (1)	(X)	Sp-Re	Jul 22 1912	29°Vi13'D	29°Vi13'D
Mon (9)	SSq Nod (8)	(X)	Sp-Re	Jul 25 1912	14°Ge57'D	29°Ar57'R

On November 19, 1911 progressed annual Mercury is trine annual Neptune. She was notified that she would be awarded the Nobel Prize around mid-October and was most likely planning her trip and writing her Nobel Prize lecture and acceptance speech at this time. On December 12 the progressed annual Ascendant squared annual Pluto at the Midheaven. She delivered her lecture and accepted her Nobel Prize the day before. Of note, the *progressed* annual Ascendant was exactly square the progressed annual Pluto on December 11, 1911, when she received the Nobel Prize.

During the first two months of 1912, the major progressed annual aspects are progressed Moon conjunct Mars on January 31 and progressed Moon semi-square Neptune on February 23, 1912. As noted by Eshelman, aspects of the annual Moon often indicate health concerns. Mars rules the return 8th house of intensive medical therapy. Neptune rules the return 6th house of illness and by ricochet, the return 12th house of depression and hospitalization.

Marc Penfield's Accident

According to *AstroDataBank*, noted astrologer Marc Penfield was born in Chicago, Illinois, at 8 PM CWT on November 8, 1942 (see Figure 10). While having his morning tea at a North Hollywood restaurant near his home on July 30, 2004, at 8:08 AM, Penfield was struck by a truck that veered out of control and smashed through the café window. He was "nearly cut in two"[20] and was fortunately rushed to the hospital where he underwent life-saving surgery, including the removal of his spleen and half of his pancreas.

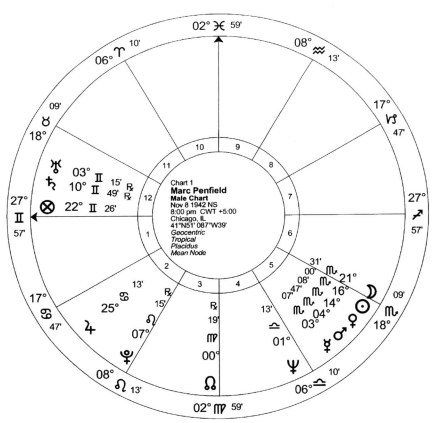

Figure 10: Marc Penfield Natal

Morin always begins by studying the birth chart. Do we see evidence of a potential life-threatening accident requiring surgery in the natal chart? The Gemini Ascendant rules the body and the Ascendant-ruler Mercury is conjunct Mars in Scorpio, which squares Pluto in Leo at the cusp of the 3rd house of traffic and transit. The stressful natal Mercury/Mars/Pluto configuration raises the possibility of a violent event involving surgery at some time in his life because natal Mars rules the natal 8th house of surgery by exaltation. Natal Neptune squares the Ascendant and gives the potential for bodily harm due to negligence. Natal Uranus conjunct Saturn in the 12th house (hospitalization) with Uranus also tightly square to the meridian suggests a propensity to accidents in a public setting. Ascendant-ruler Mercury disposes natal Saturn and Uranus in the natal 12th, and ties the natal Saturn/Uranus conjunction to the natal Mars/Pluto square.

The primary directions for the months surrounding the accident are telling. Calculated by *Solar Fire* with the Placidean method at the Naibod rate, they are all stressful:

Primary Directions

Ura (10)Qnx Mar (5) (X)	Pm-Na	May 3 2004	068°54'	04°Sc47'
Mon (4)SSq Plu (2) (X)	Pm-Na	May 17 2004	256°56'	07°Le15'
Mer (3)SSq Jup (2) (X)	Pm-Na	Jun 19 2004	273°45'	25°Cn13'
Sat (10)Qnx Ven (5) (X)	Pm-Na	Jul 16 2004	062°08'	14°Sc08'
Jup (12)Opp Mon (6) (X)	Pm-Na	Aug 2 2004	023°35'	21°Sc31'
Mon (4)SSq Ven (5) (X)	Pm-Na	Aug 11 2004	257°08'	14°Sc08'
Ura (10)Qnx Mer (5) (X)	Pm-Na	Aug 25 2004	069°09'	03°Sc07'

The quincunxes of primary directed Uranus to natal Mars and Mercury are especially prominent because they also exist in the natal chart and are triggered into action by the secondary progressed 2003 Solar Return at the mean quotidian rate on the day of the accident.

Looking at the non-precessed tropical Solar Return in effect during the year of the accident (see Figure 11, the return chart cast for North Hollywood, CA), we find Aquarius rising, making Saturn and Uranus the rulers of the 2003 annual Ascendant, so that the 2003-2004 return year is one in which the natal potential of the Saturn/Uranus conjunction can manifest. The annual Aquarius Ascendant occupies the natal 8th house of surgery. Saturn rules the 8th house of the natal chart and also the 1st (the body) and 12th houses (hospitalization) of the return chart. The planet Uranus, which occupies the 12th of the natal chart, has moved to the 1st house of the return chart.

Mercury is prominent in the Solar Return by its conjunction with the Midheaven; hence this will be a year in which the role of natal Ascendant-ruler Mercury (conjunct natal Mars and square natal Pluto) is likely to manifest.

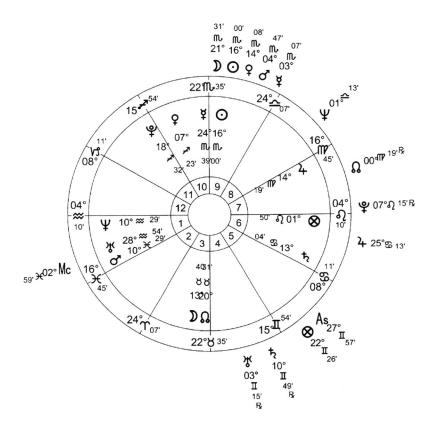

Figure 11: Penfield Natal on 2003 Solar Return

Neptune (inattention, strange circumstances) is also prominent in the Solar Return 1st house close to the annual Ascendant and square the Sun. In his natal chart Neptune squares the Ascendant, making this a year when the potential of the natal Neptune/Ascendant square is also able to manifest. Measured on the Prime Vertical, annual Neptune conjoins the return Ascendant and forms a paran-square with annual Mercury ruler of the return 8th house.

   If we superimpose Penfield's natal chart onto the non-precessed Solar Return for North Hollywood, California (Figure 11), we find annual Uranus (accidents) and annual Mars (force) conjunct the natal Midheaven in the annual 1st house. In addition, the natal Moon is aligns with the annual meridian with natal Pluto on the annual horizon, similar to the paran configuration in the Solar Return of illusionist Roy Horn the year that he was bitten by his tiger. Although natally Penfield's Moon forms a trine to Pluto along the Prime Vertical at his Chicago birthplace, when we relocate his birth chart to California, the natal Moon in the relocated chart lies on the Descendant in paran-square to natal Pluto, just inside the relocated 4th house. Because Penfield was residing in North Hollywood (where the accident took place), it is valid to use this relocated paran-square in delineating his Solar Return for the year. In fact, those who wish to elect a favorable location to spend their annual Solar Return would do well to consider which paran configurations might form at the new location in both their relocated return and relocated natal charts.

Penfield's *precessed* Solar Return for 2003 (not shown) has an 11° Sagittarius 30' Ascendant in North Hollywood, with Ascendant-ruler Jupiter in the 9th opposed by Mars in the 3rd house. Annual Pluto rises close to the Ascendant and squares Jupiter in the 9th house. Annual Saturn debilitated in Cancer tightly conjoins the precessed annual 8th house cusp, showing the potential for a life-threatening condition. Saturn in the precessed return chart rules the Aquarius 3rd cusp of local travel and also disposes annual 3rd-ruler Uranus (accidents) in the annual 3rd. Annual Mercury (the natal Ascendant-ruler) occupies the precessed return 12th house and conjoins the return 12th cusp. The precessed Solar Return Sun at 16° Scorpio 51' applies to conjoin the precessed return 12th house cusp.

A total solar eclipse occurred in the second degree of Sagittarius on November 23, 2003, just 15 days following Penfield's 2003 Solar Return. This eclipse fell in his natal 6th house of health matters where it squares the annual Ascendant-ruler Uranus in both the eclipse and return charts and also opposes his natal Uranus in the natal 12th house, suggesting a "bolt from the blue" that would have a major impact on his health. The planet Jupiter rules the Sagittarius total solar eclipse, so the role of Jupiter becomes especially important in the Solar Return where Jupiter is debilitated in Virgo, conjunct the annual 8th house cusp, and opposite annual Mars in the annual 1st house. Jupiter also carries with it a natal semi-square to Saturn, which occupies the natal 12th and rules the natal 8th house.

As for timing, we can progress the non-precessed Solar Return to July 30, 2004 – the date of the accident – an interval of 265 days after the 2003 Solar Return. Looking up the correction factor in our progression table in the Appendix[21], we find that the progressed Solar Return for the accident must be cast for 6:25:47 AM PDT on November 9, 2003 (Figure 12). Placing Penfield's natal planets around the return chart progressed to the morning of the accident is striking. The progressed annual Ascendant on the date of the accident closely conjoins natal Mars, which is part of a T-square with progressed Pluto at the

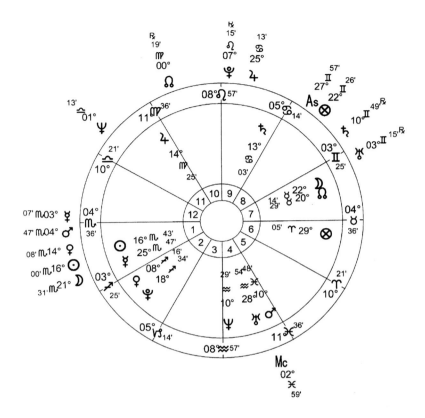

Figure 12: Penfield Natal on Solar Return Progressed to Accident

progressed annual Midheaven and with natal Neptune at the progressed annual IC. The progressed annual 8th house cusp closely conjoins natal Uranus which is quincunx natal Mars. The progressed return Ascendant-ruler Mars is almost exactly square natal Saturn in the progressed annual 8th house. Also noteworthy is the transiting Sun crossing over the positions of both natal Pluto and the progressed annual Midheaven on the day of the accident.

NOTES

1. Celeste Teal, *Predicting Events with Astrology*, Llewellyn Publications, 1999.
2. Mary Shea, *Planets in Solar Returns*, ACS Publications, 1992, p.8.
3. Mary Shea quoted at http://www.maryshea.com/sr.html. This is an excellent site for an overview of her ideas about Solar Returns.
4. Mary Shea, *Planets in Solar Returns: Yearly Cycles of Transformation and Growth* (Revised Edition), Twin Stars, Unlimited, 1998, pp. 8-9.
5. James A. Eshelman, *Interpreting Solar Returns*, ACS Publications, 1985, p.3.
6. James A. Eshelman, ibid, p.16.
7. An informative essay about Cyril Fagan by Ken Bowser can be found at http://www.radical-astrology.com/irish/fagan/bowser.html
8. James A. Eshelman, ibid, p.14.
9. The East and West points are intersections of three great circles: the Horizon, the Prime Vertical, and the Celestial Equator. The Vertex is the point in the western part of the chart where the Ecliptic crosses the Prime Vertical. The Antivertex is the point where the Ecliptic meets the Prime Vertical in the east.
10. Users of *Solar Fire Deluxe* can cast the chart along the Prime Vertical by selecting the "Harmonic Chart" option (F6) and then choosing "Z-Analogue Prime Vertical."
11. James A. Eshelman, ibid, p.65.
12. Lynn Bell, *Cycles of Light – Exploring the Mysteries of Solar Returns*, CPA Press, London, 2005.
13. Raymond A. Merriman, ibid, p.52.
14. James A. Eshelman, ibid, p.103.
15. An overview of Fagan's ideas can be found at http://www.westernsiderealastrology.com/cyrilfagan/cyrilfagan.asp
16. Raymond A. Merriman, *The New Solar Return Book of Prediction*, Seek-It Pulbications, 1998, p.15.
17. Raymond A. Merriman, ibid, p.20.
18. Raymond A. Merriman, ibid, p.82.
19. 29 min 28 seconds added to the time of the Solar Return (7:34:46 PM) gives a new time of 8:04:14 PM to cast the progressed Solar Return.
20. Marc Penfield, in a personal communication in October of 2007, discussed his birth data and the details of the accident. He told me that he now uses a rectified birth time of 8:03 PM, but I have used his birth certificate data in this text.
21. The span of 265 days after the Solar Return is equivalent to a lapse of 17 hours 21 minutes 56 seconds after the precise moment of the Solar Return (1:03:51 PM PDT). Essentially we are doing a mean quotidian secondary progression of the 2003 Solar Return chart to the date of the accident – July 30, 2004.

13

Solar Returns When the Birth Time

is Unknown

Not infrequently the astrologer must work with unknown birth times. Some individuals can offer the date but not the time of their birth. In addition, data about the founding of cities, nations, and institutions often cite only the date of inception without a specific time. If an approximate time is known, the astrologer can attempt a rectification to derive a birth chart that best fits the events that have befallen the individual or entity being studied. When the time is simply unknown, the astrologer must resort to a *symbolic* chart that captures the spirit of the date in question. A common method for constructing a symbolic chart is to cast the horoscope so that the Sun, or another symbolically significant planet, is highlighted by its exact conjunction with one of the angles, especially with the Ascendant or Midheaven.

Charts with an Unknown Birth Time

The Sun is the most important "planet" in a Solar Return. The entire field of Sun sign astrology is based on the notion that the Sun provides accurate generalizations about persons born during the Sun's transit through a particular sign of the zodiac. When the birth time is unknown, I have found that the sunrise chart for the birthday provides a convenient and often compelling Solar Return that can be interpreted by itself and by superimposing it on the natal sunrise chart to spot major themes for the year ahead. The start of a new day at sunrise is analogous to the emergence of a new individual at birth. Timing techniques are not reliable with annual charts based on the sunrise birth chart because the exact time of birth is unknown. In addition, the Part of Fortune in a sunrise chart is not meaningful because, by definition, it will have the same zodiacal longitude as the Moon.

The Sunrise Chart
We can learn a great deal about astrology by studying the charts of people and events in the news. I have randomly selected stories from the frontpage and

sports pages of the news to include in this chapter. Commonly a date and location of birth of noted individuals are available from the media, but their birth time is not mentioned. As mentioned above a helpful and often surprisingly insightful technique is a sunrise chart for the location where the person was born. The Solar Return lends itself well to the sunrise chart because it too is based on the exact location and the tremendous astrological significance of the Sun.

After experimenting with sunrise charts for many years, I have come to view them as a generic chart for anyone born on a particular day. Sunrise charts are like the alien pods in the film *Invasion of the Body Snatchers*. In the movie these alien pods take on the general features of the people they are about to absorb, but the distinguishing characteristics of the person cannot be recognized until the very moment of transfer of the personalities. The technique of sunrise charts is so useful that I find it valuable to study the sunrise chart as an adjunct to the actual chart of people with known birth times.

A Shooting in Miami

On Thursday night, July 28, 2005 in Miami, Florida, armed robbers shot Philadelphia Eagles American football defensive end Jerome McDougle. Three teenager thugs confronted the football player as he approached his parked car and proceeded to demand his watch and wallet. During the mugging the teens fired three gunshots, one of which penetrated McDougle's stomach, fortunately missing his vital organs. The athlete was airlifted to Jackson Memorial Hospital in Florida where he underwent emergency surgery.

The Natal Promise in the Sunrise Chart

Jerome McDougle, a South Florida native who had played college football at Miami, was born on December 15, 1978 in Pompano Beach, Florida, time unknown.[1] In his natal chart, set for sunrise (see Figure 1), we see an abundance of planets in Fire signs, suggesting energy, enthusiasm, and athletic ability. Natal Mars is exalted in Capricorn, giving disciplined physical energy and competitive drive – a great placement for a football defensive end. Is there any natal indication of potential violence? The natal Moon rules the sunrise chart's 8th house (surgery, death) and occupies the 7th house (open enemies), where it opposes Mars (firearms) in the 1st house (the body). The 8th ruler Moon also sesqui-squares Uranus, raising the possibility of sudden unexpected events that can cause a need for surgery or pose a risk of sudden death.

Because we do not have an accurate birth time, we cannot rely on the secondary progressed angles of the sunrise chart to reflect this violent incident. We can, however, progress the birth planets, other than the fast-moving Moon, because their positions vary only slightly during a single day. There is a suggestion of violence in a semi-square of secondary progressed Venus to natal Pluto (perfecting October 5, 2005). In the natal chart, Pluto (potential violence) occupies the 10th house, which is ruled by Venus. McDougle was shot on the eve of training camp and was unable to begin his training for the new season. This violent incident certainly did disrupt his career.

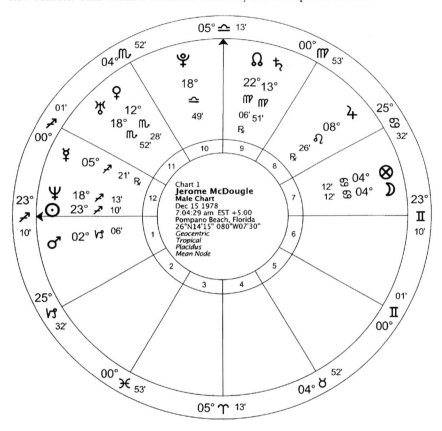

Figure 1: Jerome McDougle Sunrise Natal Chart

McDougle's Solar Return

Taurus rises in the 2005 Solar Return of the sunrise chart for his birthplace (see Figure 2). The annual Ascendant-ruler Venus occupies the 7th house of partners and open enemies. Venus, as Solar Return Ascendant-ruler, highlights the importance of the secondary progressed aspect linking Venus to Pluto in 2005. Annual Pluto is also emphasized by its conjunction to the Sun in the

Solar Return chart. The 8th house (death, surgery) of the Solar Return chart is strongly tenanted, containing the return Sun, Pluto, and Mercury. Solar Return Pluto, a natural ruler of 8th house matters, closely conjoins the natal sunrise chart Ascendant, making 2005 Plutonian year.

Annual Saturn in the annual 4th house is the most angular planet in the 2005 Solar Return. Saturn lies close to the IC and is retrograding toward an exact conjunction with that angle. An angular and prominent annual Saturn typically suggests hardship, delays, and difficulties. Return Saturn also highlights the natal sunrise 8th house because both return Saturn and the return IC closely conjoin the natal 8th house cusp. Any astrologer can plainly see a potential for surgery and a possible brush with death in this repeated 8th house symbolism.

Superimposing the natal sunrise chart on the 2005 Solar Return (Figure 2) further highlights the importance of McDougle's 8th house in 2005. His

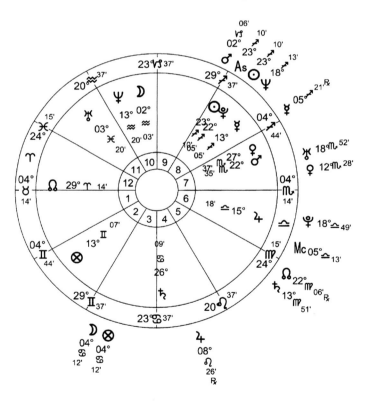

Figure 2: McDougle Natal Chart on 2005 Solar Return

natal 12th house (hospitalization, hidden enemies) falls upon the Solar Return 8th, with the natal Sun, Ascendant, Neptune, and Mercury all occupying the annual 8th (danger to one's life). The natal 8th-house ruler Moon forms a close quincunx with the annual 8th house cusp.

Big Ben's Motorcycle Accident

Now we turn to the sunrise chart of another American football player. On Monday morning, June 12, 2006, at 11:17 AM[2] Pittsburgh Steelers quarterback Ben Roethlisberger, the youngest to lead an American football team to the Super Bowl victory, injured his face and head in a motorcycle accident in downtown Pittsburgh. Foolishly he was riding without a helmet. Roethlisberger was rushed to Mercy Hospital where he underwent seven hours of surgery to repair his multiple facial fractures, broken jaw, fractured right sinus cavity, and broken nose. He also lost two teeth, chipped several others, and he suffered a 9-inch laceration to the back of his skull. Fortunately there was no serious damage to his neck, brain, or spinal cord.

Benjamin Roethlisberger, nicknamed Big Ben, was born March 2, 1982, in Findlay, Ohio (time unknown, see Figure 4). His parents had divorced when he was 2 years old, and his mother died in a car accident in 1990 when he was 8 years old. Ben's 1990 Solar Return for his birthplace has an Ascendant of 6° Aquarius 15', which almost exactly conjoins his natal sunrise chart 12th house cusp of grief and sorrow for the year of his mother's passing. His Solar Return in 1984 (the year of his parents divorce) has Uranus, the planet of divorce, almost exactly on the IC, a symbol of home and family (Figure 3).

The 2006 Solar Return (Figure 4) of Roethlisberger's sunrise chart for Pittsburgh (his residence[3]) has annual Pluto conjunct the return Ascendant, return Mars conjunct the annual Gemini (travel) 6th house cusp (health matters), return Saturn conjunct the annual 8th house cusp (surgery), and return Uranus conjunct the Sun near the 3rd house cusp (local travel).

Superimposing his 2006 Solar Return onto his natal chart (Figure 4) and vice versa (Figure 5), we see the following striking connections:

- The annual Ascendant/Pluto conjunction falls on natal Neptune in the 10th of career.
- Annual Uranus (accidents) conjoins the natal Ascendant and the natal Sun.
- The annual Midheaven conjoins natal Mars and natal Saturn in the natal 7th.
- Annual Saturn exactly conjunct the natal 6th house cusp.
- Annual Mars conjoins the natal Moon in the natal 3rd of local travel.

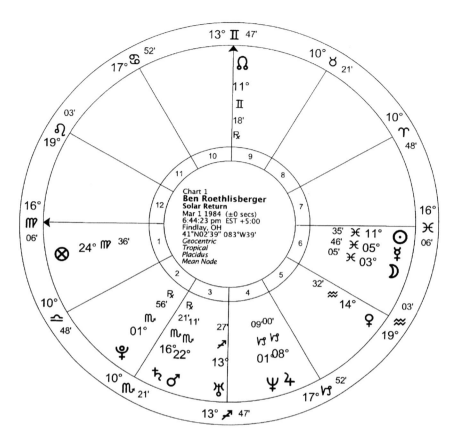

Figure 3: Roethlisberger Solar Return of his Sunrise Birth Chart for 1984, the Year of his Parents' Divorce

- The natal Moon exactly conjoins the annual 6th house cusp, where it conjoins annual Mars and opposes natal Uranus at the annual 12th house cusp.

Factors such as these suggest the risk of accidental injury (Mars opposite Uranus) involving vehicular travel (3rd house) and resulting in hospitalization (12th house). At the very moment of the accident transiting Mars at 5° Leo 21' was conjunct annual Saturn at 5° Leo 24' early in the Solar Return 8th house (surgery). Mars had moved from the cusp of the annual 6th house, where it opposed natal Uranus on the day of the Solar Return, to the conjunction of annual Saturn on the day of his injuries. This transiting Mars/annual Saturn

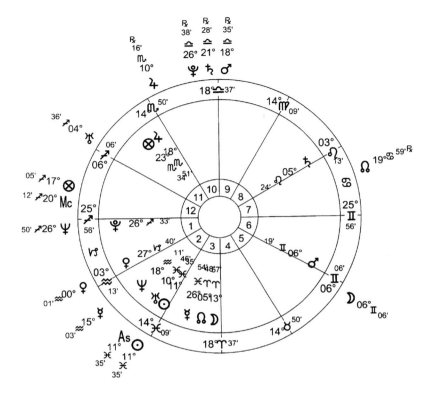

Figure 4: Roethlisberger Natal Chart on 2006 Solar Return (the year of his motorcycle accident)

conjunction in the annual 8th became exact at 1:20 PM EDT on June 12, 2006, while he was on the operating table.

On the Thursday afternoon immediately following the Monday morning accident, Roethlisberger issued the following statement to the general public. I have astrologically annotated his public apology with some key features of his 2006 Solar Return:

> "In the past few days, I have gained a new perspective on life [annual Pluto in Sagittarius conjunct Solar Return Ascendant]. By the grace of God, I am fortunate to be alive, surrounded by loved ones and lifted by the prayers and support of so many [natal Neptune conjunct Solar Return Ascendant]. I am sorry for any anxiety and concern my actions have caused others, specifically my family, the Steelers organization, my teammates and our fans [annual Moon

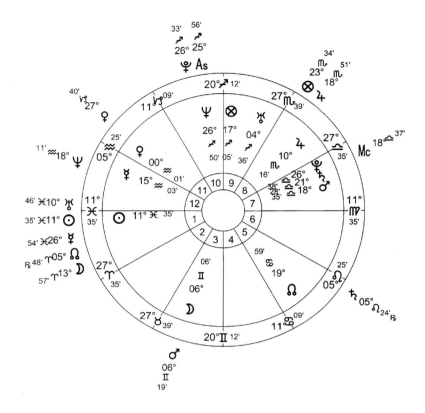

Figure 5: Roethlisberger 2006 Solar Return on Natal Chart

conjunct Solar Return IC and opposite natal Saturn; also natal Moon conjunct Solar Return 6th house cusp]. I recognize that I have a responsibility to safeguard my health in the off season so I can continue to lead our team effectively [natal Saturn conjunct Solar Return Midheaven, and natal Pluto elevated in the Solar Return 10th house near the annual Midheaven]. I never meant any harm to others nor to break any laws. I was confident in my ability to ride a motorcycle and simply believed such an accident would not happen to me [natal Mars conjunct Solar Return Midheaven, and annual Uranus conjunct Solar Return Sun]. If I ever ride again, it certainly will be with a helmet."[4]

Ben Curtis' Stunning Victory in the British Open Golf Tournament

For a change of pace let's look at a happy moment in the life of another sports champion named Ben. On Sunday July 20, 2003, golf fans were stunned when a relatively unknown 26-year-old PGA (Professional Golfers' Association) Tour rookie named Ben Curtis won the British Open Championship at the Royal St. George's Golf Club, Kent, England. Curtis was the first athlete to win a major modern professional golf competition on his first attempt. A former Kent State All-American, he was ranked a mere 396 in the Official World Golf Ranking at the time of his victory. Newspaper accounts reported his birth date as May 26, 1977 in Columbus, Ohio. At the time of the 2003 British Open tournament Curtis was living in Stow, Ohio, and working at the Mill Creek golf club in Ostrander, Ohio.

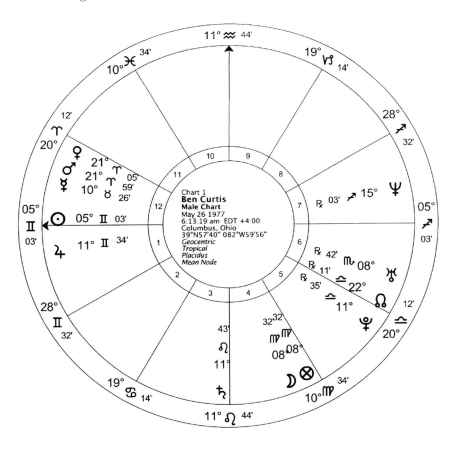

Figure 6: Ben Curtis Sunrise Natal Chart

Curtis has an interesting natal sunrise chart (Figure 6). The Sun conjoins natal Jupiter, which lies in Gemini in the 1st house, enhancing his manual dexterity. Natal Jupiter sextiles Saturn (his Midheaven ruler) on the IC and almost exactly trines Pluto in the 5th house of sports. I cast his 2003 Solar Return for Ostrander, Ohio (Figure 7), on the assumption that he spent Monday, May 26, 2003 practicing at the Mill Creek golf club, not far from his home. The annual chart is striking for the Sun (awards, honors) in the 10th conjunct the Midheaven (career) and also for Uranus (the unexpected) conjunct the Descendant (rivalries). The natal Jupiter/Pluto trine is repeated in the Solar Return. According to Morin's principle of similarity, 2003 is a year when the natal potential of that trine is likely to manifest. This Jupiter/

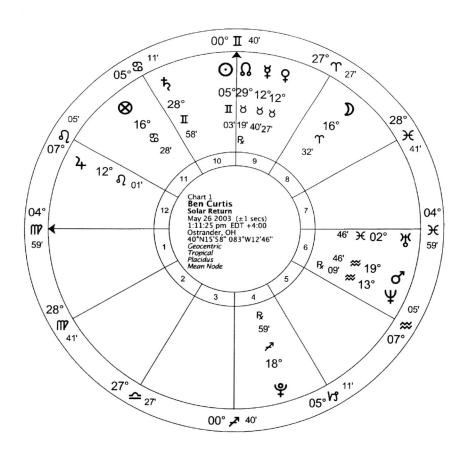

Figure 7: Ben Curtis 2003 Solar Return

Pluto trine forms a grand trine with the annual Moon, which rules the Solar Return 11th house of hopes and wishes.

If we superimpose the charts, we find that the annual Midheaven conjoins the natal Ascendant, marking an important year for his career. In addition, annual Jupiter conjoins the natal IC and natal Saturn (ruler of the natal Midheaven of career) and annual Jupiter also sextiles both natal Jupiter and natal Pluto. On the day of his victory transiting Jupiter at 21° Leo 51' exactly trined natal Mars, which is closely conjoined to Venus in his birth chart.

A Sunrise Chart for the White House

In her book on eclipses, Celeste Teal discusses her use of the chart of the White House in mundane astrology[5]. The White House has come to represent the doings of the executive branch of the United States government, especially the Chief Executive, and "is known around the world as a symbol of the power and influence of the United States."[6] Although the cornerstone for the White House was set on October 13, 1792, Teal notes that the White House was not inhabited until President John Adams and his wife Abigail moved in on Saturday November 1, 1800. Teal uses noon[7] on that date to cast the chart, but a sunrise chart is also quite informative.[8]

The 2000 Solar Return (Figure 8) for the White House sunrise chart (in effect during the terrorist attacks of September 11, 2001) has annual Uranus (unexpected events) prominent in the 10th conjunct the Midheaven and square the Sun. Annual Saturn is debilitated, being retrograde in Taurus, and conjoins the Solar Return Ascendant from the 12th house of afflictions and secret enemies – the "joy" of Saturn.[9] Annual Pluto in Sagittarius (religious fanaticism) is angular (within 7° of the Descendant) in the annual 7th of open enemies and conjoins annual Venus, ruler of the annual 12th house (Taurus intercepted in the 12th). A year when Saturn, Uranus and Pluto are all angular in the Solar Return is likely to be highly stressful. Annual Jupiter is also angular in the 1st and is debilitated being both retrograde and in detriment in Gemini. Annual Ascendant-ruler Mercury is combust the Sun in the unfortunate annual 6th house and closely squares annual Neptune (deception, secret activity) in the return 9th house of foreigners.

When we superimpose the 2000 Solar Return onto the "natal" sunrise chart of the White House (Figure 9), we again see an angular annual Uranus – this time almost exactly conjunct the natal IC. Annual Uranus in the natal 4th (foundations, buildings, real estate) squares natal Mars (ruler of the natal Ascendant) in the natal 7th of wars and open enemies. Stressful Mars/Uranus aspects can symbolize sudden conflagrations.

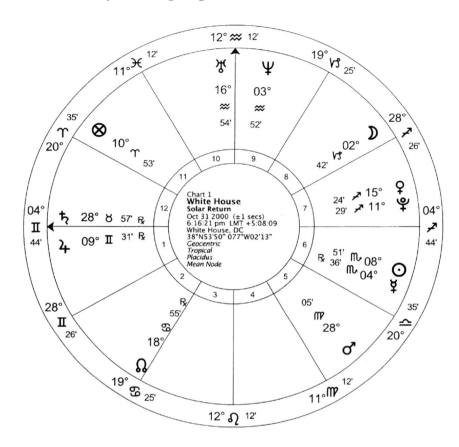

Figure 8: White House Solar Return in effect on "9-11"

The annual Ascendant conjoins the natal 8th cusp (death, destruction) in the natal 7th of war and open enemies. The annual Ascendant-ruler, Mercury, occupies the natal 12th house of conspiracies and secret enemies. Annual Mars, ruler of the natal Ascendant, conjoins natal Uranus – an explosive combination similar in meaning to the Mars/Uranus square. Annual Jupiter opposes annual Pluto (abuse of power) across the natal 2nd/8th house axis, suggesting problems with the economy as well as a destructive or life-threatening event. The first solar eclipse of the Solar Return year took place on Christmas Day of 2000 at the 5th degree of Capricorn in the annual 8th house, suggesting a national preoccupation with death and dying in 2001.[10] With hindsight we are able to see the terrorist attack of 9-11 in these astrological configurations.

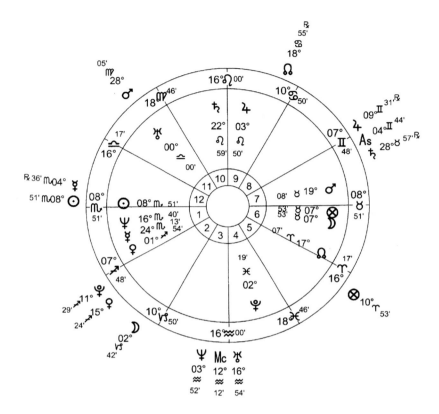

Figure 9: White House 2000 Solar Return on Natal Sunrise Chart

A Symbolic City Chart – The Disaster in New Orleans

Having looked at several sunrise charts for events with unknown birth times, let us now consider some alternative methods. On Monday August 29, 2005 hurricane Katrina hit New Orleans, leaving a wide path of destruction in its wake. The next day pair of levees broke, sending floodwaters into the streets and inundating much of the city, which had to be completely evacuated. A disaster of this magnitude should appear in the Solar Return chart.

Marc Penfield[11] speculates that New Orleans was founded on February 10, 1718. Penfield's source reported that the city was founded between February 9th and February 11th, 1718, and Penfield suggests a symbolically "rectified" chart for the founding of New Orleans at 12:13 PM on February 10th just as the Sun is crossing the Midheaven.

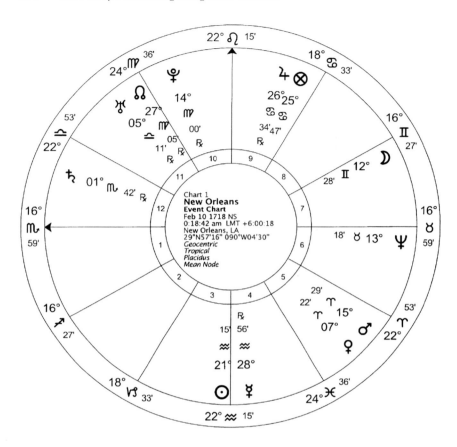

Figure 10: Symbolic Chart for Founding of New Orleans – Sun on the IC

One could also erect a symbolic chart for the foundation of the city for the time when the Sun crosses the Imum Coeli (I.C.) or cusp of the 4th house, which symbolizes foundations. It is interesting to consider the following speculative chart for the founding of New Orleans: February 10, 1718 at 0:18:42 AM LMT (see Figure 10). This chart has a prominent Neptune conjunct the Descendant and Saturn in Scorpio in the 12th house, suggesting a risk of flooding. In fact, one year after its founding, New Orleans was almost destroyed by a flood as transiting Saturn in the 12th opposed natal Neptune across the Ascendant/Descendant axis of the chart. The 1719 Solar Return for New Orleans has return Saturn at 13° Scorpio 29', almost exactly opposite natal Neptune at 13° Taurus 17'.

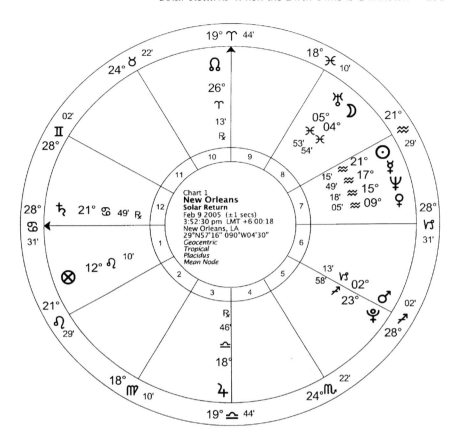

Figure 11: 2005 Solar Return for New Orleans

Looking at the Solar Return of this speculative chart for 2005 (Figure 11), we see that Cancer (a Water sign) rises and the Ascendant-ruler Moon in Pisces (a Water sign) occupies the return 8th house (death) and is about to conjoin annual Uranus (sudden unexpected events). The Sun almost exactly conjoins the Solar Return 8th house cusp. The closest aspect made by the Sun is an applying quincunx to annual Saturn in Cancer (a Water sign) in the annual 12th house of sorrow and undoing. The symbolism certainly fits the events of late August 2005 wrought by hurricane Katrina. If we look at the secondary progressions of the Solar Return chart, we find that the secondary progressed Sun formed an exact quincunx to annual Saturn on August 28, 2005 just as Katrina was about to make landfall in New Orleans.

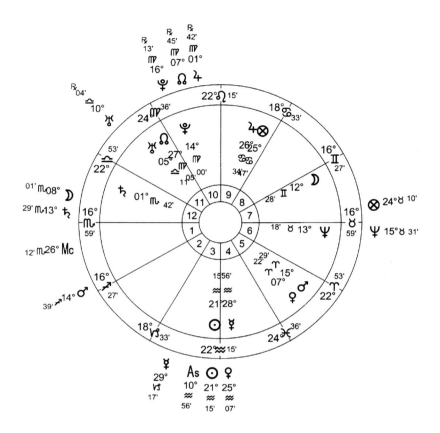

Figure 12: First Major New Orleans Flood, the 1719 Solar Return on Natal Chart

In 1719, a year after its founding, New Orleans was nearly destroyed by a flood. The colonial authorities then realized that "the city could not build enough levees to protect itself, and authorities passed a law mandating that all land owners outside the city had to build levees along their narrow, river-facing plantations."[12] Looking at the 1719 Solar Return for our speculative chart of New Orleans (Figure 12) we see that Aquarius rises, making Saturn the ruler of the return chart. Solar Return Saturn sits on the natal Ascendant and almost exactly opposes natal Neptune (sea water) from its position in the natal 12th House (sorrow).

Evangeline Adams' USA Chart and the US Entry into World War II
The gifted astrologer Evangeline Adams used a chart for the USA set for
Philadelphia on July 4, 1776 with a birth time of 3:03 AM[13] (see Figure 13).
On the basis of this speculative chart Adams was able to predict the 1942
entry of the United States into World War II as early as 1931 by noting the
ingress of Uranus into Gemini in 1942, an historical astrological marker for
the US entry into war. For years I puzzled about how Adams arrived at this
3:03 AM birth time. There is no historical evidence to support her belief that
the signers of the Declaration of Independence ratified their decision at that
early morning hour, so she must have based her chart on astrological reasoning.

My first thought was that Adams had used a symbolic method. A glance
at her USA chart reveals that the Gemini Ascendant conjoins the planet
Mars in the 1st house. Mars (assertion, independence, war) on the Ascendant
is apt because the Declaration of Independence was an act of war against

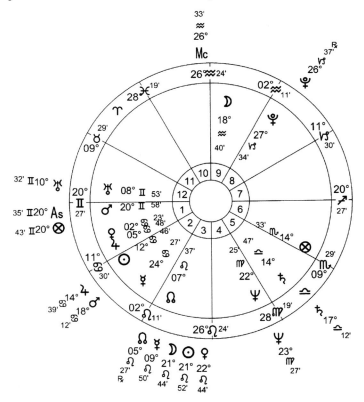

Figure 13: Adams 3:03 AM USA Chart with Aug 14 1776 Solar Eclipse
Outside

England. The planet Uranus (rebellion, freedom), also in Gemini, rose at
2:19 AM on July 4, 1776 – which may be the origin of the popular 7° Gemini
30' rising chart (around 2:13 or 2:14 AM) with Uranus conjunct the USA
Ascendant.[14] Regardless of the exact degree of Gemini on the Ascendant,
American astrologers of the 18th and early 19th century believed that the United
States was ruled by Gemini.

In Adams' 3:03 AM chart Uranus rules the Aquarius 10th house of
government and occupies the 12th house of secrecy. Again the symbolism works
because the proceedings of the Continental Congress were carried out in secret
(12th house) and were kept hidden so that the signers would not be hanged by
the British for their behind-the-scenes activities. In addition, Uranus having
just risen, with Mars rising conjunct the Ascendant, mirrors the lyrics of the
national anthem "the land of the free (Uranus) and the home of the brave
(Mars)."

It made sense that Adams was using a symbolic chart, but I could not
understand why she chose 3:03 AM instead of 3:05 AM when Mars exactly
conjoined the Ascendant. Her 3:03 AM Ascendant lies at 20° Gemini 26'
with Mars a tiny distance away at 20° Gemini 58'. Why the two-minute
difference in birth times? After experimenting with several charts I discovered
a plausible reason in the eclipses of 1776 and especially the eclipse that was
current during the summer months when the Declaration was being signed by
the delegates of the thirteen colonies.

The Declaration of Independence was primarily the work of Thomas
Jefferson with some revisions by Ben Franklin and John Adams (an ancestor
of Evangeline). At the July 2, 1776 meeting of the Continental Congress in
Philadelphia, the Lee Resolution for independence was adopted by 12 of the
13 colonies. New York did not vote at that time. Having adopted the Lee
Resolution, the Congress went on to discuss and modify Jefferson's Declaration
of Independence until July 4, 1776 when twelve of the thirteen colonies finally
ratified the document.

New York did not officially approve the actions of the Continental
Congress until July 9, 1776. Then, on July 19th the Congress ordered that the
Declaration of Independence be "fairly engrossed on parchment" and "signed
by every member of Congress." According to the records of the Continental
Congress, it was not until August 2, 1776, that "the declaration of
independence being engrossed and compared at the table was signed." In fact,
even on August 2nd not all of the 56 delegates who eventually signed the
document were present. The signing of the Declaration of Independence was
an ongoing process that continued for the remainder of the summer and into
the fall of 1776.

Realizing that the signing of the Declaration was a significant event that spanned the summer months of 1776 and that eclipses are essential tools of mundane astrology, I checked whether there was an eclipse around the official time of the signing on August 2, 1776. Sure enough on August 14, 1776, there was a partial solar eclipse whose Ascendant in Philadelphia was at 20° Gemini 35' – virtually identical to the 20° Gemini 27' Ascendant used by Evangeline Adams in her USA chart (see Figure 13). It dawned on me that Evangeline Adams must have used the Ascendant of the August 14th eclipse to construct a symbolic chart for the Declaration of Independence. In this way Adams was able to combine the planetary positions of the date that twelve of the thirteen original colonies initially ratified the Declaration of Independence (July 4th) with the Ascendant of the solar eclipse in effect during the official signing (August 2, 1776) and during the ongoing process of signing the Declaration, which continued for the remainder of the summer.

Do we see the United States entry into World War II in the 1941 Solar Return of the Adams 3:03 AM USA chart in effect during the bombing of Pearl Harbor (see Figure 14)? Aries rises in the 1941 Solar Return and the annual Ascendant-ruler Mars occupies the return 12th house of secret enemies. The natal USA Midheaven closely conjoins the annual 12th house cusp, warning of secret harmful activities that could affect the government. Natal Saturn, which rules the natal 9th of foreigners, conjoins the annual 7th cusp (wars, alliances) and also occupies the annual 7th house (open enemies). Natal Jupiter, which rules the natal 7th house of war, almost exactly opposes the Solar Return Midheaven (the government), which occupies the natal 7th house of war.

The annual Moon, which disposes the USA Sun, is afflicted in Scorpio (the sign of its fall) and occupies the Solar Return 8th house of death. This afflicted annual Moon applies to oppose the annual planets Saturn and Uranus as well as two troublesome fixed stars. Recall that Morin looked at fixed star contacts in delineating Solar Returns. In the 1941 Solar Return of the Adams 3:03 AM USA chart, annual Saturn at 24° Taurus 50' conjoins the malefic fixed star Caput Algol at 25° Taurus 20'; and annual Uranus at 28° Taurus 49' conjoins the fixed star Alcyone of the Pleiades at 29° Taurus 10'. The astrologer Alvidas wrote in 1902 that when Uranus is directed to the Pleiades, the native "will be much disturbed by his enemies."[15] Even more striking is that on December 7, 1941, during the attack on Pearl Harbor, the secondary progressed annual Moon had moved to 29° Taurus 11', exactly opposite Alcyone of the Pleiades, traditionally associated with sorrow, violent death, and losses due to fire.

Caput Algol (the head of Medusa severed by Perseus) is traditionally associated with misfortune, sudden death, violence, and beheading. Alcyone

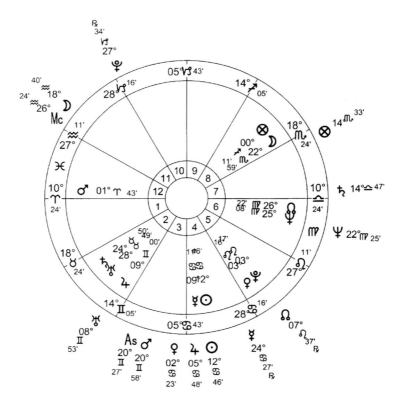

Figure 14: Adams 3:03 AM USA Chart on 1941 Solar Return

of the Pleiades, linked to bereavement, is sometimes called the star of the weeping sisters – it gives you something to cry about. Regarding these two fixed stars, Vivien Robson dramatically labeled Caput Algol "the most evil star in the heavens" and said that Alcyone, when combined with Uranus, can indicate "accidents and troubles, unexpected losses often through fire or enemies...violent death."[16] The reader may wish to review the 1997 Solar Return of Princess Diana in which both these fixed stars were also quite active in her Solar Return during the year of her death.[17]

NOTES

1. Source of birth data is ESPN: http://sports.espn.go.com/nfl/players/profile?statsId=6351.

2. The time of the accident from http://en.wikipedia.org/wiki/Ben_Roethlisberger#Motorcycle_accident: "On Monday, June 12, 2006, at 11:17a.m. EDT (UTC-4), Roethlisberger was involved in a motorcycle accident near the intersection of 10th Street and Second Avenue near downtown Pittsburgh".

3. According to http://news.steelers.com/article/83557/ (October 25, 2007), "Ben resides near Pittsburgh with his two dogs, Zeus and Hercules. His parents, Ken and Brenda Roethlisberger, continue to reside in Findlay, OH ..."

4. Roethlisberger's statement appeared in all the major news media in the United States. A copy can be found online at http://www.wpxi.com/sports/9378286/detail.html

5. Celeste Teal, *Eclipses*, Llewellyn, 2006, pp 50-51.

6. Quote from the White House Historical Association at http://www.whitehousehistory.org/04/subs/04_b_1800.html

7. Many astrologers use noon charts, especially in mundane astrology. For symbolic mid-day charts, however, I prefer a symbolic chart with the Sun exactly on the Midheaven.

8. It may be a coincidence but the sunrise chart for the White House (November 1, 1800 at 6:31:48 AM LMT Washington, DC) has the same Ascendant as Marc Penfield's Scorpio rising chart for the USA (July 4, 1776 at 2:21 PM LMT in Philadelphia). The Ascendants of these two charts are 8° Scorpio 51' and 8° Scorpio 35' respectively, a difference of a mere 16' of arc. In addition, when the Scorpio rising USA chart of 2:21 PM is progressed to April 12, 1861 (the start of the American Civil War), Mars of the Scorpio rising chart has moved to 16° Leo 06' exactly conjunct the Midheaven of the White House sunrise chart (within 06' mintues of arc). Furthermore, if we rectify the Scorpio rising chart to July 4, 1776, at 2:22:20 PM LMT (a birth time that is one minute and 20 seconds later) so that it has precisely the same Ascendant (8° Scorpio 51') as the White House chart, then Venus (7th ruler of war) of the White House chart progressed to the start of the Civil War exactly opposes the Midheaven of the Scorpio rising chart (within 02' of arc)! The 7th-ruler (war) of the USA chart opposite its Midheavean (the government) is an apt symbol for a civil war.

9. In *Christian Astrology*, William Lilly wrote of the 12th house: "Saturn doth joy in that House, For naturally Saturn is Author of mischief."

10. In the year 2000 *StarIQ.com* invited me, along with several other astrologers, to offer predictions for 2001. I used the Christmas 2000 as

the basis for my predictions (see http://www.stariq.com/Main/Articles/
P0001922.HTM). Here is a quote from what I wrote:

> "The year 2000 ends with a partial solar eclipse on
> Christmas Day. Comparing the year 2000 Christmas
> eclipse to the U.S. Gemini-rising chart, I would make the
> following predictions for 2001. The eclipse takes place in
> the U.S. natal Eighth House, suggesting that the nation's
> economy will dominate the news during the coming year.
> With the eclipse chart's Sun, Moon and Mercury all
> opposing the natal U.S. Venus and Jupiter in the Second
> House of money, we can expect a significant economic
> downturn, most likely a recession within the first six
> months of 2001. The Eighth is also the house of death.
> With the eclipse chart Midheaven for Washington D.C.
> in the Eighth House and the eclipse chart Saturn in the
> nation's Twelfth House of loss and sorrow, there is a
> likelihood of the death of an important national figure
> and a period of national mourning in 2001." At the time I
> had no idea that the national mourning would relate to
> the events of 9-11.

11.   Marc Penfield, *Horoscopes of the Western Hemisphere*, ACS Publications,
       1984, pp. 106-107.

12.   Craig E. Colten, Urban Geographer, Rebuilding New Orleans, http://
       www.lsu.edu/lsupress/Home/InTheNews/BlogArchive.htm.

13.   Evangeline Adams, *Astrology for Everyone*, copyright 1931 by Evangeline
       Adams, New York, Dodd, Mead & Co., reissued in 1960, p. xix.

14.   Another interesting symbolic Gemini rising chart puts the midpoint of
       Mars/Uranus on the Ascendant at Independence Hall in Philadelphia
       (39° N 57' 11.9", 75° W 9' 48.2"). This Mars/Uranus midpoint rising chart
       is cast for 2:41:23 AM LMT on July 4, 1776 and has an Ascendant of 14°
       Gemini 56' and a Midheaven of 21° Aquarius 49'. The charts for America's
       entrance into various wars typically have close hits (conjunction, square,
       or opposition) to the angles of this "midpoint rising" USA birth chart.

15.   Alvidas, *Science and the Key of Life*, Volume 4, Astro Publishing, 1902, p. 258.

16.   Vivian E. Robson, *The Fixed Stars and Constellations in Astrology*, 1923, pp
       181-184.

17.   An excellent online source of detailed information about fixed stars can
       be found at http://www.winshop.com.au/annew/.

14

A Cookbook of Aspects in Solar Returns

For the sake of completeness, this chapter presents some keywords for delineating astrological aspects in Solar Returns. Most important are those annual aspects that perfect within 24 hours of the moment when the Sun returns to its natal position. The first 24 hours of the Solar Return year can be projected onto the entire year, using the formula "a day for a year." The effect of annual aspects that become exact within the first 24 hours can be timed, using this formula, for a particular date during the year ahead. There are several sets of aspects to consider, including:

• Transit to transit aspects made by the transiting planets with each other within 24 hours after the moment of the Solar Return.

• The first 24-hour transits to return planets made by the transiting planets during the first 24 hours after the Solar Return to the planets and points in the Solar Return chart.

• Solar Return to natal aspects made by the annual planets to the birth chart.

• The first 24-hour transits to natal aspects made by the transiting planets during the 24 hours after the Solar Return to the planets and points in the birth chart.

• One can also consider aspects between the Solar Return and the progressions and directions of the natal chart.

In addition to looking at the Ptolemaic and minor aspects, it can be useful to consider parallels of declination and parallels of latitude, and also any conjunctions with the antiscia and contra-antiscia of the planets and points of the Solar Return and natal charts. The following list of keywords is meant to trigger your astrological imagination into producing full-blown delineations. Not every possibility can be covered in such a presentation. Remember that the planets in any chart have the following significations, all of which must be taken into account:

•   Planets have intrinsic meanings related to their essential nature. The keyword list presented here deals with this single facet of planetary signification and completely ignores the four remaining modes of signification listed below. Jean-Baptiste Morin would turn over in his grave if he knew I was presenting a list of delineations based solely on the general significations of the planets without regard to their specific determinations in the chart.

•   Planets carry the significations of the house that they occupy in the chart.

•   Planets carry the significations of any houses that they rule by domicile, exaltation, or triplicity in the chart.

•   The role of a planet also depends on the aspects that it makes with other planets and points in the chart. For example if a 1ˢᵗ house planet squares a 10ᵗʰ house planet, then any time the 1ˢᵗ house planet is triggered, it will also automatically produce a 10ᵗʰ house effect.

•   The role of a planet is determined by its antiscion and contra-antiscion contacts. For example, for a person with Libra rising, if Venus lies at 10° Aries in the 7ᵗʰ house and Saturn lies at 20° Pisces (the contrascion of 10° Aries) in the 6ᵗʰ house, then any time Venus is triggered in the 7ᵗʰ, Saturn in the 6ᵗʰ is also activated, perhaps manifesting as a period of illness or problems with pets or co-workers.

The following list of delineations of aspects is divided into "positive" and "negative" comments marked as (+) and (-) respectively. In reality this division is artificial because one man's loss is another man's gain and because both polarities of the meaning of the aspect can manifest simultaneously depending on the overall synthesis of current astrological factors. The benefic planets, Venus and Jupiter, commonly produce advantageous effects, even with hard aspects, but success may come at a price. The malefic planets, Mars and Saturn, typically cause some degree of hardship, even with harmonious aspects; there is no free lunch. Generally, however, the soft aspects produce the more beneficial responses and the hard aspects produce the more stressful ones.

If two planets stressfully aspect each another in the birth chart, even a harmonious aspect in the Solar Return will tax the native because any Solar Return aspect involving these same two planets will automatically reactivate their natal configuration. The effects of conjunctions must be judged on the basis of how the energies of the two planets combine; for example, Saturn with Venus can make you serious about having fun, as in being sure to use birth control during recreational sex.

The list on the next pages can be used when studying a chart in isolation and also when comparing superimposed charts. Bear in mind that this listing is at best partial and incomplete because it deals only with the intrinsic meanings of the planets, ignoring their other determinations by the houses, antiscia, and aspect connections in the natal and return charts. Delineations of planetary aspects will be misleading if they take into account only the general nature of the planets without considering their specifically determined roles in the natal and annual charts. Both Morin and Cardan were critical of the use of the general meanings of planets according to their essential nature or "substance." Instead Morin advocated judging the chart strictly on the basis of the planetary meanings that are specifically determined by the houses, antiscia, and aspects in the birth chart and the revolutions.

For the sake of brevity I have listed planetary pairs in the order of the first planet's distance from the Sun, and I have not distinguished which of the two planets is applying to the other. It makes a huge difference, however, whether a fast planet is applying to a slow one, or vice versa. The reader is referred to Rob Hand's excellent book *Planets in Transit* for detailed delineations of all possible transiting planet combinations.

Aspects Involving the Ascendant
At the moment of birth, the Ascendant in the east marks our unique entry into the world as a viable organism. The Ascendant represents our personal sunrise and symbolizes our physical body, vitality, life force, self-assertion, personality, identity, attitudes, and interests. Directly across the horizon in the west lies the Descendant, which signifies those with whom we have one-to-one relationships, be it as a partner or an adversary whom we meet in court or on the battlefield. Aspects involving the Ascendant affect our selves, our bodies, our health, our initiatives, our partnerships, and our relationships with others. Planets conjunct the Descendant (our personal sunset) directly oppose the Ascendant and can take a toll on our health and vitality.

ASC/Sun:
(+) new beginnings, personal achievements, recognition, honors, praise, celebrity, good health, vitality, creative ability, the will to achieve, confidence, charisma, sociability, sense of independence, personal integration, contacts with authority figures, opportunity to marry.
(–) excessive pride, hubris, identity crisis, notoriety, legal disputes, wanting to be the center of attention, putting yourself first alienates others, stressful relationships, marital problems, disadvantage come through relations with

other people, lowered vitality, health concerns (especially if the Sun opposes the degree of the Ascendant).

ASC/Moon:
(+) changes involving one's body or personality, feelings about health and fitness, security needs are met, popularity, public approval, benefits come through women, positive relationships, sociability, domestic or residential changes proceed smoothly, family matters go well, opportunities for travel.
(–) moodiness, fluctuating emotions, feelings of insecurity, problems related to or specific to women, lack of popularity, stressful changes involving home and family, inharmonious relations with your mother, worries about one's health.

ASC/Mercury:
(+) positive exchanges of ideas, good news, favorable communications, learning that goes smoothly, good relations with young people, opportunities to travel.
(–) bad news, gossip, misunderstandings, troublesome communications, anxiety, restlessness, worry, problems with transportation, accidents due to carelessness.

ASC/Venus:
(+) harmonious relationships with others, sociability, popularity, an agreeable attitude, a pleasant personality, fun, romance, friendship, financial gain, artistic endeavors, comfortable living, good health, pregnancy, childbirth, marriage.
(–) relations with people of bad taste, misplaced affections, difficulties in love relationships, breakups, indolence, self-indulgence, being overly emotional, poor finances.

ASC/Mars:
(+) energy, drive, competitive spirit, ability to assume a leadership role, assertiveness, strong motivation, personal initiative, love of challenge, efforts at self-improvement, events involving young men in your life.
(–) type-A behavior, undue haste, overexertion, feeling stressed, over-excitability, quarrels, anger, strife, heated arguments, battles for leadership, confrontations with others, stressful contact with those who use tools or weapons, health difficulties, accidents, risk of injury, involvement with violent individuals, exposure to violence, a serious illness or death in the family (especially Solar Return Mars in the sorrowful 12th conjunct the natal Ascendant).

ASC/Jupiter:
(+) opportunities for growth, prosperity, social contacts, popularity, wise counsel, beneficial associations with others, the benevolent interest of persons

of influence, success through teamwork, a positive attitude, increased tolerance of diversity, good health, self-confidence, favorable journeys, foreign travel, romance, higher learning, publishing, spiritual pursuits, positive changes in relationships.

(–) exaggerated self-importance, boasting, overestimation, bad advice, irrational exuberance, legal difficulties, overindulgence, health problems due to excess.

ASC/Saturn:

(+) self-discipline, character building, perseverance, professional accomplishment, being formally recognized for a job well done, enjoying the company of mature or older people, gaining experience from interactions with others, increased personal maturity and authority, earning the respect of others, serious study, added professional responsibilities, assuming a managerial role in an organization. Saturn conjunct any angle of the Solar Return marks an important year for career matters.

(–) lowered vitality, fears about one's health, restrictions and hardships in relationships with others, feeling inhibited or overburdened, dealing with obstructions and obstacles, depression, burnout, problems with bones or teeth, worries about one's father or an older individual, illness (especially Saturn opposite the Ascendant, which signifies the body).

ASC/Uranus:

(+) inventiveness, originality, exciting or electrifying events, quick responsiveness, contacts with new and exciting people, making new friends, unexpected or unusual love affairs, dealings with modern technology, possible change of residence or environment.

(–) sudden upsets, shocking events, disruptions, nervous tension, excessive excitability, perverse behavior, disquiet, unrest, unpleasant surprises, exciting but troublesome love affairs, sudden breakups in relationships, electrical problems, separation, divorce, accidents.

ASC/Neptune:

(+) compassionate understanding, altruism, charitable undertakings, vivid imagination, romantic journeys, travel abroad, dream vacations, spiritual pursuits, visionary or mystical experiences, engaging with others in artistic or musical endeavors.

(–) gullibility, confusion, disillusionment, deception, hypersensitivity, renunciation, irresponsibility, disappointment in dealing with others, uncertainty in partnerships and committed relationships, self-undoing, mysterious ailments (especially if Neptune opposes the Ascendant).

ASC/Pluto:

(+) personal influence, dramatic change, ambition, personal transformation, the end of one phase of life and a new beginning, striving for success, the desire for power and control, increased authority over others, research, investigation, depth understanding, eliminating emotional baggage, clearing out the old to make way for the new.

(–) a radical change in life circumstances, a health crisis, being domineering or dictatorial with others, the wish for excessive control over others, power struggles, coercion, abuse, manipulation, exploitation, heated controversies, property damage, theft, financial loss; exposure to violence, injuries, danger, or accidents; the need for surgery, the death of a partner, the risk of death.

Aspects Involving the Midheaven

The Midheaven (MC) lies due south at the pinnacle of the chart in the spot where the Sun shines brightest at midday, providing the greatest illumination and public visibility. The Midheaven symbolizes our public persona, community standing, reputation, vocation, career, life direction, destiny, the result of our actions in the wider world, our mother, and positions of authority or respect that make us stand out in the community. Opposite the Midheaven, directly across the meridian axis in the north, lies the Imum Coeli (IC) or "bottom of the sky," which represents our home, family, parents, father, base of operations, past influences, final endings, and our return to the earth from which we came. Aspects involving the Midheaven affect our career, public standing, life objectives, home, landed property, family, parents, and conditions related to the end of life.

MC/Sun:

(+) progress, success, ambition, victory, achievement, recognition, prestige, honors, creativity, advancement through merit, the will to succeed, clarification of professional objectives, help from superiors, notable change in worldly status or reputation.

(–) lack of progress, unclear objectives, power struggles, job stress, conflicts at home and at work, difficulties with influential people.

MC/Moon:

(+) career changes, strong feelings about career, desire to nurture others, family support for career changes, favorable publicity, social work, domestic and residential changes proceed smoothly, travel, benefits coming through women, advantageous happenings involving the women in your life.

(–) fluctuating life goals, stressful career changes or setbacks, unsettled conditions at work or at home, troubles through female employees, career goals conflict with family obligations, concerns about your mother or other women in your life, job stress may take a toll on your health.

MC/Mercury:

(+) thinking clearly about vocational goals, communicating well at work and in the family, learning new job skills, success in business, scholastic honors, ability to put your ideas in writing, positive relationships with young people, ability to clarify family matters, opportunities to travel.

(–) lack of clarity about professional objectives, miscommunications, misunderstandings, difficult salesmanship, poor communication causes problems at work or at home, problems with transportation, young people are a source of stress or friction, an adverse change of residence.

MC/Venus:

(+) popularity, honors, advancement, increased income, artistic success, domestic or job opportunities, favors from superiors, tact and diplomacy are beneficial, a friend or loved one helps with your career goals, ability to work harmoniously as part of a team, negotiating a favorable contract, family happiness, redecorating or remodeling one's home, marriage.

(–) financial strain, loss of income, conceit or vanity hamper career goals, frivolous or excessive spending, lack of teamwork, impeded domestic or career objectives.

MC/Mars:

(+) energetic pursuit of domestic and career objectives, quick decisiveness, taking charge, leadership ability, having a competitive edge, love of challenge, success through bold action, desire to work independently, ability to undertake new enterprises, desire to have a child.

(–) wrongly applied energy, over-enthusiasm, an excess of heat, impulsiveness, overexertion, headstrong action, domestic strife, failure to take into account the needs and feelings of others, putting yourself first creates conflict, haste makes waste, illness or accident involving a man in your life.

MC/Jupiter:

(+) professional advancement, career opportunities, job promotion, prestige, beneficial changes in career, assistance from influential people, good advice, increased income, gain through litigation, domestic happiness, joyous events in the family.

(–) diminished prestige, an exaggerated sense of your own importance, poor judgment, unwise decisions, biting off more than you can chew, unsound advice, over-optimism, misplaced trust, legal troubles, financial loss, problems due to excess.

MC/Saturn:
(+) expertise, honor, stability, the realization of one's ambitions, fulfilling one's destiny, a sense of genuine accomplishment, determination to succeed, achieving a life's goal, coming of age, establishing one's reputation as an authority, being rewarded for past actions, assuming a prestigious position, serious study, being respected as an elder, events involving one's father or a old person.
(–) setbacks, frustrations, professional delays, impediments to career matters, diminished prestige, struggling against the odds in career and domestic matters, rejection, feelings of inferiority, lack of motivation, loss of income, obstacles block your path, confronting opposition, family matters are burdensome, concerns about or possible loss of a parental figure.

MC/Uranus:
(+) sudden events, new ventures, originality and inventiveness help advance professional goals, unexpected opportunities, unexpected changes in career, benefits through networking with friends, work involving modern technology, possible change of residence.
(–) professional upsets, loss of status, impulsive decision making, haste makes waste, unwise risk-taking, separations at home or on the job, trouble caused by friends, problems with electricity or modern gadgets, a sudden or unexpected turn of events disrupts career and domestic life, accidents.

MC/Neptune:
(+) idealistic life objectives, spiritual goals, careers involving unreality, ability to use one's imagination and intuition in the workplace, dreamy conditions, mysterious circumstances affecting home or career, travel to exotic places, ability to go with the flow; work involving chemicals, large animals, places of confinement or contemplation, the sea.
(–) poorly defined life objectives, lack of purpose, unreliability, work-related stress, disillusionment on the job, confusion about career goals, deception, scandal, victimization, underhanded activities, loss of reputation, evasion of responsibility, forced resignation, self-undoing, disappointment, illness of a parent.

MC/Pluto:
(+) radical changes involving career and worldly status, entering a new phase in one's professional life, the ability to achieve success, power over others, group leadership, assuming an influential role in one's profession, notoriety, fame, recognition, authority, prominence, organizational ability, benefits through investigation and research, an extreme high or low point in one's career (especially Pluto conjunct the annual Midheaven).

(–) financial loss, damage to home or property, the need for repair, breakdown of appliances or equipment, abuse of power, professional crisis, upheaval, power struggles, confronting the consequences of past misdeeds, antisocial behavior; professional goals are impeded by the opposition or spitefulness of others, powerful forces beyond your control affect your career and/or domestic life.

Aspects Involving the Sun

The Sun is the giver of life, the cosmic father, the "king" and center of our solar system. It represents our vitality, strength, creativity, leadership ability, self-esteem, honor, influence, authority, need for attention, and ability to shine. The Sun enlivens and illuminates whatever house or planet it touches. Anatomically the Sun is connected to the heart and the spine. It often signifies important men in our lives.

Sun/Moon:
(+) feeling good about personal accomplishments, harmonious relationships, real estate transactions, vivid dreams, helpful intuitions, inner balance, new attachments, integration of masculine and feminine energies; the conjunction or New Moon is the beginning of a new cycle.

(–) stress, testing, inner tension, lowered vitality, health problems; the opposition or Full Moon is a time of completions.

It is useful to consider the eight phases of the lunation cycle when studying the Solar Return Moon.[1] Just as the most visible lunar effects are the ocean tides, the Solar Return lunar phase can indicate your personal emotional tide for the year ahead. Generally the waxing phase from the New to the Full Moon is a period of birth, new growth, and increase; it is a good time to start something and make it grow. The waning phase from the Full Moon to the next New Moon is a time for bringing something to completion, followed by a period of decline and decrease; it is a good time for projects that require harvesting, quitting, retreat, removal, clearing out, or letting go. The Dark Moon refers to the period of transition from the waning to the waxing Moon when the Moon is invisible in the sky; it is a time of release, mourning for that which has ended, looking inward, regeneration, and renewal.

MOON PHASE ASPECT	MOON/SUN	SIGNIFICANCE
New Moon	Sun/Moon Conjunction (0°)	New beginnings, rebirth, a fresh seed, a new cycle of awareness, enhanced intuition, your personal first day of spring.
Crescent Moon	Semi-square (45°)	Growth. Emerging awareness of one's individuality. Gathering energies, pushing through obstacles.
First Quarter	Square (90°) (half-Moon)	A crisis point. The need to deal with the friction and adjustment that accompany individuation. A time for integration, finalizing plans, and making progress.
Gibbous Moon	Sesqui-quadrate (135°)	A time for analysis and evaluation, appraisal of personal progress, applying energy toward completing and perfecting projects.
Full Moon	Opposition (180°)	A time of climax, maturity, and completion. The culmination of the efforts and initiatives begun at the time of the New Moon.

Disseminating Moon	Sesqui-quadrate (135°)	A time to put to use what you have created and to share what you've learned with others.
Third Quarter	Square (90°) (half-Moon)	A time of crisis and disintegration. The need to engage in conscious action, to reduce excess, and to eliminate what is no longer needed to make room for fresh growth at the next New Moon.
Balsamic Moon	Semi-square (45°)	The conclusion of a lunar cycle. Time to reap what you have sown and carry out your mission. Dealing with karmic forces. You benefit from introspection, rest, recuperation, reflection, and meditation. Time to let go of the past and embrace the future.

Sun/Mercury:
(+) clear thinking, adaptability, creative ideas, positive communications, good news, the ability to organize, commercial matters, literary or scholastic success, common sense, opportunities for travel, favorable for siblings and young people. (−) nervousness, restlessness, lack of clarity, boastfulness, gossip, inattention to detail, talking too much.

Sun/Venus:
(+) love, harmony, romance, good fortune, advancement, pleasurable activities, success in social affairs, new attachments, charm, attraction, close personal relationships, popularity, artistic endeavors, increased income, favors from women, spending on luxury items, making a good impression, engagement, marriage.

(–) conspicuous consumption, disappointment in love, lack of harmony, excessive pleasure seeking, being too eager to please, health suffers from overindulgence, over-spending.

Sun/Mars:

(+) energy, passion, vigor, vitality, heat, enthusiasm, strength, courage, ambition, leadership, assertiveness, increased libido, the urge to take action, personal initiative, taking charge, going after what you desire, advancing your interests through drive and initiative.

(–) needing to struggle to attain your goals, battling the odds, overstrain, quarrelsomeness, aggression, impulsive behavior, the use of force, conflicts with males, excess libido, heart problems; problems that are caused by fire, impulsiveness, passion, haste, or unregulated energy.

Sun/Jupiter:

(+) advancement, good fortune, pride, achievement, success, honor, praise, distinction, opportunity, enjoyment, vitality, good health, personal growth, confidence, blessings, happiness, religious aspirations, philosophical interests, long-distance travel, the ability to win, assistance from influential people, marriage, the birth of a child, an important period in one's life.

(–) narcissism, arrogance, boastfulness, over-confidence, materialism, extravagance, financial loss, overspending, lawsuits, overindulgence, exhaustion, the price of success, too much of a good thing.

Sun/Saturn:

(+) ambition, seriousness, prudent decision making, determination, devotion to duty, patience, accomplishment, accumulated wisdom, productive discipline, consolidating gains, working hard toward a goal, reward for steady effort, accepting responsibility, solitary pursuits, involvement with older or more experienced persons.

(–) a time of testing, career setbacks, thwarted ambitions, fall from power, added responsibility, pessimism, depression, hardship, self-denial, bad luck, delays, sacrifice, limitations, loss, frustrations, inhibitions, paying the piper, being overly cautious, poor health, debilitation, illness, heart problems, isolation, concerns about one's father or other male figure.

Sun/Uranus:

(+) originality, creativity, innovation, unusual contacts, novel experiences, progressive ideas, dynamic leadership, positive changes regarding home and career, finding new solutions to problems, improved circumstances, humanitarian activities, new friendships, fresh surroundings, travel.

(–) sudden setbacks, unanticipated changes in circumstances, erratic behavior, unexpected disruptions, a bolt from the blue, tension, impulsive action, rebelliousness, difficulties caused by friends, separations, accidents, concerns about one's father or other male figure.

Sun/Neptune:
(+) compassion, imagination, creativity, inspiration, heightened sensitivity, valuable hunches, spiritual illumination, mysticism, refinement, enjoyment of art and music, the ability to let go, long journeys, caring for those less fortunate.
(–) confusion about one's self, disappointment, frustration, renunciation, financial loss, scandal, gullibility, deception, exploitation, escapism, illness, a period of confinement or seclusion, problems caused by drugs or alcohol, concerns about a significant man in one's life.

Sun/Pluto:
(+) personal transformation, self-assertion, intense experiences, assuming a position of power or leadership, the urge to reform self and others, singleness of purpose, sudden advancement, increased libido, building new life structures, dealing with life and death issues, clearing away that which is outworn or useless.
(–) crises, extremes of behavior, career setbacks, compulsive sexuality, abuse, vindictiveness, dangerous circumstances, exposure to violence, near-death experiences, demolishing old structures to make way for the new, being swept up by powerful forces that one cannot control, damage to possessions, the need for surgery or invasive therapy.

Aspects Involving the Moon

The Moon, the cosmic mother, receives and reflects the light of the Sun. The Moon is connected with mothers, childbearing, menstruation, mother's milk, alimentation, nurturing, home, family, receptivity, habits, protective urges, feelings, security needs, emotional responses, change, fluctuations (the phases of the Moon), the ocean tides, the subconscious mind, public opinion, common people, and important women in our lives. Anatomically the Moon is linked to the womb, the stomach, and the breasts. In Solar Returns the annual Moon always has reference to one's state of health during the year.

Moon/Moon:
(+) emotional security, nurturing and being nurtured, being in touch with one's feelings.
(–) stress in one's emotional life, feelings of insecurity, emotional hyper-reactivity.

Moon/Mercury:
(+) thoughtfulness, good judgment, adaptability, educational opportunities, communications with women and family members, travel, journeys, visiting one's mother, efforts to understand one's emotional life, a good balance of thinking and feeling; favors writing, speaking, learning, and teaching.
(–) nervousness, gossip, lies, unreliable communications, talking too much, changing views, instability, difficulties related to travel.

Moon/Venus:
(+) affection, popularity, sociability, cheerfulness, harmony, romance, friendship, artistic appreciation, cultural pursuits, domestic happiness, increased income, improved finances, pregnancy, the arrival of children, pleasant experiences involving women, benefits to one's mother, favorable marriage and love relationships.
(–) moodiness, disharmony, indifference, laziness, self-indulgence, conflicts in close relationships.

Moon/Mars:
(+) passion, assertion, desire for change, energy, vigorous action, forcefulness, drive, initiative, increased libido, emotional climaxes, love of adventure, actions motivated by strong feelings, travel, marriage.
(–) inner tension, restlessness, acting on impulse, problems caused by undue haste, quarrels, conflicts with a spouse or partner, domestic discord, trouble involving women.

Moon/Jupiter:
(+) popularity, prestige, social success, involvement in large enterprises, interactions with foreigners, family happiness, generosity, religious experiences, accurate intuitions, prophetic dreams, good publicity, favorable interactions with the public, material gain, educational advancement, travel, expansion involving home and family, benefits come through women or family members, reminiscing about the past.
(–) wastefulness, excessive emotionality, over-optimism, snobbishness, marital problems, religious conflict, bad publicity, poor judgment, legal difficulties.

Moon/Saturn:
(+) serious feelings, emotional stability, steady application of effort, controlled emotions, orderliness, circumspection, discipline applied to home and domestic matters, contacts with older people.
(–) isolation, depression, dark emotions, ill health, restrictions, feeling blocked, delays, withdrawal, introversion, lack of support, losses related to landed property, separation from a loved one, worry about one's mother or other family

member, illness or hardship involving an important woman in your life, difficulty balancing domestic or romantic interests with the demands of a career.

Moon/Uranus:
(+) desire for independence, love of novelty, help from friends, unexpected popularity, sudden success, fresh experiences, new contacts, emotional experimentation, an unusual romance, a change in circumstances, occult interests, sudden changes affecting the women in your life.
(−) unpredictable emotions, unsettling changes, overstrain, unrest, bad publicity, breakup of a romance, emotional outbursts, unanticipated loss of emotional support, unforeseen estrangements, sudden separations or troubles involving a significant woman in your life, accidents in the home.

Moon/Neptune:
(+) compassion, sensitivity, spiritual or idealized love, creative imagination, artistic and poetic endeavors, enjoyment of music, vivid dreams, psychic experiences, helpful intuitions, empathy, an idealized woman, meeting the domestic partner of your dreams, long journeys.
(−) exploitation, self-deception, escapism, co-dependency, uncertainty, confused feelings, emotional disappointment, instability, unrealistic rose-colored glasses, cravings for sensation, sadness or grief involving a woman, separation from one's mother, a secret love affair, lack of emotional security, misguided attempts to deal with loss.

Moon/Pluto:
(+) intense feelings, making radical changes, emotional transformation, boldness, profound personality change, intensive pursuit of a goal, falling deeply in love, taking command of family matters, leadership within a group, in-depth investigation, managing finances, involvement with a powerful woman.
(−) a highly stressful time, emotional upheaval, compulsive behavior, explosive reactions, a health crisis, the need for intensive medical or surgical treatment, domestic problems, jealousy, resentment, emotional abuse, manipulation by others, a controlling woman, worries about one's mother, a death in the family.

Aspects Involving Mercury
Mercury, the quick winged messenger of the gods, is the planet of mental activity, rational thought, words, news, analysis, information processing, communication, speaking, writing, learning, teaching, students, young people, language, movement, mobility, travel, speed, flight, dexterity, transport, commerce, sales, curiosity, variety, cleverness, and wit. Anatomically Mercury is connected to the tongue, the nervous system, the hands, and the lungs.

Mercury/Mercury:
(+) clear thinking, intellectual activity, good news, ability to focus and communicate well, positive relations with young people; favors learning, travel, sales, commerce, and mental pursuits.
(–) muddled thinking, restlessness, scattered energy, miscommunications, difficulty with young people, travel problems.

Mercury/Venus:
(+) thinking about love, enjoyable communications, artistic or poetic appreciation, desire for pleasure, creative writing, ease of expression, opportunities for pleasant travel, income from mental pursuits.
(–) hypersensitivity, vanity, indolence, miscommunication with a woman.

Mercury/Mars:
(+) high energy, putting thoughts into action, forceful thinking, advancement through the exercise of initiative, incisive speech, debate, winning an argument, adventurous travel, academic progress, energetic movement, involvement in sports or exercise, an enterprising young person, increased activity in one's local community.
(–) overwork, barbed words, anger, sarcasm, quarrels, controversies, disputes, irritable speech, precipitate action, impulsive decisions, engaging in risky sports, hazardous or too rapid movement, busy-ness, travel accidents, febrile illness in a child, overheated circuits.

Mercury/Jupiter:
(+) benefits from mental activity or information processing, increase in knowledge, common sense, good news, a wealth of ideas, favorable communications, opportunities to travel, gains through the use of computers; favors writing, learning, teaching, education, publishing, successful litigation.
(–) imprudence, negligence, arrogance, over-optimism, poor judgment, undisciplined thinking, over-spending, depleted finances, troublesome lawsuits, excessive travel, being overwhelmed by communications.

Mercury/Saturn:
(+) deep thinking, concentration, attention to detail, profound learning, serious communications, success with writing or education, consolidation of knowledge, travel for a serious purpose, the need to speak or study in connection with one's career.
(–) depressing news, reserve, delays, pessimism, mental depression, slow mental reactions, boredom, narrow-mindedness, tedious paperwork, separations, difficult or delayed travel.

Mercury/Uranus:
(+) sudden insights, bright ideas, originality, inventiveness, exciting news, desire for novelty, weird communications, unexpected or exciting travel, unanticipated publicity or involvement with the media, studying avant-garde topics.
(−) scattered energies, diffuse thinking, excitement, upset, gossip, nervous conditions, strange or rebellious behavior, poor judgment, wrongheaded thinking, rash movements, accidents or disruptions while traveling.

Mercury/Neptune:
(+) imagination, idealism, inspirational thinking, sensitivity, creative imagination, interest in artistic or literary expression, intuition, precognition, compassionate understanding, spiritual awareness, communications about otherworldly topics, travel over water .
(−) wishful thinking, hypersensitivity, confusion, self-deception, gullibility, fraud, not seeing clearly, miscommunication, scandal, an uncertain journey, misguided travel, nebulous conditions affecting young people.

Mercury/Pluto:
(+) profound changes in one's thinking, depth understanding, research, probing investigation, a powerful intellect, compelling communications, public recognition, intense experiences with young people or while traveling, a transformational journey, thoughts about the afterlife, a profound look beneath the surface.
(−) invasive gathering of information, vindictive gossip, excessive zeal, obsessions, impatience, wrong ideas, mental instability, danger involving young people, news of a death, travel connected with death and dying, a near-death experience.

Aspects Involving Venus
Venus, the goddess of love and the lesser benefic, usually brings with her some joy. She governs affection, fun, romance, lovers, courtship, mating, beauty, harmony, cooperation, elegance, refinement, luxury, peace, comfort, delight, sexual enjoyment, parties, gatherings, socializing, self-indulgence, money, gifts, favors, the fine arts, decoration, fashion, and adornment. Anatomically Venus is connected to the kidneys, the venous system, and the female sex organs.

Venus/Venus:
(+) good luck, harmony, peace, social contacts, love, romance, gifts, favors, increased income, adornment, appreciation of beauty, personal appearance, sensual pleasure, indulgence, sexual intimacy.

(–) incompatibility, vanity, discontent, overindulgence, excessive spending, frivolous pursuit of pleasure, sex without love.

Venus/Mars:
(+) artistic impulses, passion, sensuality, social contacts, enjoyment, falling in love, sexual relationships, marriage, income from enterprise and initiative.
(–) problems in your sex life, outbursts of passion, impulsive spending, disharmony in close relationships, disappointments in love, infidelity.

Venus/Jupiter:
(+) good fortune, honors, advancement, lucky breaks, social contacts, fun times, enjoyment, ease, comfort, popularity, success, good times, a pleasant vacation, financial gain, romance, happiness in love, pleasant indulgences, spending on luxury items, getting engaged, getting married.
(–) indolence, lack of ambition, conceit, wastefulness, self-indulgence, extravagance, too much of a good thing, overspending.

Venus/Saturn:
(+) control of emotions, sacrifices for the sake of love, disciplined work pays off, getting serious about love and finances, dutiful connections with others, stable affections, responsible relationships, romantic involvement with an older person, reliable friends, improved income from career.
(–) inhibitions in close relationships, rejection, depression, emotional disappointment, chilled affections, suffering in a love union, separation from one's beloved, financial losses, decreased income.

Venus/Uranus:
(+) ingenuity, artistic creativity, sudden change in finances, honors, distinctions, new friendships, exciting contacts with others, love at first sight, sudden romance, an exciting love affair.
(–) unpredictability in close relationships, infidelity, one-night stands, sudden breakups, disrupted affection, separation from an important woman, unexpected financial losses or outlays.

Venus/Neptune:
(+) good taste, popularity, sociability, inner joy, delightful emotional experiences, romantic or idealized love, creative imagination, artistic or spiritual inspiration, improved finances, emotional sensitivity, pleasant journeys, good luck in Neptune-ruled ventures.
(–) "the grass looks greener on the other side," disillusionment, end of a love affair, gullibility, financial loss, deception in love, using sex as an escape, health problems related to indulging one's sensual appetites, illness of a loved one.

Venus/Pluto:

(+) transformation in relationships, being madly in love, profound artistic sensibility, socializing, romantic attachment, an intense love affair.

(−) lowered resistance, sorrow, fatal attraction, sexual compulsivity, emotional disappointments, the end of a love affair, an unfortunate love affair, the death of someone toward whom you feel emotional attachment.

Aspects Involving Mars

Mars, the god of war and the lesser malefic usually carries a sting. He governs libido, virility, the male sex drive, activity, assertion, aggression, the use of force, initiative, stimulation, energy, passion, impulse, boldness, courage, competition, rash action, quick reactions, anger, conflict, fighting, self-preservation, heat, tools, construction, guns, weapons, sharp instruments, fire, cuts, burns, accidents, surgery, penetrating wounds, athletic events, and the energetic use of the body. Anatomically Mars is connected to the muscular system, the blood and arteries, and the male sex organs. The astrological glyph of Mars symbolizes an erect phallus.

Mars/Mars:

(+) assertion, energy, boldness, initiative, enthusiasm, passion, competitiveness, love of sport and adventure, decisiveness, daring, fondness for challenge, starting new enterprises, a pioneering spirit, strong motivation, being a go-getter, enjoyable sex.

(−) overwork, conflict, strife, disputes, disagreements, bad judgment, impulsive behavior, not finishing what you start, acting too "macho," hypersexuality, cuts, burns, wounds, accidents.

Mars/Jupiter:

(+) personal achievement, ambition, confidence, enthusiasm, high energy, passion, desire for freedom, successful self-expression, creative activity, ability to concentrate single-mindedly on a goal, athletic success, good powers of recuperation, beneficial use of the muscular system of the body, increased libido, the urge to travel, long journeys, betrothal, marriage.

(−) undue haste, financial loss, dissipation of assets, exaggeration, immoderation, lack of restraint, reckless behavior, ill-advised risks, unbridled libido, unregulated energy, becoming overheated, exhaustion, strong beliefs lead to intolerance, people of influence suppress one's initiatives, rebelliousness, conflicts about philosophy or religion, difficulty while traveling, legal troubles.

Mars/Saturn:
(+) constructive use of force, focused effort, disciplined energy, persistence, endurance, the building of structures, achieving ambitions through determined effort, success at dangerous tasks.

(–) difficult confrontations, destructive use of force, damage to property, frustration, reduced energy, being blocked from forging ahead, being between a rock and a hard place, disputes, separations, strained relationships, illness, injury, blows, falls, violence, collisions, accidents, dental problems, the need for surgery, hardship due to heat or fire, "I can't get no satisfaction."

Mars/Uranus:
(+) assertiveness, originality, outbursts of energy, pioneering instincts, highly charged activity, progress through unconventional means, unexpected electrifying events, novel experiences, sudden passions, unanticipated sexual encounters, the desire for freedom, the urge to be independent, the breaking up of old conditions.

(–) undue haste, self-will, restlessness, tension, carelessness, impetuous actions, unconventional behaviors, wrongly applied initiative, lack of tact, friction with others, arguments, problems caused by sudden release of pent-up energy, electrical problems, malfunctioning motor vehicles, confronting unexpected violence, fires, burns, wounds, muggings; accidents or injuries involving fire, explosions, weapons, machinery, motor vehicles, or electrical devices.

Mars/Neptune:
(+) inspired initiatives, idealistic enthusiasm, being motivated by one's dreams, psychological understanding, spiritual insights, religious zeal, idealized sexual encounters, long-distance travel, retirement from one's job, promotion of Neptune-related ideas.

(–) poor planning, misguided or deceitful actions, fraud, slanderous accusations, exploitation, victimization, unwitting exposure to violence, being in the wrong place at the wrong time, confrontations with unsavory characters, sorrow related to misdirected force, problems stemming from drugs or alcohol, substance abuse, illness, weakness, depleted energy, inattention, accidents.

Mars/Pluto:
(+) tremendous power, courage, self-assertion, determined effort, reserves of strength, inner drive, daring, a fighting spirit, confidence, leadership, ability to direct immense force or energy to achieve one's goals.

(–) precipitate or extreme actions, applying too much force, throwing caution to the wind, acting without regard for consequences, exposure to violence as either victim or perpetrator, ruthlessness, domination, fanatical behavior, hazardous activity, victimization, explosiveness, jealousy, vengeance, a hot temper, an excess of testosterone, arguments, danger, injury, wounds, surgery, accidents, contact with death.

Aspects Involving Jupiter

Jupiter, the supreme god of the Roman pantheon and the greater benefic, expands and increases whatever it touches in the chart. Jupiter is associated with increase, growth, opportunity, abundance, good fortune, prosperity, wisdom, professionalism, generosity, excess, optimism, confidence, advancement, improvement, risk-taking, broadmindedness, tolerance, social impulses, travel, long journeys, religious strivings, philosophy, higher learning, publishing, the law, and the expansion of one's horizons. In delineating the hard aspects of Jupiter, keep in mind that more is not always better. Anatomically Jupiter is linked to the liver, the hips and thighs, and the sciatic nerve.

Jupiter/Jupiter:
(+) good luck, optimism, gains, confidence, wisdom, happiness, generosity, opportunities, educational advancement, expanded social life, travel.
(−) lack of discipline, problems due to excess, too much of a good thing, over-exaggeration, irrational exuberance, conflicts caused by one's belief system, biting off more than you can chew.

Jupiter/Saturn:
(+) wisdom, good judgment, consolidation in professional affairs, career opportunities, increased responsibility, steady progress toward a goal, material gain, advanced training, travel for education or duty.
(−) discontent, overwork, stressful life changes, unstable finances, missed opportunities, resistance to achieving your goals, material gains at a spiritual cost.

Jupiter/Uranus:
(+) unexpected good fortune, lucky breaks, sudden inspirations, originality, optimism, recognition, career opportunities, desire for independence, novel learning, unanticipated changes in one's belief system, sudden or unusual journeys.
(−) impulsiveness, unanticipated disruptions, lack of stability, poor judgment, exaggerated eccentricities, inner tension, ill-advised efforts to break free of limitations.

Jupiter/Neptune:
(+) enhanced spirituality, expanded emotionality, religious instincts, idealism, altruism, popularity, increased compassion, a rich imagination, intuitive

awareness, success related to a large institution, opportunities for unstructured travel; favors artistic, spiritual, and theatrical endeavors.

(–) gullibility, impressionability, hypersensitivity, demoralization, carelessness, over-idealization, irresponsibility, fanciful thinking, poor judgment, flights of imagination, unwise efforts to escape, fanatical pursuit of a dream, exaggerated reaction to loss.

Jupiter/Pluto:

(+) major life changes, great enthusiasm, self-assurance, exuberance, transformation, regeneration, penetrative ability, understanding in depth, assuming a role of power or leadership, desire to reform self and others, successful investments, wise financial management, support from powerful people, gain through inheritance, sexual opportunities.

(–) bigotry, intolerance, explosiveness, unbridled appetites, actions based on fanatical beliefs, abuse of power, conflicts with authority, overindulgence, waste, extravagance, speculative losses, death due to excess or extreme behavior.

Aspects Involving Saturn

Saturn, sometimes called Father Time or the Grim Reaper, works in an opposite manner to the expansion and exuberance of Jupiter. Saturn's action is to regulate, solidify, structure, shrink, contain, limit, test, inhibit, slow, delay, obstruct, constrict, depress, restrain, define, harden, contract, pressurize, consolidate, solidify, chill, and crystallize. Saturn represents patience, endurance, solidity, delay, hard reality, maturity, parental or authority figures, high standards, persistence, seriousness, practicality, frugality, deprivation, discipline, responsibility, rules, regulations, awareness of limits, hardship, structure, frustration, tolerance, organization, dogma, respectability, self-control, lessons learned, old age, and the just rewards for one's labors. Anatomically Saturn is linked to the structural and limiting elements of the body – the bones, knees, skin, and teeth.

Saturn/Saturn:

(+) maturing, settling down to work, becoming your own person, getting serious about career goals, gaining wisdom, assuming significant responsibilities. The conjunction of Saturn with its natal position marks the Saturn return, a time of major significance in one's life.

(–) feeling frustrated and overburdened, a time of testing, turning points in one's career development, feeling burned out.

Saturn/Uranus:

(+) sudden professional opportunities, career changes, consolidating progressive or innovative ideas, focused inventive ability, perseverance, ability to overcome difficulties, breakup of limiting structures; "no pain, no gain."

(–) unrest, emotional strain, restricted freedom, difficult decisions, irritability, rebelliousness, unexpected changes in career, the sudden shattering of a life structure, accidents involving inertia or gravity, separations in long-standing relationships.

Saturn/Neptune:

(+) disciplined imagination, intuitions advance career, practical idealism, devotion to an ideal, slow but steady progress, willingness to sacrifice to achieve one's goals.

(–) failure of imagination, renunciation, emotional inhibition, unrealistic career goals, unsound investments, crumbling foundations, undermining circumstances, mysterious ailments, insidious or hard-to-diagnose illness, worries about parents, dissolution of previously stable life structures, deterioration of property, water damage, self-deception or confusion in professional matters.

Saturn/Pluto:

(+) major changes in your life work, the achieving of ambitions, painstaking discipline, success through patient effort, heavy responsibilities, thorough research, working hard to achieve success, greater appreciation of human mortality.

(–) overwork, acting on compulsion, dealing with the effects of ageing, paying the piper, confronting the reality principle, setbacks, falling from power, collapse of formerly reliable structures, drastic changes involving career, near-death experiences, depression, enforced restrictions, others oppose your success, problems with laws or governmental regulations, poor health due to falls or gravity, troubles caused by egoism or ruthless behavior, concerns about death and dying, apocalypse now.

Aspects Involving Uranus

Uranus, the Rebel, acts like a live wire or an electrifying bolt of lightning striking a point or planet in the chart. Uranus appears never to have gotten over the shock of having his genitals unexpectedly cut off by his son Saturn (Cronos). The sudden and unexpected action of Uranus is to awaken, innovate, disturb, shock, startle, jolt, and galvanize – shattering the crystalline realities of Saturn to make room for a fresh perspective and a new life experience. Uranus is connected with novelty, disruption, divorce, sudden and shocking change, instability, the shattering of life structures, unusual events, love of freedom, iconoclasm, disdain for restriction, the need to change things, originality, innovation, self-will, uniqueness, deviation from the norm, invention, eccentric behavior, unconventionality, perversity, rebellion, progressive ideas, electricity, electromagnetic waves, and modern science. Anatomically Uranus is associated with the nervous system and the ankles.

Uranus/Uranus:
(+) excitement, sudden opportunities for change, the need to re-evaluate life objectives, positive breakthroughs, electrifying events.
(−) breakdown of outmoded structures, unexpected unwelcome change, crises, stress, tension, accidents, electrical problems.

Uranus/Neptune:
(+) spiritual awareness, artistic inspiration, changes in one's beliefs, altered states of consciousness, craving for excitement, desire for new or unusual sensual experiences, inner vision, psychic experiences, long journeys, invigorating spiritual retreats
(−) the fading of an illusion, moodiness, sudden loss of a dream, setbacks due to a craving for emotional stimulation, strange insights, secrets revealed, lack of vitality, mental instability, confusion, willful isolation, wrongheaded escapism, loss of a friend, unexpected confinement.

Uranus/Pluto:
(+) unanticipated major changes, inner awakening, desire for independence, intense application of effort, an urge to reform self and others, discoveries made through painstaking research, sudden elimination of outworn aspects of one's life.
(−) unanticipated major disruptions, sudden confrontations with mortality, impatience, excessive self-will, upsets, accidents, extreme efforts to break free of limitations.

Aspects Involving Neptune
Neptune, the god of the oceans, acts like a universal solvent dissolving the clear boundaries set up by Saturn. Neptune is connected with compassion, spirituality, intuition, imagination, altered states of consciousness, inspiration, creativity, music, poetry, fiction, glamour, esthetic sensibility, merging, dreams, illusion, altruism, idealism, sacrifice, mysticism, psychic experiences, otherworldliness, and transcendence. Negatively, Neptune shrouds us in fog, mist, confusion, anxiety, disillusionment, scandal, treachery, deceit, isolation, intoxication, hypersensitivity, unreality, misguided actions, pipe dreams, make-

believe, escapism, denial, blindness, or lack of clarity. Anatomically Neptune is associated with the feet and the lymphatic system.

Neptune/Neptune:
(+) favors art, music, poetry, and spiritual endeavors; transcendence.
(–) confusion, foggy thinking, lack of clarity, not seeing clearly, self-deception, scandal.

Neptune/Pluto:
(+) in-depth appreciation of ideals and spiritual matters, a transcendent approach to mortality, spiritual regeneration, pursuit of peculiar interests, intense emotional experiences.
(–) disillusionment, loss, fanatical ideals, impracticality, the death of an illusion, worries about dying, confusion about spiritual matters, life-altering changes, cravings for drugs or alcohol.

Aspects Involving Pluto
Pluto, the powerful god of death and the underworld, has to do with the cycle of death, destruction, birth, renewal, and regeneration. It acts to intensify whatever it touches and to clear away that which is outworn, decayed, and useless to make way for evolution, new growth, and development. Pluto is associated with crises, life-changing events, rebirth, reform, lifestyle change, radical or forced transformation, personal evolution, breakdown, repair, renewal, healing, power, control, domination, abuse, jealously, strong emotion, compulsion, underworld activity, sexual urges, buried resources, hidden matters, penetration, delving beneath the surface, investigation, depth understanding, purification, elimination purging, decay, garbage, refuse, destruction, and the clearing away of debris. Anatomically Pluto is linked to the organs of sex and elimination.

Pluto/Pluto:
(+) profound inner change, personal transformation, repair, restoration, reformation.
(–) crisis, inner turmoil, breakdown, radical change, stressful reform, surgery, death.

Aspects Involving House Cusps
Rather than create a separate list of all the possible aspects formed by the planets with the house cusps, I will present a table with a few keywords for the planets and houses. The reader can mix and match ideas from the column of planetary keywords with those of the house keywords to create an appropriate delineation. For example, suppose one finds Venus square the cusp of the 5th

Planet	Planetary Keywords	House	House Keywords
Sun	Vitality, illumination, being at the center, importance, influence, ego, will power, creativity, honor, authority, the father	1st	One's body, life force, personal initiatives, appearance, sense of identity, self-expression, outlook on life. Lilly says, "Mercury doth also joy in this house, because it represents the Head, and he the Tongue."
Moon	Moods, emotions, intuition, changes, fluctuations, caring, nurturing, reactivity, women in general, the mother, domestic concerns, the past	2nd	Income, money, possessions, ownership, values, personal resources, talents
Mercury	Thought, communication, the rational mind, wit, decision making, curiosity, learning, teaching, travel, quickness, mobility, variety, diversity, commerce, young people	3rd	Communication, writing, news, correspondence, local travel, mobility, siblings, kin, neighbors, one's immediate environment. Lilly says that the 3rd house "is the joy of the Moon; for if she be posited therein, especially in a moveable [cardinal] sign, it's an argument of much travel, trotting and trudging, or of being seldom quiet."
Venus	Love, tenderness, money, gifts, favors, beauty, affection, fun, emotional attachments, harmony, sensual pleasure, sexual union, adornment, self-indulgence, nubile women	4th	Home, landed property, family, parents and grandparents, the father, domestic life, base of operations, ancestral traditions, final endings, the grave
Mars	Conflict, energy, assertion, anger, impulse, activity, drives, initiative, passion, libido, construction, adventure, competition, strife, weapons, fires, cuts, wounds, surgery, virile men	5th	Creativity, fun, children, pregnancy, love affairs, recreational sex, pleasures, games, sports, show business, gambling, risk-taking. Lilly writes that Venus "doth joy in this house, in regard it's the house of Pleasure, Delight and Merriment; it's wholly unfortunate by Mars or Saturn, and they therein show disobedient children and untoward."
Jupiter	Optimism, success, gain, growth, wisdom, opportunity, advancement, social urges, protection, expansion, good luck, humor, exuberance, excess	6th	Service, health, illness, harvesting, diet, food, hygiene, daily routine, techniques, adjustments, pets, servants, co-workers. Lilly says that Mars "rejoices" in the 6th house, probably because he signifies fevers.

house in the Solar Return. A potential interpretation would be that this year you will be spending more money (Venus) than you would like (square) on children or love affairs (5th house). More extensive lists of keywords for the planets and houses can be found in Chapters One and Three of this text.

Saturn	Responsibility, maturity, structure, discipline, delays, authority, contraction, coldness, obstruction, hardness, caution, insecurity, privation, hard work, lessons learned, wisdom	7th	Marriage, partnerships, one-to-one relationships, lawsuits, rivals, open enemies, contractual agreements, dealings with the public
Uranus	Sudden change, novelty, originality, disruption, revolution, shocks, upheaval, innovation, excitement, freedom, liberation, casting off restraints, independence, shattering old structures, accidents, electricity, modern science	8th	Death, inheritance, money owed to others, taxes, partner's resources, regeneration, in-depth investigation, probing, life-threatening illness, surgery, intensive medical therapy, clearing away refuse
Neptune	Idealism, imagination, spirituality, sacrifice, merging, sensitivity, intuition, fog, confusion, blind spots, uncertainty, dissolution, deception, escapism, disappointment, mystery, poetry, the oceans	9th	Long journeys, foreign lands, expanded horizons, publishing, forecasting, preaching, propaganda, religion, in-laws, belief systems, philosophy, publishing, the Law, the Church, higher education. According to Lilly, the Sun "rejoices" in the 9th house.
Pluto	Power, control, crisis, the underworld, extremes, intensity, rebirth, reform, transformation, evolution, dominion, penetration, obsession, regeneration, elimination, decay, breakdown, repair, empowerment, getting rid of the old to make way for the new	10th	Career, vocation, destiny, status, reputation, the mother, public persona, one's influence in the larger community, professional undertakings, authority, the boss, objectives in life, the result of our actions in the community. Lilly states that "either Jupiter or the Sun do much Fortunate this House when they are posited therein; Saturn or the South Node usually deny Honor."
		11th	Friends, groups, social aspirations, hopes, wishes, support, succor, good fortune, humanitarian concerns
		12th	Sorrow, loss, troubles, illness, undoing, solitude, confinement, secret enemies, behind-the-scenes activities, spirituality, sacrifice, imagination, the subconscious mind, hospitals, prisons, retreats. Lilly says, "Saturn doth joy in that House, for naturally Saturn is Author of mischief."

NOTES

1.   Useful sources of information on lunar cycles include the following books: Dane Rudhyar's *The Lunation Cycle*, Demetra George's *Finding Our Way through the Dark*, and Daniel Pharr's *Moonwise*.

15

Pulling It All Together

This final chapter pulls together the various principles discussed in previous sections of the book and presents an outline for delineating a tropical non-precessed Solar Return. The use of this outline is illustrated with an actual case example. Because the Solar Return condenses an entire year of significations into a single chart, it contains a wealth of information that may require great patience to unpack. The astrologer does best to proceed in a stepwise manner to unravel the underlying structure of the Solar Return against the backdrop of the nativity. A systematic approach helps in mining all the treasures buried in the annual chart.

The fundamental principle of forecasting with the Solar Return is that certain potentials of the natal chart will manifest in a year when there exits a concordance between the annual chart and the nativity, the current natal directions and progressions, the current eclipses, the Lunar Returns, and the ongoing transits. Morin's words bear repeating: "the revolution either brings forth or inhibits the effect of the nativity, and it can only bring it forth from a similarity of figures…"[1] In fact, the more you work with solar revolutions, the more profoundly you will understand the potentials of your birth chart.

Below is an outline of the key factors – drawn from our study of Morin, Volguine, and modern authors – for systematically analyzing a Solar Return. In practice it is too time-consuming to examine all of these factors for each chart, but they are included here for completeness. It will also allow the reader to judge the usefulness of each technique against the evidence of a real case example. As with the rest of astrology, no single factor should be read in isolation. We must always synthesize the entire chart, and in the case of Solar Returns, synthesize the annual chart in the context of the birth chart. In addition, the Solar Return must be read in the context of the information gathered from other forecasting tools such as directions, progressions, eclipses, Lunar Returns, and transits. The reader should feel free to modify or amend this outline to suit her or his personal style and experience.

An Outline for Delineating a Tropical Solar Return

I.   **The Solar Return Ascendant**

a.   The zodiacal sign of the annual Ascendant. The sign rising in the Solar Return identifies major themes in the year ahead. Matters related to the *natal* houses(s) highlighted by the annual rising sign will come to the fore.

b.   The genders of the annual and natal Ascendants. Gender refers to the   classification of signs as either masculine (the Fire and Air signs) or feminine (the Earth and Water signs). When our annual and natal Ascendants are of the same gender, we feel more in consonance with our natal charts. When they are of opposite genders, we feel out of synch with the energies of our birth chart as represented by the natal Ascendant. According to Morin, the Ascendant represents the life force and essential disposition of the native.

c.   Aspects between the annual and natal Ascending degrees, and the whole sign aspectual relationship of the two Ascending signs. If the annual Ascendant closely conjoins one of the natal angles, it will be a very significant year. When the Ascendants form harmonious aspects (sextile, trine), there is a sense of consonance. When they form stressful aspects (square, opposition), one can expect a dynamic and challenging year. When the ascending signs are disjunct – either adjacent or in quincunx (150 degrees apart) – one can expect stress and possible health problems.

d.   Close aspects between the annual Ascendant and any natal or annual planets. Because the Ascendant is the key point in the chart, any aspects it makes are highly significant. In Merriman's view the annual horizon axis signifies our perception of reality, self-expression, dominant activities, and relations with others in the year ahead. Aspects involving the Ascendant combine the meanings of the horizon axis (self and others) with the significance of the aspected planet. One must consider the meaning of the planet *per se* together with its significance due to its specific roles in the natal and annual charts.

II.   **The Planetary Ruler(s) of the Solar Return Ascendant**
(Morin used as Ascendant-rulers those planets that either ruled or were exalted in the sign ascending. He also studied the dispositor of the planet ruling the Ascendant, which is sometimes called the "secondary ruler" of the Ascendant.)

a.   The Solar Return house placement of the annual Ascendant-ruler(s).

b.   Aspects between the ruler(s) of the Solar Return Ascendant and the annual and natal planets and cusps. Because the Ascendant is a key factor in the Solar Return, its ruler(s) become quite important. The placement and aspects of the Ascendant-ruler(s) are always significant.

III. The Sun

a. *The Solar Return house containing the Sun.* Because we are dealing with a solar revolution, the Sun takes on special significance. The annual house position of the Sun and the Sun's aspects to the annual planets become very important.

b. *Aspects between the Sun and the annual planets and angles.*

c. *A prominent, well aspected Sun in the annual chart implies vitality and good health.* In addition, one must also always look to the annual Moon, its placement and aspects, to judge health matters in the Solar Return chart. In addition, Morin taught that any planets occupying or ruling the 1ˢᵗ, 8ᵗʰ, or 12ᵗʰ houses have special significance for matters of health or life.

IV. The Solar Return Moon

Symbolizes feelings, receptivity, fluctuations, and vulnerability. Its state in the return also relates to one's health and personal relationships.

a. *A prominent but stressfully aspected annual Moon often suggests health problems and low vitality.* The state of the Moon must always be judged in the context of the state of the Sun and the rest of the annual chart. Paran-squares between the annual Moon and annual Pluto are common in years of a health crisis.

b. *The zodiacal sign, house, and aspects of the annual Moon in the Solar Return chart reflect the types of people who will play an important role in your life.*[2]

V. Solar Return Planets Conjunct the Angles (10 degree orb) have special prominence in the year ahead.

It is a long-standing tradition that angular planets have especially prominent effects. The tighter the orb, the more powerful the influence. Angularity is the cornerstone of interpreting the sidereal Solar Return, and angular planets should be given much weight in delineating the chart. Also consider that two planets conjunct the horizon and/or meridian axes will form a paranconjunction, paran-square, or paran-opposition on the Prime Vertical, even if no zodiacal aspect exists between them.

VI. Annual planets in the Solar Return 1ˢᵗ house

Annual planets that occupy the Solar Return 1ˢᵗ house show the nature of the individual's significant activity and psychological reactions during the coming year

(Volguine). Similarly, planets in the Lunar Return 1ˢᵗ house show the nature of the native's activity and psychological reactions during the coming month, that is, until the start of the next Lunar Return.

VII. The Natal Chart Superimposed on the Solar Return Chart

a.   *House emphasis by the number of planets occupying each house*. The more planets in a house, the more significant that house becomes in the year ahead. Merriman judges the overall tone of the year by identifying which type of house – angular, succedent, or cadent – contains the largest number of combined annual and natal planets. He overlays the birth chart on the Solar Return and includes both natal and annual planets in his count. It is also useful to superimpose the Solar Return onto the natal chart to judge house emphasis.

b.   *Conjunctions of any planets with annual house cusps (5 degree orb)*. *The cusps are the power points of the houses*. Morin and Volguine found that conjunctions of planets with house cusps are extremely important. The tighter the orb, the more significant the contact.

c.   *Which natal houses are superimposed on which annual houses (pay special attention to houses containing planets)*. Volguine published an elaborate set of delineations for the overlay of annual and natal houses.

VIII. The Solar Return Superimposed on the Natal Chart (See the discussion of item VII above.)

a.   *House emphasis by number of planets in each house*.
b.   *Conjunctions of any planets with natal house cusps (5 degree orb)*.
c.   *Which annual houses are superimposed on which natal houses (pay special attention to houses containing planets)?*
d.   *Annual planets in the natal 1ˢᵗ house show which planetary influences are about to rise to the horizon of the birth chart*.

IX. The Solar Return Midheaven and its Ruler(s)

a.   *A close conjunction of the annual Midheaven with any natal angle suggests an important year, especially as regards career and family matters*. The Midheaven is a powerful angle, second only to the Ascendant in strength. Merriman notes that the meridian axis symbolizes one's profession, home, family, domestic concerns, and one's sense of purpose in life.

b.   *Close aspects between the annual Midheaven and any natal or annual planets*. Such aspects combine the meanings of the meridian axis (vocation, home, family) with the significance of the planet(s) being aspected. One must consider the meaning of the planets *per se* together with their significance deriving from their roles in the natal and annual charts.

c.   *The house placement and aspects of the Midheaven-ruler are significant with regard to one's professional life.*

X.   Planetary Aspects

a.   *Close aspects between annual planets, especially those that will perfect by transit within 24 hours of the Solar Return.* Because the 24 hours following the Solar Return are mapped onto the coming year of life, any annual aspects that perfect during the 24 hours after the Sun returns to its natal position are highly significant in forecasting.

b.   *Close aspects between natal and annual planets.* Such aspects release the potential of the natal planet to manifest in the year ahead.

c.   *Comparison of the genders of the zodiacal signs occupied by the same planet in the natal and annual charts.* Comparing the genders of the signs occupied by same planet gives an indication of how that planetary energy resonates between the annual and birth charts during the coming year.

d.   *Aspects that a house-ruler forms with the house cusp and the planets contained within that house.* Studying the aspects formed between a house-ruler and the corresponding house cusp or any planets within that house gives an indication of how the matters signified by that house resonate – whether harmoniously or discordantly – between the annual and birth charts. One can also consider the aspect formed between the sign of the house cusp and the sign containing the planet ruling that house.

e.   *Parans* – planets simultaneously conjunct the horizon and/or meridian axes form paran-conjunctions, paran-squares, or paran-oppositions when measured along the Prime Vertical.

XI.   Eclipses

a.   *Eclipses, especially solar eclipses.* In natal astrology we often study the prenatal eclipse as well as ongoing eclipses, solar and lunar, during the life of the individual. With Solar Returns I have found repeatedly that the first solar eclipse to occur after the time of the solar revolution is especially telling when superimposed on the Solar Return chart. An eclipse that occurs within the week or so before the Solar Return is also highly significant. My practice is to cast the eclipse chart for the same location as the Solar Return and to pay special attention to the placement in the annual chart of the eclipse, its dispositor, and the Ascendant and Ascendant-ruler of the eclipse chart.

XII. Timing

> *a.   The natal chart's primary, Ascendant-arc, and solar arc directions that are active during the current Solar Return year.* Morin looked chiefly to the primary directions of the birth chart to identify central themes for the year ahead. Modern astrologers use other methods of direction and also secondary progressions of the birth chart for the same purpose.
>
> *b.   The secondary progressed annual Moon and Solar Return planets.* Merriman looks at all exact aspects that the progressed annual Moon forms with the natal and annual planets and angles, and with their antiscia or solstice points. I use the computer program *Solar Fire* to do a "dynamic report" for the secondary progressions of the Solar Return – the "progressed to radix" and "progressed to progressed" options – for the year ahead. This report lists specific dates when the secondary progressed annual aspects become exact during the coming year.
>
> *c.   The mean quotidian secondary progressed Solar Return chart, especially the angles, according to the Conversion Table in the Appendix.* To progress the annual chart, find the number of days that have elapsed since the Solar Return date. Look up the corresponding time interval in the Conversion Table and add that time interval to the original time of the Solar Return. Be sure to adjust the date if the time takes you past midnight. Erect the progressed annual chart using the calculated "progressed" time. This method is available as the mean quotidian secondary progression in *Solar Fire*.
>
> *d.   The transits of the Sun to the annual house cusps during the year.* Because it is a *Solar* Return, the transits of the Sun through the houses of the annual chart highlight major themes that change as the Sun transits houses of the chart. Conjunctions of the transiting Sun with annual house cusps often mark events related to that house.
>
> *e.   The daily progressed Lunar Return.* This is a method I developed based on the theory of diurnal charts and Morin's idea that the directed Moon should make a complete revolution in the course of a lunar month. Basically it produces daily progressed angles and house cusps by advancing the Lunar Return chart by 24 hours 17 minutes 9 seconds for each complete day that has elapsed since the Lunar Return. This method resembles the use of lunar mansions.
>
> *f.   Morin's methods of directing the Solar and Lunar Returns.* In my own practice I use the above methods for timing and have not used Morin's techniques for directing the return charts.

XIII. The Precessed Tropical Solar Return

Look at the precessed annual chart, especially any planets that closely conjoin the Solar Return angles or intermediate house cusps. Combine the meaning of the planet with the meaning of the cusp. Note the role the planet plays in the natal and annual charts through house rulership and disposition of other planets. In my experience precessed tropical Solar Returns strongly highlight key events of the year; or as Marc Penfield is wont to say, in precessed Solar Returns major events stick out like sore thumbs.

XIV. The Lunar Returns

Morin studied the Lunar Returns to pinpoint in which month an event promised in the Solar Return will occur. He looked for similarities in signification among the natal, annual, and Lunar Return charts.

XV. Additional Considerations

(Almost any astrological technique can be applied to the Solar Return.)

a. *Fixed Stars*. Morin routinely studied fixed stars in his Solar Return delineations.

b. *Arabic Parts*. I generally consider the Part of Fortune (PF) and Emerson's Point of Death. For daytime births, PF = ASC + Moon – Sun and for nighttime births, PF = ASC + Sun – Moon. Emerson's Death Point = MC + Saturn – Mars.

c. *Chiron and the Asteroids*. I generally do not include these when studying Solar Returns because there is already enough detail with the standard ten planets. Remember that Morin got excellent results using only the seven visible planets. More is not necessarily better but the reader may wish to experiment with asteroids, dwarf planets, and the like.

d. *Midpoints*.

e. *Converse Solar Returns*. Converse returns count astrological birthdays backwards in time. For example, if you were born in the year 2000, your fifth Solar Return would occur in 2005 but your converse Solar Return would have occurred in 1995. For lack of time I generally do not look at converse returns but I suspect they would be informative as are other converse techniques in astrology.

f. *Firdaria, profections, and other medieval techniques*.[3] Morin disdained these medieval techniques and dismissed them as superstitions. Nonetheless, some modern astrologers, like Robert Hand and Robert Zoller, have worked to resurrect these medieval methods. Tables of firdaria are given in Appendix B for readers who wish to experiment with them. Annual profections were not discussed in this book but essentially amount to directing the entire chart by 30 degrees or one zodiacal sign per year, which equates to 2°30' per month. A variant of this technique is to advance the Ascendant to the next house cusp each year.

Using the Outline to Delineate a Solar Return

My friend Don

My wife and I had a close friend Don, a psychologist who lived and worked in the Washington, DC area. Beginning in the year 1975 Don spent every Thanksgiving with us. During those visits I would typically spend time with him reviewing his Solar Return, transits, and secondary progressions for the

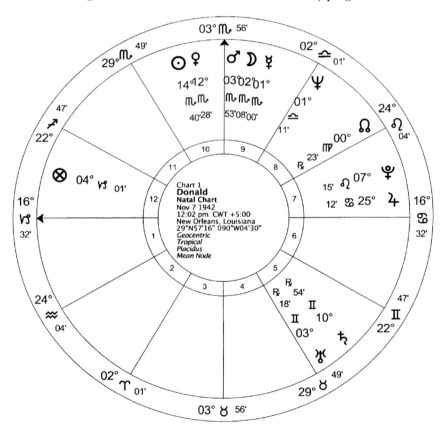

Figure 1: Don's Natal Chart

year ahead. The Solar Return was especially appropriate because Don's birthday was in early November, not long before his annual visit. During the 2000 Thanksgiving holiday we were very busy and did not find time for our usual astrological reading. As a result, Don returned to Washington, DC, without our having reviewed his astrological chart for the year. According to his birth certificate, Don was born on November 7, 1942 at 12:02 PM CWT in New Orleans, Louisiana (Figure 1).

In late December of 2000 Don mentioned in a phone call that he was having bowel problems and had scheduled an appointment with his doctor for early January of 2001, just after the Christmas holidays. On Friday evening January 5, 2001, Don telephoned me to say that he had just been diagnosed with colon cancer. As it turned out, the cancer had metastasized to various parts of his body and he was not a candidate for surgery.

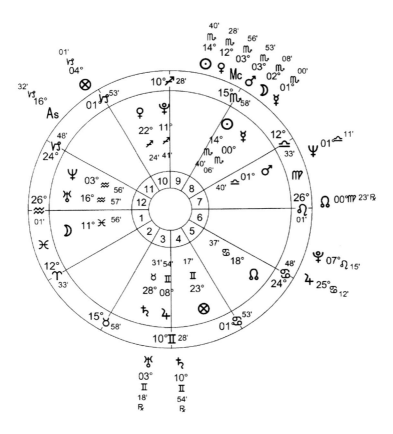

Figure 2: Don's Natal Chart Superimposed on his 2000 Solar Return

Over the coming months Don underwent chemotherapy, including several experimental approaches at a research hospital, but his condition continued to worsen. He died in Bethesda, Maryland, on Monday November 26, 2001 around 5:30 AM, just 20 days after his 2001 Solar Return (not shown) which had its 8th house cusp at 17° Capricorn 28' conjunct his natal Ascendant. To this day I regret having missed the opportunity to review Don's 2000 Solar Return with him. Had I seen his Solar Return during the Thanksgiving holiday, I certainly would have advised him to see his doctor, though even by then it may have been too late. My friend Don was the inspiration for my writing this book, and it seems fitting to end with a belated study of his 2000 Solar Return.

I.   **The Solar Return Ascendant**

a.   The zodiacal sign of the annual Ascendant. Don's annual Aquarius Ascendant suggests an unusual and surprising year, perhaps involving high tech or experimental approaches. The news about colon cancer certainly struck like a Uranian bolt of lightning.

b.   The genders of the annual and natal Ascendants. Don's natal Capricorn Ascendant is feminine (yin) whereas his annual Aquarius Ascendant is masculine (yang) – matters do not flow smoothly and he feels out of synch.

c.   Aspects between the annual and natal Ascending degrees, and the whole sign aspectual relationship of the two Ascending signs. There is no close aspect between the annual and natal Ascendants. In fact, they are disjunct, being of adjoining signs (Capricorn and Aquarius), and form no Ptolemaic aspect (sextile, square, trine, or opposition). The annual and natal Ascendants falling in inconjunct signs (one or five signs apart) form a stressful relationship since they have no aspectual connection. Health problems are commonly associated with disjunct relationships (being 30 or 150 degrees apart).

d.   Close aspects between the annual Ascendant and any natal or annual planets. The closest connection is a stressful quincunx between the annual Ascendant and natal Jupiter, which is conjunct the cusp of the annual 6th house, suggesting an illness due to some type of growth or expansion. Since Pisces is intercepted in the 1st house, Jupiter co-rules the annual 1st house (the body). There is a close square between the annual Ascendant and annual Saturn in the Solar Return 3rd house. Saturn rules the annual 12th of illness as well as the annual Aquarius Ascendant (the body and life force). The annual Ascendant-ruler Saturn squaring the annual Aquarius Ascendant indicates stress and potential health problems.

II.   The Planetary Ruler(s) of the Solar Return Ascendant

With Aquarius rising, the annual Ascendant-rulers are Saturn and Uranus. With Pisces intercepted in the annual 1ˢᵗ house, Jupiter and Neptune co-rule the Solar Return 1ˢᵗ house. By exaltation, Venus rules Pisces and also rules the annual 1ˢᵗ house.

a.   *The Solar Return House placement of the annual Ascendant-ruler.* Annual Saturn occupies the Solar Return 3ʳᵈ house (communication, local travel) and annual Uranus occupies the Solar Return 12ᵗʰ house (sorrow, hospitalization) of the Solar Return. Annual Jupiter, also in the Solar Return 3ʳᵈ house (commuting), conjoins the annual IC of final endings. Annual Neptune joins annual Uranus in the Solar Return 12ᵗʰ house of illness. Arranging his chemotherapy involved an enormous amount of telephone calling and commuting. Natal Venus occupies the annual 8ᵗʰ house where it is combust the Sun and square to annual Uranus in the return 12ᵗʰ.

b.   *Aspects between the ruler of the Solar Return Ascendant and the annual and natal planets and cusps.* The modern Ascendant-ruler Uranus in the annual 12ᵗʰ house closely squares the Sun in the annual 8ᵗʰ house (death, life-threatening illness). Annual Venus, which rules the annual 1ˢᵗ house by exaltation and disposes the annual Ascendant-ruler Saturn (in Taurus), is closely conjunct the natal 12ᵗʰ house cusp of illness and confinement.

III.   The Sun

a.   *The Solar Return House containing the Sun.* The Sun occupies the annual 8ᵗʰ house of death, legacies, and life-threatening illness. Don was concerned with all these issues this year.

b.   *Aspects between the Sun and the annual planets and angles.* The Sun makes a favorable trine with the annual Moon but forms a stressful square from the annual 8ᵗʰ house to chart-ruler Uranus in the annual 12ᵗʰ house.

c.   *A prominent, well aspected Sun in the annual chart implies vitality and good health.* The Sun is not in a prominent position, since it lies near the end of the annual 8ᵗʰ house and conjoins the cadent Solar Return 9ᵗʰ house cusp. The Sun has mixed aspects – trine the Solar Return Moon but square the annual Ascendant-ruler Uranus (surprising disruptions) in the unfortunate 12ᵗʰ house.

IV.   The Solar Return Moon

Symbolizes feelings, receptivity, fluctuations, and vulnerability. The state of the Moon in the return is related to health and relationships.

a.   A prominent but stressfully aspected annual Moon suggests health problems and low vitality. Don's annual Moon is prominent in the 1st house of the Solar Return. The Moon has mixed aspects. The annual Moon makes a favorable trine to the Sun but also forms a stressful almost exact square to annual Pluto at the Solar Return Midheaven and a close square to the conjunction of natal Saturn/annual Jupiter on the annual IC of final endings. In fact, the annual Moon is part of a powerful and extremely stressful T-square pattern as it squares the opposition of annual Pluto to the natal Saturn/annual Jupiter conjunction along the meridian axis. Had I noticed this angular T-square in November, I would have encouraged Don to see a doctor as soon as possible.

b.   The zodiacal sign, house, and aspects of the annual Moon in the Solar Return chart reflect the types of people who will play an important role in your life. The doctors and research scientists who treated Don are most likely symbolized by the Sun, Pluto and Saturn.

V.   Solar Return Planets Conjunct the Angles *(10 degree orb) have special prominence in the year ahead.*

The most angular planets in the Solar Return are annual Pluto, annual Jupiter, and natal Saturn. Annual Uranus is also angular since it lies 9 degrees from the annual Ascendant. Of these four planets, Pluto, Saturn, and Uranus have a generally malefic significance. Jupiter is generally favorable but lies in Gemini, the sign of its detriment. In addition, Jupiter rules the 12th house of the birth chart, and natal Jupiter almost exactly opposes the 12th house of the Solar Return.

VI.   Annual Planets in the Solar Return 1st House

Annual planets that occupy the Solar Return 1st house show the nature of the individual's activity and psychological reactions during the coming year. The annual Moon lies in Pisces in the annual 1st house in a tight T-square with annual Pluto and natal Saturn. This was a highly emotional and depressing year with many personal changes.

VII.   The Natal Chart Superimposed on the Solar Return Chart

a.   House emphasis by number of planets in each house. A total of seven planets plus the natal Midheaven lie in the annual 8th house, creating an overwhelming emphasis on 8th house matters. In terms of the general tone of the year, there are seven planets in succedent houses, seven in cadent houses, and six in angular houses. This is a fairly balanced distribution. The natal Ascendant and Midheaven however, lie in succedent houses of the annual chart, giving a modest emphasis to a succedent type of year with a focus on conditions that may be hard to change. The succedent houses (2, 5, 8, 11) are generally connected to highly emotional matters – money, love, sex, death, and friendship.

b.   *Conjunctions of any planets with annual house cusps (5 degree orb).* Annual Pluto conjoins the Solar Return Midheaven; annual Jupiter in Gemini conjoins the Solar Return IC; and the Sun conjoins the annual 9th cusp. Natal Saturn, ruler of the natal Ascendant (the body), conjoins the annual IC (final endings). Natal Jupiter conjoins the annual 6th house cusp (illness). Natal Venus conjoins the annual 9th house cusp.

c.   *Which natal Houses are superimposed on which annual houses (pay special attention to houses containing planets).* Most prominently the natal 9th and 10th fall on the annual 8th house. Don would do much traveling to a research hospital for experimental chemotherapy. His illness and treatment also profoundly affected his professional life.

VIII.   The Solar Return Superimposed on the Natal Chart

a.   *House emphasis by number of planets in each house.* In contrast to the natal superimposed on the annual chart, there is no outstanding house emphasis. The 9th house, however, has four planets, probably reflecting his many trips to the research hospital as well as the many hours he spent reflecting on his worldview and philosophy of life in the context of his terminal illness.

b.   *Conjunctions of any planets with natal house cusps (5 degree orb).* Annual Venus, which rules the Solar Return 1st house by exaltation, conjoins the natal 12th cusp of illness and hospitalization. Annual Saturn conjoins the natal 5th house cusp and opposes the natal 11th house cusp – he felt cut off from his friends and unable to enjoy life because of his illness. Annual Mars conjoins the natal 9th house cusp – he would certainly do a lot of stressful traveling to doctors and hospitals during the year. Annual Mercury, which rules his natal 6th house of illness as well as his natal 8th house of death, stands out "like a sore thumb" as it conjoins the natal Midheaven. His illness and concerns about death certainly took a toll on his professional life.

c.   *Which annual houses are superimposed on which natal houses (pay special attention to houses containing planets)?* The Solar Return Ascendant conjoins the natal 2nd house cusp, closely opposing the natal 8th house cusp. Morin viewed the house cusps as powerful points and would have regarded the 8th cusp of death opposing the Ascendant (the body) as highly significant. Issues of finances, his last will and testament, and

matters related to death and dying were certainly of concern this year.
d.   *Annual planets in the natal 1ˢᵗ house show which planetary influences are about to rise to the horizon of the birth chart.* Don has annual Neptune (dissolution) and annual Uranus (shocking events) rising in the natal 1ˢᵗ house, with annual Neptune square annual Saturn[4] and annual Uranus square the Sun.

IX.   **The Solar Return Midheaven and its Ruler(s)**

a.   *A close conjunction of the annual Midheaven with any natal angle suggests an important year, especially for career and family matters.* This does not apply in this case.

b.   *Close aspects between the annual Midheaven and any natal or annual planets.* The annual Midheaven conjoins natal Pluto – there were radical changes in his professional life because of his cancer. Annual Midheaven opposes annual Jupiter and natal Saturn, which conjoin the annual 4ᵗʰ cusp of endings.

c.   *The house placement and aspects of the Midheaven-ruler are significant with regard to one's professional life.* Jupiter rules the Solar Return Midheaven and opposes the annual Midheaven because it conjoins the annual IC of endings – this is the year that Don had to close his psychology practice due to his illness and thus end his career.

X.   **Planetary Aspects**

a.   *Close aspects between annual planets, especially those that will perfect within 24 hours of the Solar Return.* The closest aspect to perfect during the 24 hours after the Solar Return was a stressful sesqui-square between annual Mars and annual Uranus. By secondary progression this perfected on April 27, 2001. At that time Don was undergoing experimental chemotherapy. The annual Moon had just squared annual Pluto prior to the Solar Return, suggesting a period of intense emotional upheaval. Annual Saturn (in the natal 4ᵗʰ of endings) was square annual Neptune in the natal 1ˢᵗ (the body); Saturn square Neptune is often associated with insidious debilitating illness.

b.   *Close aspects between natal and annual planets.* The closest aspect is a stressful conjunction of annual Mars with natal Neptune, often associated with depleted energy. The annual Moon, a general signifier of health, is closely square natal Saturn – a depressing influence. Annual Jupiter, ruler of the natal 12ᵗʰ of bodily afflictions, conjoins natal Saturn, which in turn is being opposed by annual Pluto, signifying a period of being forced to let go and surrender. Annual Uranus occupies the natal

1st house (the body) and squares the Sun (ruler of the natal 8th of life-threatening illness).

c.   *Comparison of the genders of the zodiacal signs occupied by the same planet in the natal and annual charts.* The following table compares the genders of each planet in the two charts and gives the relationships of the signs they occupy. There is a 50/50 split of genders but the most common relationship between annual and natal signs containing the planets is the inconjunct.

Planet	Annual chart + = yang, - = yin	Natal chart	Same or Opposite Genders
Sun	Scorpio (-)	Scorpio (-)	Same, conjunct
Moon	Pisces (-)	Scorpio (-)	Same, trine
Mercury	Scorpio (-)	Scorpio (-)	Same, conjunct
Venus	Sagittarius (+)	Scorpio (-)	INCONJUNCT
Mars	Libra (+)	Scorpio (-)	INCONJUNCT
Jupiter	Gemini (+)	Cancer (-)	INCONJUNCT
Saturn	Taurus (-)	Gemini (+)	INCONJUNCT
Uranus	Aquarius (+)	Gemini (+)	Same, trine
Neptune	Aquarius (+)	Libra (+)	Same, trine
Pluto	Sagittarius (+)	Leo (+)	Same, trine
ASC	Aquarius (+)	Capricorn (-)	INCONJUNCT
MC	Sagittarius (+)	Scorpio (-)	INCONJUNCT

d.   *Aspects that a house-ruler forms with the house cusp and the planets contained within that house.* This process can be quite detailed and time-consuming, and I give it less weight than other techniques mentioned. For example, annual Saturn rules the 12th house and forms a favorable trine with the annual 12th cusp. More significant, however, are annual Neptune in the 12th (square annual Mercury in the return 8th) and annual Uranus in the 12th square the Sun in the annual 8th.

XVI. Eclipses

a.   *Eclipses, especially solar eclipses.*

There were two solar eclipses during Don's 2000 Solar Return year. The first eclipse on Christmas Day 2000 has an Aries Ascendant in Washington, DC. Mars rules the eclipse Ascendant and occupies the annual 8th house of intensive medical therapy, where eclipse Mars conjoins annual Mercury, ruler of the Solar Return 4th house of endings. The second eclipse of June 2001 is a total solar eclipse falling in a cardinal degree (0° Cancer), which makes it extremely powerful. This total solar eclipse, falling in Don's annual 4th house of endings, activates the Solar Return square aspect between the annual 8th house Sun and the annual 12th house Uranus by forming a sesqui-square to each of those planets – thus activating 4th, 8th, and 12th house issues in the summer of 2001. The Ascendant of the total solar eclipse falls in the Solar Return 6th house conjunct its cusp. Mars of the total solar eclipse chart conjoins annual Venus, ruler of the Solar Return 8th house, and opposes annual Mercury, ruler and occupant of the Solar Return 4th house of final endings.

Solar Eclipses During Don's 2000 Solar Return Year

Date	Type	Position	Hard Contacts
Dec 25 2000	Solar Partial	4° Capricorn 15'	Square annual Mars
June 21 2001	Solar Total	0° Cancer 11'	Square annual Mars Sesqui-square annual Sun Sesqui-square annual Uranus

XI.   Timing

  *a.   The natal chart's primary, Ascendant-arc, and solar arc directions
  chart that are active during the current Solar Return year.* Using *Solar Fire*,
  I calculated the following primary mundane directions of Don's *natal*
  chart starting with his birthday in 2000. Just a week before he received
  the diagnosis of colon cancer his primary directed Uranus (at the natal
  solar rate) sesqui-squared his natal 8th house ruler, the Sun, in the natal
  10th – consistent with unexpected shocking news about his health and
  life. Primary directed Venus (at the natal solar rate), ruler of the natal
  4th of endings, conjoined the natal Moon's North Node in the natal 8th
  house during March 2001 when he was undergoing intensive
  chemotherapy. Primary directed Venus in the 8th house also went on to
  square natal Uranus in August 2001 when it became clear that even
  the experimental chemotherapy was not succeeding. His death on
  November 26, 2001 occurred two months after the primary directed
  Ascendant (at the natal solar rate) squared natal Pluto, a natural signifier
  of death, and about a month before his primary directed Saturn (at the
  natal solar rate) sesqui-squared natal Pluto.

Primary Mundane Directions (at the natal solar rate):

Ura (1) Sqq	Sun (10)	(X)	Pm-Na	Dec 29 2000	303°13'	14°Sc39'
Ven (8) Cnj	Nod (8)	(X)	Pm-Na	Mar 12 2001	145°09'	00°Vi23'
Ven (8) Sqr	Ura (5)	(X)	Pm-Na	Aug 1 2001	145°35'	03°Ge17'
Mon (8)Sxt	Mer (9)	(X)	Pm-Na	Sep 8 2001	152°21'	01°Sc00'
Asc (5) Sqr	Plu (7)	(X)	Pm-Na	Sep 26 2001	069°34'	07°Le15'
Sat (1) Sqq	Plu (7)	(X)	Pm-Na	Dec 20 2001	294°34'	07°Le15'

  *b.   The secondary progressed annual Moon and annual planets. (Merriman
  considers all exact aspects the progressed annual Moon forms with the natal and
  annual planets and Angles as well as with their antiscia or solstice points.)*

  In April of 2001, around the time when the progressed annual Mars
  sesqui-squared Uranus, Don learned that the traditional chemotherapy
  was not effective, and he was placed on an experimental protocol. In
  September of 2001, at the time the progressed annual Moon squared
  Venus (ruler of his annual 8th house), Don realized that the experimental
  chemotherapy was also not being effective and he began to prepare
  himself for death, which came on November 26, 2001. His natal
  Ascendant closely conjoins the annual 8th house cusp (at 17° Capricorn
  28') of his 2001 Solar Return, which took place 20 days before his
  death.

For readers who have *Solar Fire*, an easy way to time progressed aspects is to run a year-long "dynamic report" for secondary progressions of the Solar Return, beginning on the date of the return (which becomes the "radix" chart). Be sure to include all the planets and chart points that you want to progress in the "point selection" menu for progressions. Here is the *Solar Fire* "progressions to radix" dynamic report for Don's Solar Return in 2000.

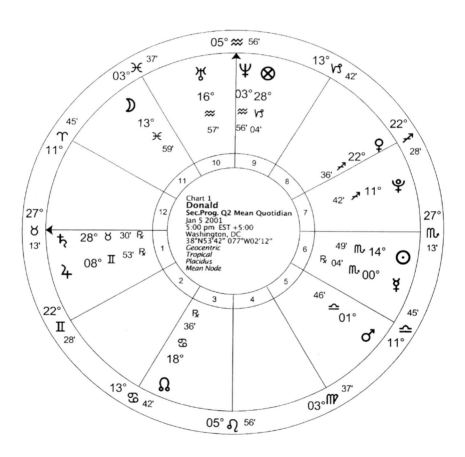

Figure 3: Don 2000 Solar Return progressed to Jan 5, 2001

Secondary Progression of Solar Return:

Mon (1) Tri Sun (8)   (X) Sp-Re Jan 25 2001   14°Pi40' D 14°Sc40' D
Mon (1) Sqq Mer (8)   (X) Sp-Re Feb 7 2001   15°Pi06' D 00°Sc06' R
Mon (1) SSx Ura (12)   (X) Sp-Re Apr 2 2001   16°Pi57' D 16°Aq57' D
Mar (7) Sqq Ura (12)   (X) Sp-Re Apr 27 2001   01°Li57' D 16°Aq57' D
Mon (1) Tri Nod (5)   (X) Sp-Re May 21 2001   18°Pi37' D 18°Cn37' R
Mon (1) SSq Nep (12)   (X) Sp-Re May 30 2001   18°Pi56' D 03°Aq56' D
Ven (10) Opp PF (4)   (X) Sp-Re Aug 2 2001   23°Sg17' D 23°Ge17' D
Mon (1) Sqr Ven (10)   (X) Sp-Re Sep 8 2001   22°Pi24' D 22°Sg24' D

c.   *The progressed Solar Return chart, especially the angles, according to the Conversion Table in the Appendix (the Mean Quotidian Secondary Progression)*

Sixty days elapsed between Friday January 5, 2001 around 5 PM, when Don was first diagnosed with cancer, and the date of his 2000 Solar Return. According to the Conversion Table we must add 3 hours 55 minutes 55 seconds to the moment of the Solar Return (1:38:27 PM EST), which gives a new time of 5:34:22 PM to cast the progressed annual chart. Alternatively we can secondary progress the Solar Return at the mean quotidian rate to January 5, 2001, around 5 PM. The progressed Solar Return Ascendant at 27° Taurus 13' completed a square to the annual Ascendant late on Thursday afternoon January 4th, the day before he received the diagnosis of colon cancer. On Friday January 5th at 8 PM (around the time Don phoned me with the news) the progressed annual 8th cusp exactly conjoined the progressed annual Ascendant-ruler Venus in the return 8th house. On Saturday, January 6[h], the progressed annual Ascendant passed over progressed annual Saturn in the 1st house. All of these progressed aspects are consistent with receiving a diagnosis of cancer at this time.

d.   *The transits of the Sun to the annual house cusps during the year.* On January 5, 2001 when Don called me with the news of his colon cancer, the transiting Sun at 15° Capricorn occupied his annual 11th house of friends. On the previous day the Sun by transit completed a sextile to its position in the annual 8th house and was applying to semi-sextile annual Uranus in the 12th house on January 6th, thus activating the annual Sun/Uranus square from the annual 8th to 12th houses during the period from January 4 to January 6, 2001. On January 14, 2001, the transiting Sun entered the annual 12th house and remained there for the following month, as Don began his intensive chemotherapy.

e.   The daily progressed Lunar Return.

Don received the news of his colon cancer on Friday afternoon January 5, 2001, slightly more than 16 days after his December 20, 2000 Lunar Return. Using the table in Chapter 9, we must add 16 days 4 hours 34 minutes 29 seconds to the moment of the original Lunar Return (12:09:25 PM EST), which gives a new time of 4:43:54 PM EST for a daily progressed chart cast for January 5, 2001. The daily progressed Lunar Return for January 5th has an angular Sun/South Lunar Node

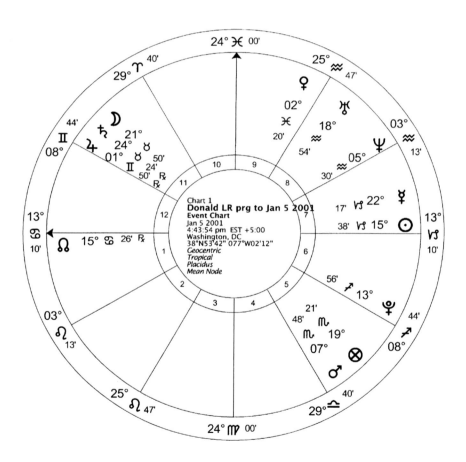

Figure 4: Don Lunar Return Progressed to Jan 5, 2001

conjunction on the progressed lunar Descendant. In Don's natal chart the Sun rules the 8th house and the Moon's North Node occupies the natal 8th house of life-threatening illness. The Moon, which rules the Ascendant of the daily progressed Lunar Return for January 5th conjoins 8th-ruler Saturn, lending a depressive cast to the day. Neptune in the 8th house of this chart lies exactly on the contrascion of Saturn (similar to Saturn being square Neptune). Rob Hand notes that stressful Saturn/ Neptune combinations can indicate "chronic illnesses that become visible only when it is almost too late to do anything about them."[5] In addition, the daily progressed Ascendant opposes Don's natal Ascendant from the natal 6th house of illness.

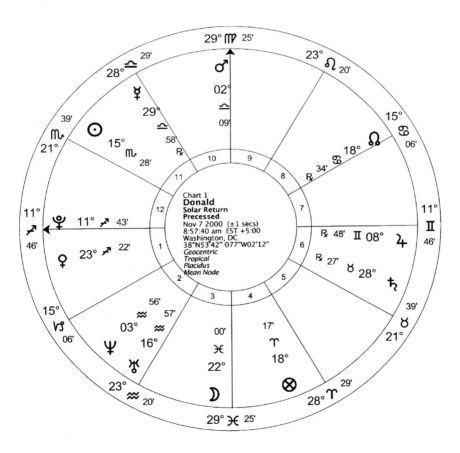

Figure 5: Don's Precessed 2000 Solar Return

f.   *Morin's methods of directing the Solar and Lunar Returns.* Because of the rigorous mathematics involved, I generally do not use Morin's techniques for directing *return* charts.

XII.   The Precessed Tropical Solar Return

Look at the precessed annual chart, especially any planets that closely conjoin the Solar Return Angles or intermediate house cusps. The precessed 2000 Solar Return has annual Pluto (dramatic change) on the Solar Return Ascendant (his body) and annual Mars conjunct the Solar Return Midheaven, highlighting the possible need for surgery or intensive medical therapy. Annual Jupiter, which rules the precessed return Ascendant (his life force) opposes annual Pluto and

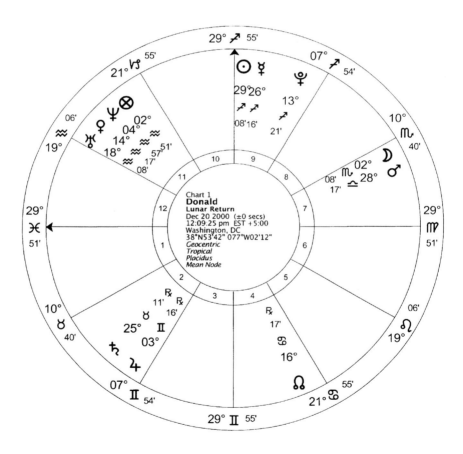

Figure 6: Don's December 2000 Lunar Return

forms a paran-square with annual Mars. There is actually a *paran-T-square* involving the annual Ascendant-ruler Jupiter (his body) in the annual 6th house in aspect with annual Mars and Pluto, joint rulers of his return 12th house (illness, hospitalization). In fact, if we were to cast this chart on the Prime Vertical, we would see a *paran-grand cross* involving annual Pluto, Mars, Jupiter and the Moon, each conjoining one of the angles. The closest paran-square in this grand cross is actually annual Pluto in paran-square with the Moon (orb 0° 34' on the Prime Vertical), which may herald a major health crisis as we saw in the charts of Roy Horn and Marc Penfield in earlier chapters.

XIII. The Lunar Returns
Morin looked to the Lunar Returns to pinpoint which month an event promised in the Solar Return would occur. He searched for similarities in signification among the natal, annual, and Lunar Return charts. Don's Lunar Return in December 2000 had an angular Sun/Mercury conjunction resting on the Midheaven. In Don's natal chart the Sun rules his natal 8th house of life-threatening illness and Mercury rules the natal 6th house of sickness. In the Lunar Return the Moon conjoins Mars, which rules the lunar 8th house cusp. Don's natal Ascendant opposes the Lunar Return North Lunar Node, which occupies the natal 8th house. In addition, the Lunar Return Ascendant conjoins the unfortunate fixed star Scheat (at 29° Pisces 22'), which is similar in influence to Neptune in square to Mars or Saturn and is associated with misfortune and loss of life.[6]

XIV. Additional Considerations
a. *Fixed Stars.* Morin routinely studied the fixed stars in Solar Returns. Caput Algol, which Robson called an evil fixed star, is frequently active in charts of major misfortune. In November 2000 Algol was at 26° Taurus 10' forming a close square to Don's annual Ascendant of 25° Taurus 59'. On January 5, 2001, when Don received the diagnosis of colon cancer, the secondary progressed annual Ascendant had moved to 26° Taurus 14'. The square from the secondary progressed annual Ascendant to Caput Algol became exact on December 20, 2000 when his bowel symptoms were becoming noticeable and he first sought medical attention. Nine days later, on December 29, 2000, his primary directed Uranus sesqui-squared the natal Sun.

b. *Arabic Parts.* Especially the Part of Fortune (PF) and Emerson's Point of Death. Don's natal Point of Death at 10° Gemini 57', which conjoins his natal 5th house Saturn, is closely conjunct his 2000 Solar Return 4th cusp of final endings at 10° Gemini 27' and opposite his annual Pluto at 11° Sagittarius 41'. Saturn and Pluto are astrological symbols associated with dying. In the 2000 Solar Return chart the annual Point of Death lies in the 6th house at 7° Leo 18' exactly conjunct natal Pluto at 7° Leo 15'. Pluto is the dispositor of the annual Sun in Scorpio in the return 8th house. Natal Pluto opposes annual Neptune in the 2000 return 12th.

c.   *Chiron and the Asteroids.* I did not look at Chiron or the asteroids in Don's charts.

d.   *Midpoints.* I did not consider the midpoints in Don's charts, though they can often add useful information.

e.   *Converse Solar Returns.* Due to time constraints I rarely look at the converse return.

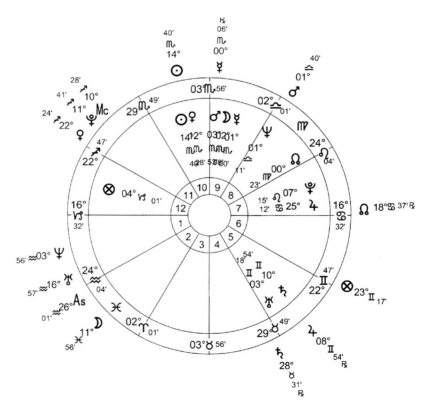

Figure 7: Don's 2000 Solar Return Superimposed on his Natal Chart

f. *Firdaria, profections, and other medieval techniques.* Don was born with the Sun above the horizon. He was passing through the Mercury subperiod of his Jupiter firdar when he was diagnosed with cancer and died of it. Jupiter does rule his natal 12th house of illness, and Mercury has rulership in his natal 6th and 8th houses, so the symbolism is fitting. In his 2000 Solar Return annual Mercury (his firdar subperiod ruler) occupies the annual 8th house and conjoins the natal Midheaven, emphasizing its key role during the year.

NOTES

1. Morin, *Book 23*, translated by James Holden, AFA, 2003, p. 130.
2. See Lynn Bell, *Cycles of Light, Exploring the Mysteries of Solar Returns*, CPA Press, UK, 2005.
3. Interested readers are referred to *Tools & Techniques of the Medieval Astrologers* by Robert Zoller, 1981. An updated and revised PDF version of Zoller's book is available from http://www.new-library.com/zoller/books/
4. Reinshold Ebertin found Saturn square Neptune to be connected with "diseases with causes difficult to ascertain" in *The Combination of Stellar Influences*, AFA, 1972, p. 186.
5. Robert Hand, *Planets in Transit*, Para Research, 1976, p. 355.
6. Alvidas (Henry Clay Hodges), *Science and the Key of Life*, Volume 4, Astro Publishing Co., Detroit, 1902, (republished by Weiser in 1977), p.171.

Appendix A

A Table to Determine the Time Interval by which to Progress the Solar Return Chart

Those who use the *Solar Fire* computer program can progress the Solar Return to any date during the Solar Return year by using the *F4* option (Transits, Directions, Progression). It is necessary first to select Preferences, Edit Settings, Progs/Dirns, and then set the Chart Angle Progression to Mean Quotidian. The resulting mean quotidian secondary progressed Solar Return is identical to one calculated using the table below, which advances the "birth time" of the Solar Return chart by 3 minutes and 56 seconds for each day of the Solar Return year.

To use the table, find, in the first column, the number of days that have elapsed during the year since the time of the Solar Return. To the right of the number of days you will see the equivalent numbers of hours, minutes and seconds that have elapsed since the time of the Solar Return. Add the time interval given in the table to the "birth time" of the Solar Return chart to calculate the "birth data" of the progressed Solar Return chart.

This table proceeds in one-day increments, that is, each subsequent 24-hour period in the coming year corresponds to a roughly 4-minute advance in the Solar Return birth time. Once you locate the day that something has occurred, you can fine-tune the progressed chart by adding roughly one minute of Solar Return "birth time" for every 6 hours of actual elapsed time on the day of the event.

# Days After SR =	Hours	Min	Sec	# Days	Hours	Min	Sec
1	0	3	56	10	0	39	20
2	0	7	52	11	0	43	16
3	0	11	48	12	0	47	11
4	0	15	44	13	0	51	7
5	0	19	40	14	0	55	3
6	0	23	36	15	0	58	59
7	0	27	32	16	1	2	55
8	0	31	28	17	1	6	51
9	0	35	24	18	1	10	47
				19	1	14	43
				20	1	18	39

# Days	Hours	Min	Sec	# Days	Hours	Min	Sec
21	1	22	35	59	3	51	59
22	1	26	31	60	3	55	55
23	1	30	26	61	3	59	51
24	1	34	22	62	4	3	47
25	1	38	18	63	4	7	43
26	1	42	14	64	4	11	39
27	1	46	10	65	4	15	35
28	1	50	6	66	4	19	31
29	1	54	2	67	4	23	26
30	1	57	58	68	4	27	22
31	2	1	54	69	4	31	18
32	2	5	50	70	4	35	14
33	2	9	46	71	4	39	10
34	2	13	41	72	4	43	6
35	2	17	37	73	4	47	2
36	2	21	33	74	4	50	58
37	2	25	29	75	4	54	54
38	2	29	25	76	4	58	50
39	2	33	21	77	5	2	46
40	2	37	17	78	5	6	41
41	2	41	13	79	5	10	37
42	2	45	9	80	5	14	33
43	2	49	5	81	5	18	29
44	2	53	1	82	5	22	25
45	2	56	56	83	5	26	21
46	3	0	52	84	5	30	17
47	3	4	48	85	5	34	13
48	3	8	44	86	5	38	9
49	3	12	40	87	5	42	5
50	3	16	36	88	5	46	1
51	3	20	32	89	5	49	56
52	3	24	28	90	5	53	52
53	3	28	24	91	5	57	48
54	3	32	20	92	6	1	44
55	3	36	16	93	6	5	40
56	3	40	11	94	6	9	36
57	3	44	7	95	6	13	32
58	3	48	3	96	6	17	28

# Days	Hours	Min	Sec	# Days	Hours	Min	Sec
97	6	21	24	135	8	50	48
98	6	25	20	136	8	54	44
99	6	29	16	137	8	58	40
100	6	33	11	138	9	2	36
101	6	37	7	139	9	6	32
102	6	41	3	140	9	10	28
103	6	44	59	141	9	14	24
104	6	48	55	142	9	18	20
105	6	52	51	143	9	22	16
106	6	56	47	144	9	26	11
107	7	0	43	145	9	30	7
108	7	4	39	146	9	34	3
109	7	8	35	147	9	37	59
110	7	12	31	148	9	41	55
111	7	16	26	149	9	45	51
112	7	20	22	150	9	49	47
113	7	24	18	151	9	53	43
114	7	28	14	152	9	57	39
115	7	32	10	153	10	1	35
116	7	36	6	154	10	5	31
117	7	40	2	155	10	9	26
118	7	43	58	156	10	13	22
119	7	47	54	157	10	17	18
120	7	51	50	158	10	21	14
121	7	55	46	159	10	25	10
122	7	59	41	160	10	29	6
123	8	3	37	161	10	33	2
124	8	7	33	162	10	36	58
125	8	11	29	163	10	40	54
126	8	15	25	164	10	44	50
127	8	19	21	165	10	48	46
128	8	23	17	166	10	52	41
129	8	27	13	167	10	56	37
130	8	31	9	168	11	0	33
131	8	35	5	169	11	4	29
132	8	39	1	170	11	8	25
133	8	42	56	171	11	12	21
134	8	46	52	172	11	16	17

# Days	Hours	Min	Sec	# Days	Hours	Min	Sec
173	11	20	13	211	13	49	37
174	11	24	9	212	13	53	33
175	11	28	5	213	13	57	29
176	11	32	1	214	14	1	25
177	11	35	56	215	14	5	21
178	11	39	52	216	14	9	17
179	11	43	48	217	14	13	13
180	11	47	44	218	14	17	9
181	11	51	40	219	14	21	5
182	11	55	36	220	14	25	1
183	11	59	32	221	14	28	56
184	12	3	28	222	14	32	52
185	12	7	24	223	14	36	48
186	12	11	20	224	14	40	44
187	12	15	16	225	14	44	40
188	12	19	11	226	14	48	36
189	12	23	7	227	14	52	32
190	12	27	3	228	14	56	28
191	12	30	59	229	15	0	24
192	12	34	55	230	15	4	20
193	12	38	51	231	15	8	16
194	12	42	47	232	15	12	11
195	12	46	43	233	15	16	7
196	12	50	39	234	15	20	3
197	12	54	35	235	15	23	59
198	12	58	31	236	15	27	55
199	13	2	26	237	15	31	51
200	13	6	22	238	15	35	47
201	13	10	18	239	15	39	43
202	13	14	14	240	15	43	39
203	13	18	10	241	15	47	35
204	13	22	6	242	15	51	31
205	13	26	2	243	15	55	26
206	13	29	58	244	15	59	22
207	13	33	54	245	16	3	18
208	13	37	50	246	16	7	14
209	13	41	46	247	16	11	10
210	13	45	41	248	16	15	6

# Days	Hours	Min	Sec	# Days	Hours	Min	Sec
249	16	19	2	287	18	48	26
250	16	22	58	288	18	52	22
251	16	26	54	289	18	56	18
252	16	30	50	290	19	0	14
253	16	34	46	291	19	4	10
254	16	38	41	292	19	8	6
255	16	42	37	293	19	12	2
256	16	46	33	294	19	15	58
257	16	50	29	295	19	19	54
258	16	54	25	296	19	23	50
259	16	58	21	297	19	27	46
260	17	2	17	298	19	31	41
261	17	6	13	299	19	35	37
262	17	10	9	300	19	39	33
263	17	14	5	301	19	43	29
264	17	18	1	302	19	47	25
265	17	21	56	303	19	51	21
266	17	25	52	304	19	55	17
267	17	29	48	305	19	59	13
268	17	33	44	306	20	3	9
269	17	37	40	307	20	7	5
270	17	41	36	308	20	11	1
271	17	45	32	309	20	14	56
272	17	49	28	310	20	18	52
273	17	53	24	311	20	22	48
274	17	57	20	312	20	26	44
275	18	1	16	313	20	30	40
276	18	5	11	314	20	34	36
277	18	9	7	315	20	38	32
278	18	13	3	316	20	42	28
279	18	16	59	317	20	46	24
280	18	20	55	318	20	50	20
281	18	24	51	319	20	54	16
282	18	28	47	320	20	58	11
283	18	32	43	321	21	2	7
284	18	36	39	322	21	6	3
285	18	40	35	323	21	9	59
286	18	44	31	324	21	13	55

# Days	Hours	Min	Sec	# Days	Hours	Min	Sec
325	21	17	51	362	23	43	20
326	21	21	47	363	23	47	16
327	21	25	43	364	23	51	11
328	21	29	39	365	23	55	7
329	21	33	35	(New SR begins)			
330	21	37	31	365.2422	23	56	4
331	21	41	26				
332	21	45	22				
333	21	49	18				
334	21	53	14				
335	21	57	10				
336	22	1	6				
337	22	5	2				
338	22	8	58				
339	22	12	54				
340	22	16	50				
341	22	20	46				
342	22	24	41				
343	22	28	37				
344	22	32	33				
345	22	36	29				
346	22	40	25				
347	22	44	21				
348	22	48	17				
349	22	52	13				
350	22	56	9				
351	23	0	5				
352	23	4	1				
353	23	7	56				
354	23	11	52				
355	23	15	48				
356	23	19	44				
357	23	23	40				
358	23	27	36				
359	23	31	32				
360	23	35	28				
361	23	39	24				

Appendix B

Sample Firdaria for Day and Night Births

The firdaria are the medieval western version of the Vedic *dashas* or the Hellenistic *time lords*. Readers who wish to explore firdaria will find below sample charts for day and night births with corresponding tables of their firdaria. The first column shows the firdar and its subperiod. The second column shows the date it goes into effect for the same day and night charts cast for January 1, 2000. The third column shows the person's age at the start of the particular firdar and its subperiods. The dates that begin the firdaria and their subperiods will vary depending on the birth date of the individual, but the age in years at which the period goes into effect will be the same for all day births and all night births.

The arrangement below is the one found in the original description by Abu Ma'shar (787-886) with the lunar nodes always governing the ages 70-75 regardless of whether it is a day or night birth.[1] To use these tables first determine whether yours is a day or night birth (the Sun above or below the horizon). Then look up your age in column three and find the corresponding planetary period/subperiod to the left in column one. You can ignore the specific dates because they only apply to someone born January 1, 2000, and are presented solely to illustrate the concept.

FIRDARIA (Al Biruni/Schoener)								
☽	Jan 1 2000	0.0	♃/♄	Apr 14 2030	30.3	♀/♂	Sep 17 2054	54.7
☽/♄	Apr 14 2001	1.3	♂	Dec 31 2031	32.0	♀/☉	Nov 9 2055	55.9
☽/♃	Jul 28 2002	2.6	♂/☉	Dec 30 2032	33.0	☿	Dec 30 2056	57.0
☽/♂	Nov 9 2003	3.9	♂/♀	Dec 31 2033	34.0	☿/☽	Nov 9 2058	58.9
☽/☉	Feb 21 2005	5.1	♂/☿	Dec 31 2034	35.0	☿/♄	Sep 17 2060	60.7
☽/♀	Jun 5 2006	6.4	♂/☽	Dec 31 2035	36.0	☿/♃	Jul 27 2062	62.6
☽/☿	Sep 18 2007	7.7	♂/♄	Dec 30 2036	37.0	☿/♂	Jun 5 2064	64.4
♄	Dec 31 2008	9.0	♂/♃	Dec 31 2037	38.0	☿/☉	Apr 14 2066	66.3
♄/♃	Jul 28 2010	10.6	☉	Dec 31 2038	39.0	☿/♀	Feb 21 2068	68.1
♄/♂	Feb 22 2012	12.1	☉/♀	Jun 5 2040	40.4	☊	Dec 30 2069	70.0
♄/☉	Sep 18 2013	13.7	☉/☿	Nov 8 2041	41.9	☋	Dec 30 2072	73.0
♄/♀	Apr 14 2015	15.3	☉/☽	Apr 14 2043	43.3	☽	Dec 31 2074	75.0
♄/☿	Nov 8 2016	16.9	☉/♄	Sep 17 2044	44.7	☽/♄	Apr 13 2076	76.3
♄/☽	Jun 5 2018	18.4	☉/♃	Feb 21 2046	46.1	☽/♃	Jul 27 2077	77.6
♃	Dec 31 2019	20.0	☉/♂	Jul 28 2047	47.6	☽/♂	Nov 8 2078	78.9
♃/♂	Sep 17 2021	21.7	♀	Dec 30 2048	49.0	☽/☉	Feb 21 2080	80.1
♃/☉	Jun 6 2023	23.4	♀/☿	Feb 21 2050	50.1	☽/♀	Jun 5 2081	81.4
♃/♀	Feb 21 2025	25.1	♀/☽	Apr 14 2051	51.3	☽/☿	Sep 17 2082	82.7
♃/☿	Nov 9 2026	26.9	♀/♄	Jun 5 2052	52.4	♄	Dec 31 2083	84.0
♃/☽	Jul 27 2028	28.6	♀/♃	Jul 27 2053	53.6	♄/♃	Jul 27 2085	85.6

Figure 1: Night Birth Firdaria for a Person born January 1, 2000 at 00:00 hrs

FIRDARIA (Al Biruni/Schoener)								
☉	Jan 1 2000	0.0	☿ ♀	Feb 21 2029	29.1	♃ ☽	Jul 28 2059	59.6
☉ ♀	Jun 6 2001	1.4	☽	Jan 1 2031	31.0	♃ ♄	Apr 14 2061	61.3
☉ ☿	Nov 10 2002	2.9	☽ ♄	Apr 14 2032	32.3	♂	Dec 31 2062	63.0
☉ ☽	Apr 14 2004	4.3	☽ ♃	Jul 28 2033	33.6	♂ ☉	Jan 1 2064	64.0
☉ ♄	Sep 18 2005	5.7	☽ ♂	Nov 9 2034	34.9	♂ ♀	Dec 31 2064	65.0
☉ ♃	Feb 22 2007	7.1	☽ ☉	Feb 22 2036	36.1	♂ ☿	Dec 31 2065	66.0
☉ ♂	Jul 28 2008	8.6	☽ ♀	Jun 5 2037	37.4	♂ ☽	Dec 31 2066	67.0
♀	Dec 31 2009	10.0	☽ ☿	Sep 18 2038	38.7	♂ ♄	Dec 31 2067	68.0
♀ ☿	Feb 22 2011	11.1	♄	Jan 1 2040	40.0	♂ ♃	Dec 31 2068	69.0
♀ ☽	Apr 14 2012	12.3	♄ ♃	Jul 28 2041	41.6	☊	Dec 31 2069	70.0
♀ ♄	Jun 6 2013	13.4	♄ ♂	Feb 22 2043	43.1	☋	Dec 31 2072	73.0
♀ ♃	Jul 28 2014	14.6	♄ ☉	Sep 18 2044	44.7	☉	Dec 31 2074	75.0
♀ ♂	Sep 19 2015	15.7	♄ ♀	Apr 14 2046	46.3	☉ ♀	Jun 5 2076	76.4
♀ ☉	Nov 9 2016	16.9	♄ ☿	Nov 9 2047	47.9	☉ ☿	Nov 9 2077	77.9
☿	Dec 31 2017	18.0	♄ ☽	Jun 5 2049	49.4	☉ ☽	Apr 14 2079	79.3
☿ ☽	Nov 10 2019	19.9	♃	Dec 31 2050	51.0	☉ ♄	Sep 17 2080	80.7
☿ ♄	Sep 18 2021	21.7	♃ ♂	Sep 17 2052	52.7	☉ ♃	Feb 21 2082	82.1
☿ ♃	Jul 28 2023	23.6	♃ ☉	Jun 6 2054	54.4	☉ ♂	Jul 28 2083	83.6
☿ ♂	Jun 6 2025	25.4	♃ ♀	Feb 22 2056	56.1	♀	Dec 31 2084	85.0
☿ ☉	Apr 15 2027	27.3	♃ ☿	Nov 9 2057	57.9	♀ ☿	Feb 21 2086	86.1

Figure 2: Day Birth Firdaria for a Person born January 1, 2000 at 12:00 noon

NOTES

1.   See http://www.astrologiamedieval.com/firdaria.htm

Appendix C

William Lilly on Solar Returns

The great British astrologer William Lilly (May 11, 1602 NS – June 9, 1681) was a contemporary of Morin de Villefranche (February 23, 1583 NS – November 6, 1656). Whereas Morin discarded as unscientific or superstitious many of the techniques he found in the medieval astrological texts, Lilly adopted them wholeheartedly. Unlike Morin, Lilly made extensive use of the Ptolemaic terms[1] (bounds) of the planets as well as the method of annual profections, which Lilly used in tandem with primary directions and solar revolutions as part of his predictive armamentarium. Let us now take a look at annual profections, which Lilly found so useful, before proceeding to an overview of his approach to Solar Returns.[2]

Annual profections are perhaps the simplest technique employed by the medieval astrologers. The method consists of advancing the entire chart (all planets, points, angles, and house cusps) at the same rate of exactly 30 degrees per year.[3] Thus, every 12 years (ages 12, 24, 36, 48, 60, 72, 84, etc.) the annual profected Ascendant returns to its natal location, and the annual profected chart is identical to the birth chart. The ruler of the profected Ascendant is highly influential and becomes the "Lord [or Lady] of the year." If two signs happen to occupy the profected 1st house, then the lordship of the year passes to the ruler of the second sign at the time of year when the profected Ascendant enters that sign during its profection at a rate of 30 degrees per year.

To illustrate annual profections, let us revisit the chart of King Gustavus Adolphus, so often used as a teaching device by Morin, and its profections at the time of the king's death in the foggy battle of November 16, 1632 NS. The November 1632 profected Ascendant in Aquarius (see chart next page) makes Saturn the Lord of this part of the year (late 1632). Saturn and Neptune (fog) occupy the natal 8th house of death. The profected Sun, which rules the natal 8th house (Leo intercepted), exactly opposed natal Saturn in the 8th within hours of the king's demise. No wonder Lilly was so impressed with this technique!

Lilly relied on profections to determine when the current primary directions would manifest. Like Morin, Lilly regarded the currently active primary directions as keys to forecasting. The annual *profections* and solar revolutions indicated for Lilly when the primary directions would make themselves felt – "for Profections of themselves without Directions are not of

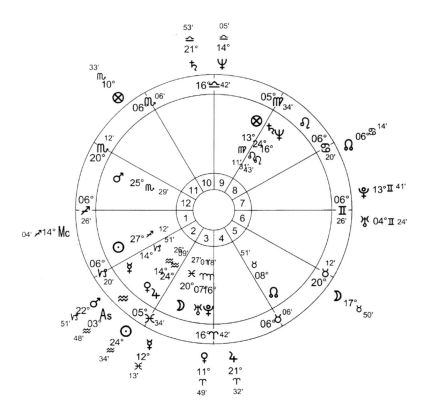

King Gustave Adolphus Nov 16, 1632 NS Annual Profection on Natal Chart

much validity, or effect little; so also Directions are less powerful and valid, when they are contradicted by *Profections* and *Transits* of a contrary influence."[4]

In the case of King Gustave, his primary directed Mars conjoined his natal Midheaven[5] in October of 1632 (at Ptolemy's rate of one degree of right ascension per year) or in April of 1633 (at the Naibod rate). In any case, primary directed Mars conjunct the natal Midheaven was active during November of 1632. Because Mars rules the natal 12th of undoing, its primary direction to the natal Midheaven signals professional defeat or disaster. Natal Mars in the unfortunate 12th partakes of a taxing T-square with natal Saturn in the 8th of death and natal Jupiter (the Ascendant-ruler) in the 2nd. This entire natal T-square was activated several times by the profected Sun (ruler of the natal 8th of death) during November of 1632, as can be seen in the following report from *Solar Fire*:

Gustavus Adolphus - Natal Chart (Na)
Dec 19 1594 NS, 7:11:33 am, LMT -1:12:12
Stockholm Sweden, 59°N01', 018°E03'

Annual Profections (Pf) of natal 8th ruler Sun to the natal T-square during
November 1632:

Sun (2) Cnj Jup (2)	(X)	Pf-Na	Nov 11,1632	NS	24°Aq09' D	24°Aq09' D
Sun (2) Opp Sat (8)	(X)	Pf-Na	Nov 15,1632	NS	24°Aq31' D	24°Le31' R
Sun (2) Sqr Mar (12)	(X)	Pf-Na	Nov 27,1632	NS	25°Aq29' D	25°Sc29' D

Lilly would have argued that when the profected Sun opposed natal Saturn
on the day of the king's final battle, it triggered into action both the natal T-
square and the primary directed Mars/Midheaven conjunction.

Lilly appears to have read the same astrological literature as did Morin,
and their approaches to delineating solar revolutions have much in common.
He agreed with Morin that "annual revolutions of the Sun are especially
effective the more closely they correspond to the natal figure."[6] Lilly summarizes
his own method on pages 736-737 of *Christian Astrology*:

> "Compare the Figure of the Birth with that of the Revolution,
> and observe how the cusps of the houses, and their Lords, and the
> principal Significators do agree or are disposed.... the *Significators*
> of the Radix ought annually, or in every year to work their effects
> by the *significations* of those houses in which they are constituted
> at the time of the Revolution..."

Lilly illustrates this principle with the following observations:

• If the Ascendant of the return agrees with, or is the same as, the natal
Ascendant, it will be a good year.
• If the ruler of the return Ascendant is combust the Sun, such combustion
"threatens many mischiefs to the native."
• The role of the Sun in the annual chart is highly significant (the Sun's
aspects and annual house position and rulership).
• A dignified annual Moon, especially with a nocturnal birth, mitigates
potential evils; but a weak or afflicted Moon has the opposite effect.
• If the annual Ascendant squares or opposes the natal Ascendant, or
falls in the sign of an unfortunate house or one signifying evil in the birth
chart, the native can expect "loss and detriment." For example if the sign on
the natal 6th, 7th, or 12th cusp rises in the Solar Return, there is a possibility of
illness or other misfortune during the year.

- If the sign on the natal 7th cusp ascends in the return, there will be "contentions and brawling," but the native may marry or want to get married. (Marriage and brawling are both signified by the 7th house.)
- Benefits generally come through the affairs of the annual house(s) containing the ruler of the natal 2nd (wealth), the Part of Fortune, or benefic Jupiter.
- When the annual Ascendant forms stressful connections with either the annual or natal malefics (Mars or Saturn), one can expect "great peril," which will manifest when the Lord of the year (the ruler of the annual profected Ascendant) "shall come to the body of that Planet who signifies the infelicity" as the profected Ascendant advances at a rate of 30 degrees per year. This was seen clearly in King Gustave's chart discussed above.
- Like Morin, Lilly stresses the importance of the similarity or contrariety of the natal and return charts: if the annual planets "are disposed contrary to the radical Geniture, though they be well disposed [in the Solar Return], yet they signify ill..." For example, it signifies ill if the birth planets are all below the horizon while the annual planets are all above the horizon; or if in the birth chart the natal planets are "cadent from their own houses" while in the return they are "in their own proper houses," etc.

For further information the reader is referred to *Christian Astrology, Book 3: Nativities*, where Lilly provides detailed examples of his use of primary directions, annual profections, and solar revolutions as tools for forecasting.

NOTES

1. Each sign of the zodiac is divided into five segments (*terms*) of unequal length ruled by one of the non-luminary visible planets – Mercury, Venus, Mars, Jupiter, and Saturn. Different versions of the terms exist. Lilly used Ptolemy's table of terms from the extant transcription of Ptolemy's original text.
2. See William Lilly, *Christian Astrology*, pages 715-734.
3. This is equivalent to advancing the chart by 0.0821 degrees per day, which is almost 5 minutes of arc per day.
4. William Lilly, *Christian Astrology*, page 719.
5. Natal Mars has a right ascension of 233°11' and the natal Midheaven has a right ascension of 195°23'. Subtracting, we see that the difference in right ascensions amounts to 37.8° or 37°48', the equivalent of about 37 years and 10 months at Ptolemy's rate. The king was 37.9 years old when he died. If we rectify the natal Midheaven to 16° Libra 35' (just 7' of arc earlier), this primary direction of Mars to the Midheaven would be exact on the date of his death at the rate of one degree of RA per year.
6. Morin, *Astrologia Gallica, Book 23 on Revolutions*, page 56.

Recommended Reading

Bell, Lynn. *Cycles of Light, Exploring the Mysteries of Solar Returns*. CPA Press, UK, 2005. Transcript of a seminar in London on the technique and use of Solar Returns.

Davison, R.C. *The Technique of Prediction*. L.N. Fowler & Co., 1971. A well-researched book on forecasting using secondary progressions; it has excellent delineations of the signs, Houses, and aspects in the progressed horoscope.

Eshelman, James A. *Interpreting Solar Returns*. ACS, 1985. A classic text on interpreting Solar Returns in the sidereal zodiac.

Freeman, Martin. *Forecasting by Astrology*. Aquarian Press, 1982. An excellent overview of various forecasting techniques including progressions, directions, transits, and returns.

Hand, Robert. *Planets in Transit*. Para Research, 1976. The most authoritative source for delineations of the aspects and house placements of transiting planets.

Houlding, Deborah, *The Houses – Temples of the Sky*. The Wessex Astrologer, April 2006. An excellent discussion of the meanings of the houses in traditional astrology.

Louis, Anthony. *Horary Astrology Plain & Simple*. Llewellyn, 1998. An introduction to traditional astrological techniques including dignities, debilities, fixed stars, Arabic parts, solstice points, etc., with a focus on horary astrology.

Mason, Sofia. *Forecasting with New, Full & Quarter Moons through the Houses*. AFA, 1980. Ms. Mason's text covers exactly what the title promises.

Merriman, Raymond A. *The New Solar Return Book of Prediction*. Seek-It Publications, 1977. Merriman's excellent delineations are based on his extensive experience with Solar Returns in the tropical zodiac. Highly recommended.

Morin de Villefrance, Jean-Baptiste. *Astrologia Gallica, Book 23: Revolutions* (Paris: 1661). Translated by James Herschel Holden. AFA, 2003. The definitive English translation of this 17th century classic on delineating Solar Returns. Essential reading.

_____ *The Morinus System of Horoscope Interpretation* (Book 21 of Morin's *Astrologia Gallica; 1661*) translated by Richard S. Baldwin. AFA, 1974. This is my preferred translation of Book 21, Morin's key text outlining his method of chart interpretation.

_____ *The Strengths of the Planets (Book 18 of Morin's Astrologia Gallica; 1661)* translated by Anthony Louis LaBruzza. AFA, 2004. This book discusses the various dignities and debilities of the planets.

Penfield, Marc. *Solar Returns in Your Face.* AFA, 1996. A collection of well-researched case studies delineated from the perspective of precessed tropical Solar Returns

Scofield, Bruce. *Astrological Chart Calculations: An Outline of Conventions and Methodology.* One Reed Publications, 2001

_____ *User's Guide to Astrology.* One Reed Publications, 1997. An excellent beginner's guide to natal astrology – concise and to-the-point.

Shea, Mary. *Planets in Solar Returns.* ACS, 1992. An approach to delineating Solar Returns from a psychological perspective.

Teal, Celeste. *Eclipses.* Llewellyn, 2006. A well-researched study of the role of eclipses in forecasting in both mundane and personal charts.

_____ *Identifying Planetary Triggers.* Llewellyn, 2000. A good overview of working with returns of the Sun, the Moon, and the planets from Mercury through Saturn.

Volguine, Alexandre. *The Technique of Solar Returns.* ASI Publishers: New York, 1978. This is Volguine's classic text on Solar Returns in the tropical zodiac, based on his many years of research.

INDEX

OTHER BOOKS BY THE WESSEX ASTROLOGER

The Essentials of Vedic Astrology
Lunar Nodes - Crisis and Redemption
Personal Panchanga and the Five Sources of Light
Komilla Sutton

Astrolocality Astrology
From Here to There
Martin Davis

The Consultation Chart
Wanda Sellar

The Betz Placidus Table of Houses
Martha Betz

Astrology and Meditation
Greg Bogart

Patterns of the Past
Karmic Connections
Good Vibrations
Judy Hall

The Book of World Horoscopes
Nicholas Campion

The Moment of Astrology
Geoffrey Cornelius

Life After Grief - An Astrological Guide to Dealing with Loss
Darrelyn Gunzburg

You're not a Person - Just a Birthchart
Declination: The Steps of the Sun
Paul F. Newman

The Houses: Temples of the Sky
Deborah Houlding

Temperament: Astrology's Forgotten Key
Dorian Geiseler Greenbaum

Astrology, A Place in Chaos
Bernadette Brady

Astrology and the Causes of War
Jamie Macphail

Flirting with the Zodiac
Kim Farnell

The Gods of Change
Howard Sasportas

Astrological Roots: The Hellenistic Legacy
Joseph Crane

Lightning Source UK Ltd.
Milton Keynes UK
11 September 2009

143631UK00001B/20/P